THE GOD OF THE WEST VERSUS THE CHRIST OF GLORY

An Exciting and Liberating Journey of Faith

By
Milton A. Reid, D.Min., D.D.

Eleven times in jail trying to make a difference

Order this book online at www.trafford.com/06-0636
or email orders@trafford.com

Most Trafford titles are also available at major online book retailers.

Note for Librarians: A cataloguing record for this book is available from Library and Archives Canada at www.collectionscanada.ca/amicus/index-e.html

ISBN: 978-1-4120-8880-0

We at Trafford believe that it is the responsibility of us all, as both individuals and corporations, to make choices that are environmentally and socially sound. You, in turn, are supporting this responsible conduct each time you purchase a Trafford book, or make use of our publishing services. To find out how you are helping, please visit www.trafford.com/responsiblepublishing.html

Our mission is to efficiently provide the world's finest, most comprehensive book publishing service, enabling every author to experience success. To find out how to publish your book, your way, and have it available worldwide, visit us online at www.trafford.com/10510

www.trafford.com

North America & international
toll-free: 1 888 232 4444 (USA & Canada)
phone: 250 383 6864 ♦ fax: 250 383 6804 ♦ email: info@trafford.com

The United Kingdom & Europe
phone: +44 (0)1865 722 113 ♦ local rate: 0845 230 9601
facsimile: +44 (0)1865 722 868 ♦ email: info.uk@trafford.com

10 9 8 7 6 5

Mrs. Reid's 1960 First Grade Class, Petersburg, VA.

Acknowledgements

There are a number of persons and institutions that I wish to acknowledge for leadership and inspiration given me in the development of this book. First and foremost, I would like to acknowledge my father, the late Reverend Moses Ananias Reid, and my sainted mother, the late Mary M. Odom Reid, for sharing with me their experience with the Risen Lord, and who inspired me to proclaim the Gospel of Jesus Christ. I acknowledge the late Dr. Vernon Johns, my first mentor, whose practical application of the Gospel first helped me to raise ideological suspicion in the traditional Black church and the late Dr. Martin Luther King Jr., for impacting my ministry in new direct actions under the Lordship of the Christ of Glory, challenging both church and state to a higher level of "being."

I acknowledge the late Dr. John M. Ellison for believing in me and for instilling in me that the preacher was more than a proclaimer but an "Interpreter of the times" in which he lives, the late Dr. Samuel Dewitt Proctor, for insisting on my going on into the Seminary upon completing the requirements for the Master's degree in Theology at Virginia Union University, J. W. Kinney, Ph.D., Dean of the School of Theology at Virginia Union University for re-directing the writings in this book and enlarging my prospective of myself and my abilities, Ms. Joyce Jenkins, my M.B.A. niece, of Queens, New York, for the investment of her time and effort to make this publication a reality. I acknowledge Minister Hope Ward of Chesapeake Virginia, for doing the first draft of the book cover drafts. She is another talented niece of mine. I acknowledge my brother-in-law and my sister Sarah and Walter Gilchrist respectively, for jogging my memory around family details, and for their encouragement in writing this book. I acknowledge the help of Dr. Wyatt Tee Walker, fellow pastor with me in Petersburg, Virginia, author of 27 books and civil rights advocate for his counsel on publishing; Mrs. Donna Waddell of Danville, Virginia for her persistence in my completing the book while I was still alive; my two wonderful daughters, Maravia and Michelle, for making it possible for me to continue this book and making my writings readable; and the School of Theology of Boston University, for guidance in my studies of Liberation Theology, giving me focus in both intellectual and practical experience applications.

I acknowledge the help of the editor of this work, a long time friend and classmate, Attorney William A. Smith, for his diligence, his patience, and legal advice; retired Coach Robert "Bob" Heard, for his technical support and computer skills that made possible my computer operations. I must acknowledge Mrs. Ruth A. Lewis, my prayer partner of many years, who has helped pray me through some mighty tough times, as a friend, a deaconess, a deacon, and above all as a disciple beloved, and finally I acknowledge my Marian, who I have renamed in our sunset years, "AA," (**Aion Agathosune, Greek for Eternal Goodness**). When we meet beyond the vale, I will still be thanking the Creator for the "goodness" He sent me, who understands me and loves me as if she never even seen or suspected a flaw. That is God's unfailing love, which we call **agape!**

It is impossible to name everyone who helped with this publication, but "Thank you, anyway."

Milton, the Disciple, Author

Contents

Dr. and Mrs. Reid visit the Ivory Coast of Africa, 1991.

FOREWORD

Thanks be to God for the day He allowed my life to intersect with that of Milton, the Disciple, a.k.a., Reverend Dr. Milton A. Reid. This occurred on the campus of Virginia Union University in Richmond, Virginia, the venerable institution from which we both graduated in 1955. Little did I realize in the more than fifty years that have transpired since our leaving alma mater Union that we would both end up in Tidewater Virginia, and that I would be witness to much of the unfolding of Milton's great, fulfilling and dynamic life.

Milton has always marched to the drumbeat he heard emanating from the God of Glory, about which he writes. Abraham Lincoln once said that we must "do right as God gives us the power to see what is right." Like many great leaders who have tasted man's jails and dungeons of injustice, including Nehru, Gandhi, Mandela, Martin Luther King, Jr. – indeed Jesus Himself was arrested, tried, convicted in four trials in one night and executed the following day – Milton has known persecution for his righteous action in causes greater than himself. Being a third-generation preacher, Milton is familiar with the part of the Sermon on the Mount that states: "Blessed are you when man reproach you and persecute you and speak against you every kind of evil, falsely, for my sake, Then be glad and rejoice, for your reward is increased in heaven; for in this very manner they persecuted the prophets who were before you" (Matthew 5:11-12, Lamsa translation). Milton's prophetic vision for the betterment of Christian living in this great country (and indeed the world) made him a natural ally of Dr. King, with whom he worked closely until the untimely assassination of this modern-day prophet in 1968.

Milton's association with Farrakhan and other 'controversial' brothers and sisters caused him to be shunned and castigated by many persons. To Milton, he was simply walking in the shoes of Jesus, the Christ, as well as Dr. King, who longed for the day when all of us – Catholics and Protestants, Blacks and Whites, Jews and Gentiles – could begin to see each other first, as brothers and sisters in the great family of man. Was not Jesus castigated for his association with 'undesirables' and did not the American government attempt to link Dr. King with atheistic Communism? Through it all my Brother Milton held his head high and his shoulders erect as he demonstrated his willingness to suffer in the ministry of bringing people closer to the worship of the God of Glory and His Principles.

In his several pastorates and the many other activities in which he engaged, Milton always enjoyed the loyal support of his precious wife, Marian, and the four children, one of who lives in Liberia. Milton still shares the treasures of his mind and life experiences each week in the New Journal and Guide newspaper and with the Bible class he teaches. God seems to be adding new persons weekly to the class.

It is my hope that this book that has been written for our posterity will inspire, encourage, educate and enrich the lives of many who would dare follow the path carved out by this giant oak of a man.

William Alfred Smith, Esquire

Opening Prayer for Global Fammily Day Breakfast by Mrs. Cross.

Dr. Milton Reid accepts the United Nations Award for the 2006 GFD Breakfast.

INTRODUCTION

"In the year of Divine Reality, I found God."

Our world today is not too dissimilar from the world into which Christ came as Savior and Lord. There exist captivity, wars, sexism, racism, exploitation, hunger, "lock- ins," and "shut-outs," the very rich and the very poor, on which the gospel has had very little effect. With the affirmation of secular humanism as a neutralizer, there is a continual falling away from the "faith that was once delivered unto the saints." God's chosen people have, for the most part, become God's frozen people. To become different from the acceptable forms of religious behavior makes one a misfit, a cultural outcast and a candidate for "Calvary." The witness of the Christian church has, in too many instances, been confined to those areas where we can be appreciated by our culture and our world, rather than to those actions of faith that reveal the Christ of Glory in our lives.

The church that was commissioned by our Lord to 'Go into the entire world and make disciples of men, teaching them to observe all things" just may not be the same church in which we pay homage to Him today. These writings have been in the working for a number of years. They tell the story of my life and are centered on my life's work as a minister of the gospel, a pastor, a civil rights activist, a student of Liberation Theology and my doctoral studies in the School of Theology at Boston University. I do not want to leave this world with unanswered questions about my ministry. I want to set the record straight in that I have had an opportunity to look back over my years and come to terms with what made me who I am. I have had the experience of "Doing Liberation" in the Black church, which I was privileged to serve for more than 59 years. This writing could be of interest to clergy students of theology, pastors, community organizers, and lay persons, who do not have to experience the setbacks that I did while attempting to "Do Liberation Theology." It seems as though I was involved in "Doing Liberation Theology" long before I even knew what it was. I have been committed to doing the work that brings about the necessary changes, not only in my life, but also in the Kingdom of God that I learned from my mentors and Jesus, the Christ of Glory.

In my witness, I have had some success as well as some failures. I see my failures as stepping-stones paving my way to the Glory of God, whom I hope to see one day soon and very soon. I agree with the late Reverend James Cleveland, "Jesus is the best thing that ever happened to me." There is no question that I have concluded that the institutional or the mainstream church, as we know it, has lost its way. The late Dr. Paul Tillich, A German Theologian had long ago reach this conclusion. He said, in essence we have to dismiss Christianity, as we know it. We have been off track so long until the "Old Paths, have become a New Way. Many ministers are in search for a comfortable package that will meet their needs and the needs of their families. The seven churches of Asia Minor, as revealed in Revelation, are an exposition about Jesus, whose Body constitutes the church. I believe that they are directive for us today in a prophetic, urgent, and relevant ministry. Note if you will, that Revelation is the last book in the Bible with a summary of finals, and a new beginning. It tells us that God shall dwell with man without warfare, hurricanes, or natural disaster, for we would have overcome the great tribulations. God shall dwell with humankind and we shall be His people and we shall live in His peace and Love. The God of the West is not the God of the Ages. He is not the same as the God of Abraham, Isaac, and Jacob. The God of the West is at war with the Christ of Glory. We are sometimes in a blasphemous relationship with God because we have created the God of the West in our image and in our likeness. He is a God that permits us to do whatever we want as long as it sustains the economics of our faith and our social well-being. You will discover through a contextual understanding of the Bible, augmented by these pages, that the Christ of Glory is both above and beyond the God of the West and demands that we be too. He is to be our Lord, our Kurios, and Redeemer.

Dr. Reid greeted by Fidel Castro in Cuba.
Received *The Medal of Friendship*.

CHAPTER I

THE GOD OF THE AGES

"In Beginning...God"(The God of gods)

Like Jeremiah, I felt God's anointed Power for my life while still in my mother's womb, as my saintly, committed and caring parents prayed for a boy child. Deeply spiritual both of my parents were steeped in fundamentalist evangelism. Michelle Avella, my youngest daughter who works in the division of Vital Records in the Health Department of the Commonwealth of Virginia, recently told me that my birth certificate was filed 15 years after I was born, and my whole existence on planet earth "was suspect." I was relieved when she told me that my mother Mrs. Mary M. Reid, and my oldest sister, Mrs. Thelma Clemons, signed it. The fact that it stated I was born Sunday January 26, 1930 at 3:00 P.M., made me a little more real. During the months of my formation in the womb, my parents prayed day and night in the bed and beside the bed for a boy child, following the birth of seven girls, my sisters, who had preceded me. They believed in a God who could not fail. They believed that he was Omnipotent, all-powerful, Omnipresent, everywhere at the same time, and Omniscient, all knowing. I grew up believing what my parents and the community of faith believed; that God was from everlasting to everlasting. I believed with the Psalmist, that "The Lord owns the earth and all it contains, the world and all who live in it. For he set its foundation upon the seas, and established it upon the ocean currents" (Psalms 24:1,2, New English Translation). Many of us were nurtured during the days when the King James Version of the Bible of 1611, was the "only viable" translation. It reads this way: "The earth is the Lord's and the fullness thereof; the world, and they that dwell therein. For he hath founded it upon the seas, and established it upon the floods"

(24:1,2, King James Version).

Across the years I have discovered many appellations for God, some of them very descriptive. I found out that El in Hebrew means God. Elshaddai means God Almighty. Elroi means God who sees me. Yahweh means am that I am. Elohim means Creator. Elolam means everlasting God. What human can define the indefinable? The Old Testament scribes, who were led to write the story of Moses' conversation with God on the foothills of Sinai, were right when they had God to answer Moses by saying, "I Am, that I am, or I am AHIAH ASHAR HIGH (that is, THE LIVING GOD); and he said, Thus you shall say to the children of Israel: AHIAH has sent me to you" (Exodus 3:14, Holy Bible Lamsa from Ancient Eastern Manuscripts).

Jesus tells us that "God is Spirit, and the people who worship Him must worship in Spirit and Truth" (John 4:24 NET). My purpose here is not to make any effort to prove God or to define Him in any religious persuasion but to share with you my faith in the "isness" of God and the "nowness" of his presence all over the Universe. While we Christians call him God in English, He is called Dieu, in French. He is called Dio in Italian, and Gott in German. He is called Allah in Arabic, and Alaha in Aramaic. He is called Dois in Spanish and Deus in Portuguese. Jesus as you know did not speak English; he spoke Aramaic, and called God Alaha (Allah) the one and only God. It wasn't long before I accepted the Triune God of Abraham, Isaac and Jacob. And to this day, because I live clothed in my right mind, I know God lives as Jesus reveals Him to us through the Scriptures and the Holy Spirit teaches us through His presence and His pleadings.

As I grew and explored "Aion," this Age of men, this world this existence, this fallen age of man, I get the feeling that somebody "nictitated or blinked." God, or the "Ekklesia," the church, that called out community of faith. The God of the Ages became to the mind of men, the "God of the West." The God of the West has been at war with the God of the Ages. This was long before Constantine the Great came to power during the three-year reign of the first black pope of the Catholic Church whose name was Pope Miltiades. He was the last Pope to be buried in the Cata Combs of Rome. It has been my privilege to visit Rome on three different occasions, and the Cata Combs, and also Paul's Prison cell down stairs in the inner chambers of the Roman Jail. These have always been places of fascination to me along with St. Peters, and the Sistine chapel. When the church "blinked," it began to pull away from the God of the ages. When the church blinked Deism began to evolve in the womb of the world. When the church blinked, humanism and atheism were at war with one another and both of them won, with Atheism crying out I have been cheated, 'there is no God'! Jesus in his prophetic vision saw this coming, and he called on the Church to be faithful. He said, "Remain faithful even to the point of death, and I will give you the crown that is life itself" (Revelation 2:10 NET) and "for where two or three are assembled in my name, I am there among them" (Matthew 18:20 NET). I think he was talking to the traditional church or the cultural church when he said, "Why do you call me Lord, Lord, and don't do what I tell you" (Luke 6:46 NET)?

As I see it, and I am looking through the eyes of the teachings of Jesus, too many of us have been worshipping and witnessing under the banner of the God of the West, who is at war with the Christ of glory. For the most part, the God of the West permits and insists on your giving allegiance to just the opposite of what the God of the Ages and the Christ of Glory would have us to do. Christ calls on us to love one another and many of us haven't come to the place where we can even like one another. The Love He is talking about is a love that will make you lay down your very life if need be for a friend. It is divinely appointed Agape Love. He tells us that we must forgive one another so that God can forgive us. We may be living in times of Eros, self-serving love, or Phileo (Philanthropia) or brotherly love, but Agape, an uncaused love, a love of divine action; being what God is, is a love that is difficult to be seen in these our "last days." I hear in Sunday school classes, "I can forgive, but I cannot forget." Jesus said, "For if you forgive others their sins, your heavenly Father will also forgive you. But if you do not forgive others, your Father will not forgive you your sin" (Matthew 6:14,15 NET). Or we hear words like "I will get even if it is the last thing I do." That doesn't sound like the Christ of Glory to me. The God of the Ages has said, "Do not avenge yourselves dear friends, but give place to God's wrath, for it is written, 'Vengeance is mine,'

I will repay" says the Lord. "Rather if your enemy is hungry, feed him; if he is thirsty, give him a drink for in doing this you will be heaping burning coals on his head. Do not be overcome by evil, but overcome evil with good" (Romans 12:19-21 NET). From the Old Testament we find these words. "Vengeance and recompense belong to me, at the time their foot will slip; for the day of their disaster is near, and the events to come are rushing on them" (Deuteronomy 32:35 NET).

Ceilings of Faith

The God of the West permits us, and yes, encourages us to define God in acceptable theological and philosophical terms that will not disturb the status quo of society, and that doesn't hurt the economy. For the most part our faith is in each other rather then in God, and we are still rising and falling in the "Charis," of God, or in the Grace of God. Our faith hits the ceiling of cultural consent and we tend to stay within those bounds. Abraham "suspended the ethical for the teleological," (he failed to do what was expected of him by his peers, and that was to slay his son out of loyalty to the gods of his day). He Obeyed God! Abraham was obeying God when he was offering Isaac up to be sacrificed. "Sometime after these things God tested Abraham. He said, "Abraham! Take your son – your only son, whom you love, Isaac- and go to the land of Moriah! Offer him up there as a burnt offering on one of the mountains which I will indicate to you"(Genesis 22:1,2 NET). Note the writer says, "After these things, God tested Abraham." How has the God of Abraham, Isaac and Jacob tested us? Was American slavery a test for Christians in the West? If so we failed the test. When God blessed the founding fathers of this nation with the insight and skills to develop a constitution and a Bill of Rights, while many of them were slaveholders, was that a test for the young nation? If it were, it was a test we failed. Chattel slavery in America was the most barbaric form of captivity known to man. It was upheld by both Church and State, as manifested by the Catholic Church, when under its ceiling of faith, it rendered its decision that said 'blacks did not have souls," which made them inhuman. The church in the West then rendered man to an ontological rejection. The Church seemed to have forgotten the great invitation extended by the

Christ of Glory who said, "Come unto me, all you who are weary and burdened, and I will give you rest" (Matthew 11:28 NET). The state accepted this non-being status on the personhood of black men and women in an infamous Supreme Court Decision in the Dred Scott Case of 1857 that denied Black persons full personhood and diminished them to 3/5's of a person. It also stated that a "black man had no rights that a white man is bound to respect." Many whites live today in the arrogance of racial stupidity and ignorance, as if to carry out the original definition in our constitution that made African Americans 3/5 of a person for voting purposes only.

When I speak of ceilings of faith I am talking about a limited faith that soars to the height of doubt, to the past findings of traditions, and won't allow you to go any further in your thinking or in your actions. When I came into the world I found the "faith of my father" and others like him, struggling under the ceiling of social injustice, particularly his peers who were opting for what we came to know as "other worldly theology." This is what the white masters taught us and many churches are still operating under that level of Christian commitment, which isn't Christian at all. We are being religious, but we are not being Christian. It didn't bother me when I was young, but it disturbs me to no end, to hear elderly saints say "Leave it in the hands of God, and God will fix it after while. The word hasn't gotten out that God gave us the challenge to do some fixing, but we are still waiting on Him! We were taught, "slaves, (some translations say servants) be obedient to them that are your masters according to the flesh, with fear and trembling in singleness of your heart, as unto Christ" (Ephesians 5:5 KJV). Modern-day translators tried to equate American Slavery with slavery in the Bible in the day of Paul. This is the kind of religious mentality that cluttered the mind of some of the translators of the writers of the Bible and the early church that affirms the thought that we are serving the God of the West, and not the God of the Ages, the Eternal Living God. We switched our God somewhere along the way and we at the same time nullified the Christ of Glory, because long ago, the church blinked in its teaching, its preaching and in its practice.

How could you otherwise explain the Reverend Pat Robertson who turned in his ordination papers as an ordained minister in apostolic succession by the laying on of hands, called of God, to run for the presidency of the United States? How do you explain his call for the assassination of President Hugo Chavez of Venezuela? Didn't Christ give his life for the entire world of fallen men? Again Robertson said that God was punishing Israel's leader, Ariel Sharon, who suffered a medical calamity, for giving back land to Palestinians that had been taken from them by Israel. There have been calls for the White House to condemn Robertson. How can President Bush condemn Robertson, when he has called for the arrest of Osama Bin Laden, "dead or alive?" To date, there has been no conclusive evidence that Osama Bin Laden was involved in the 9/11 tragedies. For the sake of common consent, let's say that he was involved. "Is there anyone so vicious, cruel, wicked, and wretched that Christ's love cannot redeem?" This is the same kind of religious mentality that supports the death penalty that supports racism; that supported slavery before Christ and during the 2,100-year witness of the church since Calvary. There is absolutely no identification with redemption in Christ because its faith only goes to the ceiling of humanistic thinking or cultural acceptance. Jesus said in his Sermon on the Mount, "For I tell you, unless your righteousness goes beyond that of the experts of the law and the Pharisees, you will never enter the kingdom of heaven" (Matthew 5:20 NET).

We need to be careful how we pronounce judgment on those who don't see Jesus as we do. God of the Ages is bigger than to be seen only through the eyes of the "religious right." He is bigger than the Republican or Democratic Party, but the God of the West is not. The God of the West is a God that was created in the "image and likeness of man." Mark tells the story of some disciples who were disturbed about a "way-out group" that was casting out demons, but were not with them. John said to him, "Teacher, we saw someone casting out demons in your name, and we tried to stop him because he was not following us." But Jesus said, "do not stop him, because no one who does a miracle in my name will be able soon afterward to say anything bad about me. For whoever is not against us is for us. For I tell you the truth, whoever gives you a cup of water because you hear Christ's name will never lose his reward" (Mark 9:38-41 NET). There is not a word of contradiction whenever Jesus speaks of Himself. He is the King of Kings and the Lord of Lords and that makes Him the Christ of Glory. Look at Jesus through the eyes of the Apostle John, who lay on his breast during the last Supper. "I am the good shepherd. The good shepherd lays down his life for the sheep. The hired hand that is not a shepherd and does not own sheep sees the wolf coming and abandons the sheep and runs away. So the wolf attacks the sheep and scatters them. Because he is a hired hand and is not concerned about the sheep, he runs away. I am the good shepherd. I know my own and my own know me-just as the Father knows me and I know the sheep. I have other sheep that do not come from this sheepfold. I must bring them too, and they will listen to my voice, so that there will be one flock and one shepherd" (John 10:11-16 NET).

Getting to Know God

I had been going to church ever since I could remember, and my mother tells me that as a child I insisted on wearing a white shirt and a necktie. I was attending Sunday school and church twice a month at the Little Zion Baptist Church in Chesapeake, Virginia. I was there when my father was ordained a deacon. I was there when he was licensed to preach in 1944, and when he was ordained in 1948. I accepted Christ at Little Zion and was baptized in a creek, a tributary of the Southern Branch of the Elizabeth River. I knew my father's God, and my mother's God. But it wasn't until I was seven years of age that I went in quest for the God of the Ages. I knew something was wrong with the social conditions under which we were living. I recall a white boy spitting in my face while passing us by as he rode to school and we walked. I brought the situation to the attention of my father who didn't give me a satisfactory answer. I later found out that Black people had to pay a poll tax and take a test as a condition of registering to vote. I questioned my father about voting and discovered that he had never paid the poll tax, had not registered and had not voted. He was trusting in the Lord to make things right and he had been waiting on the Lord. My father was more compliant and less assertive than I ever dreamed of being.

I got to know God through that experience. My father did register and pay the poll tax, and became a voting citizen. It would be nine years later when the first School bus for "colored" children was put on our route, and I was the driver. I didn't hold that job too long because I got fired for speeding and there were no children on the bus when a white man came up to me at a stop that I was to pick up students. He talked to me as if I was a piece of dirt, and I found out that I wasn't as saved as I thought I was. There was no one around to stop me so I just let him have it from my unbridled tongue. I don't know what I didn't say to that white man, and I thank God now for my memory loss, and his Grace to forgive me. When I got back to school, the principal, the Reverend F.D. Nance, called me into his office, and told me what I had done. I assured him that the bus had a governor on it, and it was locked in at 35 miles per hour. I encouraged him to drive it or have someone to drive and see. He took me up on it. They drove that bus for more than an hour, and they could not get more than 35 mph out of it.

When he made his report to that white man who had called him, he was told that if they didn't fire me, he the principal and those who took the bus on the road test would be fired. And who was this White man? He was the superintendent of schools in Norfolk County. I had discovered a way of bypassing the governor with a twist of my foot on the gas pedal. No one knew that trick except me. Poor me. While in Providence High School, that no longer exists, I was a pretty fair student. I was also a schemer. Miss Alma Ruffin, my English teacher, called on me to read a report that she had given as a homework assignment. I had forgotten to do the report. She called on several students who responded by reading their reports. When she came to me, I got up and read and read, and then I read some more. I had the attention of everybody – even the teacher. I read so much until she suspected my report. She said when I finally finished let me see your report. To the surprise of the class, I was reading from a blank sheet of paper. I am not sure now if this was before or after I was fired from the school bus. She could have expelled me, but she didn't, so I escaped being fired from class or from school. The bus incident was the first of my firings, and the only firing of which I was guilty; so don't look for any other confessions.

That spit-in-the-face incident ignited my career in civil rights. It was to last me until I met Dr. Martin Luther King, Jr., during the Montgomery bus boycott. I just did not "like" white folk. I did not see any scriptural reference any where in the Bible where God had directed me to "like" anybody. The Bible teaches that we must go beyond liking to loving. When I saw how Negroes were being treated in Alabama, and there was the young Dr. Martin Luther King, Jr., talking about non-violent love, I was drawn to him. I was interested in finding a way to "love my enemies" as I had read many times in the Bible. I didn't get my temperament from my father or my mother. They tried to like and to love everybody, for in a sense, white folk could do no wrong. They believed in them. But I found out early that some white folk could and did lie and cheat for economic gain and for anything else they wanted. My mother and my second oldest sister, who became Martha Smith, were visiting a white family across some fields and up the lane from our house. My mother called me and sent me to the store to get her a can of Tube Rose snuff. My playmate, Wallace Greene, and I went to the store. The white lady sent her daughter to the store also. We all had to walk a little over a mile to get to the store at Butts Station. Wallace and I were walking together. At no time did we get within fifty feet of this little white girl. When I got the snuff and brought it back to my mother, she thanked me. The white lady asked us where was her daughter. We didn't know. When the daughter showed up, she started crying. She told her mother that I had taken her money. My mother immediately believed her, although I had never taken anything from anybody in my life. My mother and my sister were determined to punish me to the satisfaction of our white neighbor and her daughter. They got a switch and whipped me across two fields and up the lane to our house and ordered me to "shut up" every time I would scream in unjustified pain. For a long time I was bitter toward white people. When I met Dr. King with his message of redemptive love, i.e., that unearned suffering is redemptive, that was the first relief from my burden of bitterness that I had received.

I did not really get to know God through the revival experience, nor through a traditional church worship experience, but through love actions of the civil-rights movement. In 1959, after I had been preaching for a few years, by Dr. Martin Luther King, Jr., asked me to work with him on the National Board of Directors of the Southern Christian Leadership Conference. I was the pastor of the

First Baptist Church of Petersburg, Virginia, which was located near the largest battlefield of the Civil War. That is where my real development took root in civil rights. In 1960, I organized the Virginia State Unit of the Southern Christian Leadership Conference. We helped to bring into being small groups from around the state that formed units of SCLC. We demonstrated in Petersburg, where I first went to jail for civil disobedience. This is when I really got to know Dr. Wyatt Tee Walker, a fellow pastor of the Gilfield Baptist Church who would become the first executive Secretary of the Southern Christian Leadership Conference. I also got to know the late Dr. R.G. Williams, who was pastor of the Zion Baptist Church on Byrne Street in Petersburg, who was also active in the civil rights movement along with Wyatt and me. R.G. was a good friend, a compassionate pastor, and a compulsive prankster. He played more tricks on Wyatt Tee Walker and myself than one can image, just for the fun of it. Marian declares I came to Petersburg a virgin saint, but after meeting R.G. and Wyatt Tee, she had to pray for my soul. Although the times have changed, I told her a few days ago to keep on praying, just incase I haven't been totally forgiven. Dr. Fred Boddie Senior, who was the pastor of the Tabernacle Baptist Church was also a dear friend in Petersburg, and was a strong supporter of the civil-rights movement. Just before he passed, he called me beside his bed and requested that I would deliver his Eulogy. He gave me the text and the subject. He also told me to look out for Fred Jr., his son who was young in the ministry. I said, Dr. Boddie that is a tall order…I would rather deliver the eulogy, with Fred Junior standing right there. I'll never forget his final words to me. When I told him I was leaving and would come back the next day, Dr. Fred Boddie Senior said, "Milton, come early!" I said Dr. Boddie, I have to come from Norfolk, and I will come early. He said, "Come, early." I did come early, but not early enough. When I arrived at the hospital, that I had demanded that they admit Black patients on an equal basis as other people, Dr. Boddie expired as I was coming to his room. I have made it a point, to get to wherever I was going from that day forward, I would arrive before time even if I had to wait until the doors were opened.

On four occasions I was jailed in Danville, Virginia, after being sent there by Dr. Martin Luther King, Jr. I was jailed in Edenton,

North Carolina, Albany Georgia, along with Dr. Martin Luther King, Jr. In Norfolk Virginia, I was jailed twice because I failed to do what the judge of the Circuit Court ordered me to do and that was to turn over the membership list of the church to the court, and the Church had asked me not to, at my recommendation. (This was interfering in the affairs of a local congregation, and the First Amendment protected us). By this time, I had earned an A.B degree in history in 1955, and a Master of Divinity degree in 1958 in theology, both from Virginia Union University, and a Doctor of Ministry degree from the School of Theology at Boston University in Liberation Theology in 1980.

While at Boston University, I was pastor of New Calvary Baptist Church of Norfolk, Virginia. I was the owner and publisher of the Journal & Guide Newspaper and the CEO of Lassister's Septic Tank Company. The late Mr. Raymond Lassister was Chairman of the Trustees at New Calvary and had befriended me. He made good money and was a lot of fun. We traveled for several years in January, to Puerto Rico, and the Virgin Islands. He was always laughing and joking and was married to Henrietta, who was the president of the Pastor's Aid Club. Now she was a "great president." Whenever her husband Raymond saw a pretty girl, the quintessence of beauty and the epitome of femininity, he would say, "My Lamb, Nicodemus, desired to know." Because of my heavy load, The School of Theology at Boston University did not accept me as a full student. They knew I was going to flunk. One thing about white folk, they don't like to fail in anything they do. I had been accepted as a "conditional student." About two subjects and a "paper" from completing my studies, I questioned the fact that I was about to graduate and had not been accepted as a full student. When they checked over my grades and determined that I had made a high "B" average, they sought to make it up to me by doing two things. They offered me full scholarship to attend any university in the world, to work on a Ph.D degree. The only catch to this was I had to enter the University that year. Here it is about two months from graduation and I had not even thought about continuing my education and had not applied to any university. The second thing they offered to do was to present me my Doctorate of Ministry degree during a worship service at New Calvary one

Sunday Morning. That went over pretty big. Presidents from every university around Tidewater were invited, and most of them came in their academic regalia. Dr. Norman Thomas, a professor at Boston University and head of the D.Min program of which I was a student, delivered the message. I was the first of all of the students that had entered the program in 1978 to graduate. In all of this my lovely wife Marian the Marvelous, and my children stood with me and stood by me. I am still grateful for the support of the churches that made my ministry and my education possible. Yet there was more to come.

The God of the Ages has been my witness all of my life through the Christ of Glory and His Amazing Grace. As these pages unfold, you will find my testimony "to be;" while the devil had a hold on me for a while, the ideology of Willie Lynch never did, and never will." Bishop A. J. Jones, who became my third mentor in life, came to me as the embodiment of the Holy Spirit, when he keep telling me about the "Mind of God." As I pondered this thought, I knew that it was never in the mind of God that men would be separated by race, class, or faith, in that we are all "children of Abraham," the Father of the faithful. Bishop Jones befriended me during a very critical period in my life. He was a real friend that had gone through what I was going through in my response to the calling of God. When he thought I was a little down, he would come to me or call me and pray with me. When I was in jail, he came to visit me and to pray with me. He taught me how to raise money for the church, and how to keep myself pure. I thank God for the late Bishop A. J. Jones who has preceded me on the journey home. He had been jailed and locked out of his pulpit for taking a stand for the God of the Ages and the Christ of Glory. That however did not stop him. He had a beautiful shout that didn't last long enough for me to catch on. Now I was a dancer in my day, but I never could do the Holy Dance, or whoop. I tried both of them and neither of them worked for me. The Bishop's life rekindled the fire of the Holy Spirit in him, and he passed some of that mantle on to me. I am also grateful to his widow, Bishop Loretta Jones, who carried on as pastor until her health failed. None of us came to planet earth to stay always, I hope to continue and join that number made Holy be the indwelling of the Spirit of God that sanctified us or set us apart for his divine purpose. My brothers and my sisters, I hope to see you in the glory of God's everlasting presence when this life is over. The late Brother Joe Mays used to sing, "I'm too close...to heaven."

VA Governor John Dalton assists Dr. Reid with Communion-New Cavalry.

CHAPTER II

The Historical Black Church in Exile

(This Chapter now revised. Was submitted in partial fulfillment of my doctorial paper in the School of Theology at Boston University 1980)

In its most popular usage, "exile" refers to the act of being banished or turned away. Usually one relates this meaning to the political arena where it has become commonplace to read of a dissenter of a particular system being banished or exiled to a foreign country or an isolated area. Probably the best-known Biblical use of the word exile can be found in the story of the captivity of the Israelites in a strange land. To the Black man and the Black church the word exile has an even deeper and more exacting meaning. The Black church has been and continues to be in exile because it has throughout its history been a dissenter from the doctrines of the white man and his religion. I am not sure that I have ever heard a white Southern Baptist minister preach without in some way opening the door of the church so that individuals might go to Heaven when they die, as if that is man's only call to being. We are called on to be witness for Jesus and His love in this world. Further, the word exile takes on a different meaning for the black church in that its banishment has been within and not outside of its homeland in America.

This chapter traces the Black church's struggle in exile through important historical and political events that have affected its development. Attention will be given to the Black church in slavery and birth of the independent Black church in exile. Included will be examples of the Black church doing liberation theology during critical periods in its history. Interwoven into the fabric of this chapter will be examples of Black personalities who, throughout the history of the Black church, have had a decisive influence on its direction. The Black church has been the center and the soul of Black people in their common struggle for freedom and justice for all of the years that this nation has existed. The religious life of Black people has been one of the overwhelming factors in their survival. The Black church today is for the most part in exile in a land where Black people have been held hostage by the compelling forces of psychological disorientation and inverted racism. This exile did not just begin yesterday; it can be traced back to the Black man's beginnings in America. This exile state was as real to the slaves during the demoralizing period of slavery as it is to the Black man in America today. A retrospective account will serve to explain this contention. The Black religious experience and, subsequently, the Black church were created in the context of the human struggle against slavery and oppression. The Black church was the result of the Black man's struggle to affirm his humanity despite the dehumanizing conditions of slavery and oppression. Therefore, in order to understand the dynamic movement of the Black church in bondage or in exile in its own land, we must keep in mind the social and political existence from which Black theological reflections emerged.

Black religion in America can be considered a product of slavery and, as such, had its origin with the people of African descent who were brought to this land against their will. None came here with a passport from our native Africa. To recount Black history in detail is not necessary for the purpose of my story. However, it is important to take a brief look at its characteristics as they relate to the Black church in exile. Disagreements exist as to the exact origin of slavery in America; however, the fact is clear that 20 Africans were sold in Jamestown, Virginia, in 1619, as indentured servants. Further history records that at around 1700, this indentured status had changed to slavery for the Black man and his family. Out of this condition of servitude grew the traumatic and devastating experiences that were designed by the White man to convince Blacks that they were non-humans. The forms of brutality and atrocity that were inflicted upon the slaves were used to show them that they were not human beings in the eyes of their masters. Out of this demoralizing cultural and historical situation, the slaves used their religion to try to cope with their situation as well as to oppose it. Because of the nature of the slave system, the slaves were forced to acquire new and less visible expressions in order to survive. We find some carryover of that today. I have been in enough struggles to know that there are some folk who would advise you to be quiet and let the Lord fix it for you. This less visible experience emerged as the Black church in its earliest form of exile. From its beginning America was a nation built upon two concepts that were in direct conflict. On one hand, America professed to be a nation built upon liberty and dedicated to the proposition that "all men are created equal." On the other hand, America's practice was legally defined in a constitution that recognized lawfully sanctioned and protected inequality and the total denial of liberty for Black American, who provided the economic prosperity through slave labor. The dawning of the Civil War found that the slave master had invaded the slave community with his brand of "white" Christianity. The feeling was then, and in some cases now, "If it's white, it's got to be right." This infiltration of White Christianity meant that the slaves could openly vent their religious feelings. However, this outward appearance of slave religion was a duplicate of the white master's religion and did not represent the essence of Black religion. The true essence of Black religion existed in the invisible exiled Black church of that period. Even though the slaves were allowed to worship, with certain limitations, in the churches of the masters, their desire was to survive and maintain their humanity. The slaves had a special encounter with God in the midst of the historical reality of slavery. This encounter allowed them to transform the White man's Christianity and reinterpret the scriptures in light of the Black experience. This encounter formed the foundation for the expression of the Black experiences though the Black theological perspective and of the Black church during it's founding and during the pre-Civil War period. The Black church was founded on the belief that God condemned slavery and that Christian freedom meant total emancipation.

Through the lives of men such as Richard Allen, Nathaniel Paul and Henry Highland Garnet, one can trace the early efforts of the Black church in doing liberation theology. These men were deeply committed to the principle that liberation, as the fight for justice in the world, was an important part of the Black church's mission.

There could be no separation between Black religious experience and the day-to-day struggle for freedom, justice and equality. Garnet, in an address to slaves, represented the spirit of the Black church in exile when he identified obedience to God with the struggle against slavery:

> *"Your condition does not absolve you from your moral obligation. The diabolical injustice by which your liberties are cloven down, neither God, nor angels, or just men command you to suffer a single moment, therefore it is your solemn and imperative duty to use every means, both moral, intellectual and physical that that promises success."*

This same identification of divine justice with civil rights and liberation can be found in the central theme of the civil rights struggle of the 60's. To justify his fight against injustice, Dr. Martin Luther King, Jr., referred not only to the Exodus and Jesus Christ, but also to the Prophets of the Old Testament. Quoting Amos, he states: "Away with the noise of your song! I will not listen to the music of your harps. But let Justice roll on like a river, righteousness like a never failing stream" (Amos 5:24 NIV).

The Black church's quest for liberation can be chronicled in the work and struggles of Richard Allen. Allen was an aggressive man of unquestioned integrity, whose behavior was deeply rooted in the gospel. He saw Black faith as inseparably bound with the historical struggle for freedom. Allen's experiences with the God of the oppressed gave him a new level of consciousness of his identity. Because of this he could not reconcile his personhood and status with the institution of slavery. He quickly saw the inconsistency between the white man's proclamation of religion and his practices when he and other Blacks were relegated to the gallery of the White church. Unable to live with these blatant contradictions, Allen, along with other Blacks, walked out of the White church after being pulled from their knees praying on the main sanctuary floor. This bold action on the part of Allen and his followers gave birth to the independent Black African Methodist Episcopal Church. The establishment of the AME Church contributed significantly to the development of self-determination, independence and self-respect among Blacks. The naming of the new church, Mother Bethel, was in itself a significant step toward liberation. The name was derived from two Hebrew words, "Beth' and "El," meaning "House of God." Allen chose this name to denote that it was the "first" church of God, thus negating the whole concept of the White church. Allen had taken a brave stand against White religion and the doctrines of the White church. It was he who helped Black slaves to understand that there should be no dichotomy between spiritual and physical liberation; rather liberation of the whole man was to be the focus of Black religious life.

Crucial to the development of the Black church were the work and thoughts of Nathaniel Paul. Having witnessed and experienced the atrocities and degrading misery resulting from the slave system, Paul began to raise fundamental questions about evil in the context of the gospel. In so doing, he exposed his theological suspicions that there could be no reconciliation of human suffering, bondage and injustice with the goodness and mercy of a just God. This recognition of the significance of the problem and the interim turmoil that resulted is evident in Paul's demand of an accounting from God:

> *"Tell me ye mighty waters, why did ye sustain the ponderous load of misery? Or seek, ye winds and say why it was that ye executed your office to waft them onward to the still more dismal state; and ye proud waves, why did you refuse to lend your aid and to have overwhelmed them with our billows."*

Paul finds his answer in his confidence that the God of the oppressed would indeed vindicate the suffering of the enslaved. He reflects this confidence thusly:

> *"But then there came in my mind those solemn words: 'With God one day is as a thousand years and a thousand years as one day. Trust in Him and He will bring slavery and all its outrageous atrocities to an end.' These words from the spirit world acted on my troubled soul like water on a living fire, and my aching heart was soothed and relieved, from the burden of woes." African American Struggling in Faith.*

Like many men of the period who saw liberation as the focal point of their existence, Paul's dissatisfaction with his lot in life was grounded in reality; it grew out of the social realities in which he found himself. If we can accept Segundo's definition that the hermeneutic principle involves the continuing change in our interpretation of the Bible dictated by the reality of our day-to-day situation, then we can easily see the hermeneutic principal in operation in the work of Allen, Garnet, and Paul. All three men began at the point of their experiences. Significant to this experience was the reality of slavery as a demeaning and demoralizing evil thrust upon the Black man. These men were able to raise questions about this evil in the context of the Christian faith. As Dr. James Cone would say, "they were aware of the gaps that existed between the white man's proclamation and his practice of the Christian faith. They were aware of the gaps that existed between the white man's proclamation and his practice of justice and equality." This awareness and his theological perceptions that were the results of his conversion to a belief in a "God of the Oppressed," led to the writing of his book of the same name. Out of this application came a new way of experiencing the realities that had been the source of their suspicions. Each man used his new experiences to interpret the scripture in such a way as to culminate in thoughts and actions that dealt not only with spiritual liberation, but physical liberation from slavery as well. The refusal of Blacks to accept slavery as their lot in life, the refusal to accept the racist White church as being consistent with the gospel of Jesus Christ, and the establishment of the African Methodist Church, were all manifestations of the hermeneutic principle in operation. The post-Civil War period can be considered as a time of stagnation for the Black church doing liberation theology. The Emancipation Proclamation, in its real light, was a hoax for Black Americans. Black people were given the understanding that slavery had come to an end and that they could participate in American society as human beings and not as pieces of property.

Little did many Blacks realize that the Emancipation Proclamation did not free all of the slaves, but it was directed toward those states and counties that had seceded from the Union. The majority of Blacks were to find themselves victims of a new form of slavery created by the same racist people who had kept them in bondage for over 200 years. The promise of forty acres of land and a mule were just promises and never became realities. Following the Civil War Blacks owned more than 15 million acres of land in America. But even as early as 1910, the figure was down to less than 3 million acres, and today it is even less. I was flabbergasted to find out that Ted Turner, a multi-billionaire who built perhaps the largest cable network in the world, was trying to grasp 68 acres of land on St. Helena Island, South Carolina, that belonged to the Gullah people. According to the Atlanta Journal-Constitution he already owns 1.7 million acres of land. He owns more land now than some nations. He owns 15 ranches in six western and mid-western states. According to "Worth" magazine, Ted Turner is the nation's largest private landowner; with his holdings and his ability to buy influence (not that he would dare do it. A-hem). If the past is any judge of history the 68 acres are already his. If Black people can lose millions of acres without a court fight, what do you conclude are the chances of the Gullah people against this giant? God told the children of Israel, "When you enter the land, possess it." I don't know what Ted Turner gave to the Martin Luther King, Jr., Center for Social Change, but I was there, as a former member of the board of directors, when Ted Turner was given the Martin Luther King, Jr. Award some years ago. I am happy to report that he withdrew his offer to gain the land owned by the Gullah people. Following the Emancipation Proclamation many Blacks found themselves free to do nothing because they had nothing. Many found themselves returning to the plantations from which they had so long wanted to escape. Accounts are given of instances where slave masters held back their slaves by force. Armed Whites hunted down wandering Blacks to either kill or capture them. The Emancipation Proclamation had brought a different level of freedom than the Black man had not expected. It brought freedom to the White man to declare open season on all Blacks. To kill a Black man was not murder, to rape a Black woman was not deemed a crime, and to take property away from Blacks was not considered robbery.

The Emancipation Proclamation had broken the back of the liberation movement that had developed in the exiled Black church. During this period the influence of the Black church waned. Evidence shows that the Black church was slowly reverting to the safety of the doctrines of the White church. Noted among those who spoke out was Henry McNeal Turner who never ceased to proclaim God's triumph over the evils of injustice. As a politician McNeal spoke out against the refusal of the Georgia legislature to permit the seating of Black representatives:

> *"I hold that I am a member of the body. Therefore, Sir, I shall neither fawn nor cringe before any party, nor stoop to beg them for any rights. I am here to demand my rights and to hurl thunderbolts at the men who dare to cross the threshold of my manhood...You may expel us, Gentlemen, by your votes today; but while you do it, remember there is a just God in heaven, whose all seeing eyes beholds alike the acts of the oppressor and the oppressed, and who despite the machination of the wicked, never fail to indicate the cause of justice and the sanctity of His own handiwork."*

The unfortunate halt of the Black church's liberated approach during this period after the Civil War gave the White man another opportunity to exhibit his ever-present feelings of superiority. The rise of such organizations as the Ku Klux Klan was evidence that slavery had not been abolished. Slavery reared its ugly head through such organizations that legitimized the continued dehumanization of the Black man.

The plight of the Black man during the post-Civil War period would be more affected by personalities from the secular world than from the Black church. Men such as W.E.B. Dubois, Booker T. Washington and Frederick Douglas were at the fountainhead of the struggle against injustice, while the black church relegated itself to a position of comfort. This period saw the continuing growth of the Black press as an advocate of freedom and justice and its impact on the liberation struggle. Unfortunately for the Black church, the Allen's, the Paul's and the Turners were not to be found. It was not until the civil rights movement of the 50's and the 60's that a true leader of the caliber of these men emerged.

Dr. Martin Luther King, Jr.'s entrance on the scene gave back to the Black church its place of eminence in the struggle for liberation. In King's opinion, as had been the opinion of Allen and others, there was a diametric opposition to the practice of segregation and injustice in the proclamation of Christianity. Dr. King made application of the hermeneutic principle by starting with reality. The reality was that segregation and injustice still permeated the land. His suspicion was that there existed a gap between proclamation and what confirmed practice he daily saw the White man do to Blacks. King set out to interpret the scriptures in light of his new theological reflection and proceeded to implement these reflections through methods designed to bring about the liberation of Black people from social, political, economic and religious bondage.

The brief discussion presented here could in no way encompass all of the factors or personalities that have influenced the Black church and its conditions of exile. However, one cannot get away from this discussion without facing the fact that even today the Black church remains in exile. Until the Black church is willing to accept the premise that its mission is both spiritual and physical liberation, it will remain in exile. Dr. James Cone states it this way:

> *"Sometimes because of the very nature of oppressed existence, the oppressed must define their being by negating everything the oppressor affirms, including belief in God. Black liberation as a movement began with the pre-Civil War black churches who recognized that Christian freedom grounded in Jesus Christ was inseparable from civil freedom."*

What makes the plight of the Black church and Black people so disheartening today is that we exist in large measure as if we are really in "the land of the free and the home of the brave." As we begin these early days of the new millennium, Black people are in worse condition now than we were prior to the historic Supreme Court decision of May 17, 1954. What we don't realize is that we are scattered in America and have accepted the idolatrous gods of the land formed by White people as the true and living God, who is in fact the God of the West. We tend to be color-blind in a racial bondage where color and capitalism are the primary conditions of our servitude.

The ethnic makeup of this country is diverse. It has developed to the point that it could be divided into white, black, brown, yellow, and red. I am sure there are other ethnic distinctions, but for reason of this discussion, these will do. This is a very human dilemma that former President Ronald Reagan called colorblindness. Every now and then, somebody expresses his or her brand of the truth (that misses the mark) and lays claim to colorblindness. I thank God for sight and the ability to see. The only way that I can imagine one being colorblind is to be blind. Even if you don't act on the basis of color, if you have sight, you will have to see color first, if there is color. Other minorities have grown at such a rapid rate until Blacks or African-Americans, are no longer the majority, according to the last census. While none of the other minorities came to this country on slave ships, the Native Americans were indigenous to this land that was stolen from them. They were forced to live on reservations, without "reservations." We don't read too much about this in our American history books. And, as many have said before me, if we don't tell our own story, our story will not be told. The sad thing about this entire matter is that so many Black churches that lost their zeal and their fire following the Emancipation Proclamation have copied their history through the blue eyes of their brothers of a different hue. They have bought into his kind of worship and have identified with his god, the God of the West and not the God of our Fathers. While we can boast of our new churches, with paid-off mortgages, we have formed more choirs and have more Cadillac's and Hammond organs than any other minority or majority group in the world. African Americans could really put Ford and General Motors out of business if we stopped buying Lincolns and Cadillacs. I am just as guilty about this as anyone else in America. We are not waiting any longer for our funeral to ride in a Cadillac or a Lincoln. It would be suicidal to lead a movement to get the Black preacher or church out of the luxury car movement. I think we ought to practice riding well and living well on earth. We want His will to be done on earth as it is in Heaven, don't we? However, we should never forget that our purpose is to proclaim a Christ who has power to save and to liberate and to celebrate. We have not been trained to accept captivity and proclaim a gospel compatible with pacification rather than one that deals with the revelation of liberation.

In all the years and generations of our exiled conditions, God has not been without a witness to make known our bondage and our captivity. History records the indelible contributions of men and women like Frederick Douglas, David Walker, W.E.B. Dubois,

Marcus Garvey, Richard Allen, Benjamin Quarles, E. Franklin Frazier, the Honorable Justice Thurgood Marshall, Congressman Adam Clayton Powell, Jr., Malcolm X, Carter G Woodson, Sojourner Truth, Harriet Tubman, Mary McLeod Bethune, the Honorable Louis Farrakhan, and Dr. Martin Luther King, Jr., who are among the stars that shine in our Black night of affliction. There are perhaps a zillion stars like these that are shining brightly in the universe of our midnight. Both faceless and nameless, they have testified to the world and have made invaluable witnesses of God's redeeming Love while in Black bondage. It is as if the writer of the book of Hebrews could well have been speaking of our exiled conditions and those who gave their lives in the struggle for liberation and justice when he wrote:

> *"These all died in faith, not having received what was promised, but having seen it and greeted it from afar, And having acknowledged that they were strangers and exiles on the earth. For people who speak thus make it clear that they are seeking a homeland" (Hebrews 11:13-14 RSV).*

The people of God have always been in captivity by the world. Yet God lifts up the life of the church in the hearts of those committed to doing His will and purpose. While in exile, we should get to know how we got here, and what we must do while here, for we are on our way out of this hell. I am most uncomfortable when I realize that a large portion of the Black church has become like the church in Laodicea, "neither hot nor cold." So because you are lukewarm and neither cold nor hot, I am going to vomit you out of my mouth!" (Revelation 3:16 NET). Something has happened to our zeal and our fire when it comes to the social imperatives of the gospel. Nowhere in the scripture did Jesus separate worship from healing. He was the embodiment of a holistic ministry. Jesus would be just as concerned today about HIV infections as he was about leprosy yesterday. He is just as concerned about prostate cancer as he was about inflammation, pneumonic and bubonic plagues of yesterday. The sad thing about this is that we don't see Black men in large numbers who are willing to get themselves checked out for maddening terminal illnesses. In too many instances we are still making psychological and physiological adjustments to our bondage. Some of us believe that the Lord is going to come down again and deliver us.

We went through a period following the signing of the Voting Rights Bill of 1965 when we were trying to get Blacks elected to public office from school board elections to president of the United States. In the beginning of the millennium we are now in search for the "right" black to get elected because we discovered that our struggle is not just between Black and White, but it is also between wrong and right. When a Black mayor believes that it is all right and just to pay homage to our captors of yesterday in the same way we tend to honor our liberators of today, we have a problem. The Black church finds itself conducting silent meditation at the very time it has been called "to cry loud and spare not, in telling Judah about her sins." While running for the presidency the second time, Jesse Jackson, in speaking about presidential candidates, said, "we don't just need to change pilots; we need to change directions."

Yet there is hope. With strong support from the Black church, the City of Richmond, Virginia, elected a Black majority on its city council as well as a black mayor, and witnessed the ascendancy of a chief of police, city treasurer, superintendent of schools, and chairman of the school board. The city of Petersburg, Virginia, some 25 miles south of Richmond, did about the same thing, but it only happened with strong support from the Black church. Following the March on Washington in August 1963, the Black church seems to have awakened, and in 1965, following the Voting Rights Bill, it looked like the church would never retreat although many in the Black church never woke up. We found out that you could not elect a political leader and then neglect him or her. We found out that just as we had been sold by our Black brothers and sisters on the West coast of Africa, some brothers or sisters will sell you out today in a hot minute, and then go to jail proclaiming his or her righteousness. Our social, and political situation today calls for cohesion like we have never known before. It demands redeeming love, commitment, support, and what is the best for the community of faith. This will require Bible study, prayer, town hall meetings, and the guidance of the Holy Spirit and not just leaving it all up to the person elected. Too often we hear it said in the church, "I just cannot be there, but whatever you all do it will be all right with me." That is either misplaced "blind faith" or a kind of assurance and faith that is of God. God never said that to us, yet we have responded to God as if He doesn't care what we do. Many times we have found that there are those who come to hasty conclusions that are not in the best interest of the body of Christ, but what is in the best interest of the party. The condition of our psychological bondage has made us want to take some kind of action, get out, close the meeting so we can get on to the next concern which may have nothing at all to do with our liberation.

From birth I have spent most of my years in the traditional or Black church. As we live and witness to Jesus in this dispensation, there is a passage of scripture regarding the church in Laodicea that I am still wrestling with. It says, "Listen! I am standing at the door and knocking! If anyone hears my voice and opens the door I will come into his home and share a meal with him, and he with me"(Revelations 3:20 NET). This is the invitation to forsake the traditional church and the God of the West that gave birth to our servitude. There is a knocking that is being heard, and more Black churches are hearing and heeding that invitation to open up and let Him come in. This passage ends with what I term the key to the Black church in exile. "He who has an ear let him hear what the Spirit says to the churches" (Revelations 3:22 NET). We must listen to the Spirit of the living God. I have a new appreciation for the exiles in Babylon. I used to wonder why they could not "sing the Lord's song" in a strange land. They could not sing because nothing for them and in them had changed, and nothing was happening. They could not sing in exile because perhaps they had never really sung in Jerusalem.

But something has happened for us today. God has built for Himself a church on a rock of "faith" out of a testimony with divine coaching. Something has happened. He has built a church that even the forces of hell that surround us cannot prevail against. That's why the Black church can sing in exile. Dr. J. M. Ellison, the first Black president of Virginia Union University, published his second book in 1961. The title is "They Sang Through the Crises." Although the title is suggestive of the traditional church in the dark days of slavery, when I purchased the book that's was what I was looking for. But I found that in a vicarious kind of way. There is no question that the Black church has discovered itself in exile; something both dramatic and divine has happened. The life of the exiled church has been invaded by what Rudolf Otto has called the "Holy Other." The Black church came through in the Spirit that our culture denied its members to be; "Children of God with a theological understanding of their journey." Largely because the teachings in the Black church have historically been the teachings in the White church, we had come to believe in the White man's god, the God of the West. Not all White people believe in this God of the West. There have been some real pioneers and stalwarts of the faith, who have fixed their faith in the God of the Ages and demonstrated it by their witness. Much of the Black church is in exile, but it is on the move in some instances. Recent signs have been the response to Katrina. Churches have contributed and pledged hundreds of thousands of dollars, and have taken evacuees from the coastal region and housed them temporarily in their churches, fed them, clothed them, and cared for them. "And obviously people who talk (talk the talk and walk the walk) like that are looking forward to a country they can call their own"..."But they were looking for a better place, a heavenly homeland. That is why God is not ashamed to be called their God, for he has prepared a heavenly city for them." (Hebrews 11:14, 16, LASB) Dr. Martin Luther King, Jr., would be reassured that the tail light that was burning in the church during his day is becoming the headlight that it used to be in its early history, beginning with Simon, who was forced to help Jesus bear His cross (see Matthew 27:32 NET).

Dr. Reid & Dr. King at New Cavalry, 1966.

Dr. Reid & the 1st VA State Officers of 1960 Chapter of the SCLC.

CHAPTER III

BETWEEN SUNDAYS IN BLACK THEOLOGY

"Everyday is Holy unto the Lord"

Black people are a part of a great heritage in the religious life of their communities and the nation. Historically, the Black preacher or pastor was the leader of his community. Many times he served in the role of educator, political participant, elected official, social worker, healer, and liberator of his people. He would read or have read to him from the Holy Bible, particularly the King James Version, about how God delivered Israel out of the hands of Pharaoh in Egypt. He would draw an analogy to the social existence of Black people who were either in physical slavery or psychological bondage and sometimes both. It was through the church, the center and soul of life in the Black community, that the people gathered to hear words of faith and challenge for a better life. It was in the church that social coercion, once destroyed, was rebuilt, to the extent that the church came under the control of White pastors and state legislative bodies, especially in Virginia. I served as pastor of First Baptist Church of Petersburg, Virginia, the oldest Black congregation in America, whose corner- stone dates back to 1774. It really had its start back in 1754, but the church was hampered after a fire and moved to Petersburg in 1774. Virginia passed a law that "it would be unlawful" for Black people to gather for any occasion without a White man being their immediate overseer. This occurred after the Nat Turner insurrection of 1831. We can look at points and places in recent years where Black churches have been bombed, set on fire mysteriously, refused loans or had loans foreclosed that called them to renew their covenant of faith from painful praying grounds.

The Black preacher who insists on a theological ideology outside of the traditional concept of major mainline churches is often looked upon with suspicion. This is true not only of the Black church but the White church also. Both history and the observable presence tell us that, in violation of the first amendment to the constitution, religious practice from a theological perspective that differs from the ingratiated acceptance of mainline churches is to be mediarized into order, face cultic isolation or banished from society. Seldom does one attack the system of oppression in America, no matter in whose name (Jehovah, God, Allah, Christ or any other being supreme to the believer) and thrive comfortably. As long as you are confined to what happens between the call to worship and the benediction that takes you emotionally through a corporate worship experience that says "y'all be good now until next Sunday," you are generally safe for retirement, with your last days possible in the sun, but not necessarily in the "Son," the Christ of Glory.

To move outside the system in traditional mainline churches in America you have to deal first with your religious patriotism. If the Old Testament prophets would come back for a visit and move throughout the country proclaiming the righteousness of a God unacceptable to America, they would probably meet up with their bearded friends in the newest prisons in Cuba. Yes, they would probably be called "terrorist," "Talibans," or certainly "the Al Qaeda network." To think un-American or extra-public policy, even in religious matters, will get you a hearing with the IRS, CIA, FBI, the new Homeland Security agency or the United States Attorney General. Believe me I have heard from all of the above during my unorthodox ministry

Liberation Theology in recent years emerged in Latin America, where a majority of the people is not only poor, but also oppressed. There, Liberation Theology is an interpretation of scripture that many times runs counter to the social order of governments and the socio-technical systems that have divided nations between the "haves" and the "have nots." It seeks in a number of ways to bring into being a more humane, caring, and sharing order that eases the misery and suffering of masses of people. Some theologians have advocated and used the tactics of Karl Marx to overthrow dictatorships and forced imperialism as a means of not only calling attention to the problems, but also of solving them. They see it as an evil to take necessities from the lowly masses and give luxury and comfort to the upper classes. In the technical sense of the word, Karl Marx was not a theologian. Even so, Marxism has given hope to many theologians, scholars and the oppressed of that region of the world, to the dismay of Pope John Paul, religious conservatives in the United States and our government, often seen as the oppressor.

Some one has said, "Black theologians and Marxist thinkers, while they share similar goals, do not start from the same perspective. They do not employ the same methodology, and neither do they form any kind of alliance to reach their goals." It would be helpful to examine both. In the first place, Black theology and/or Liberation theology are not added to either Marxism or Liberation Theology in Latin America. Just as with most theological thought-wells that spring forth nurturing and refreshing streams of pure water, Black theology was born out of the social context of a divinely felt need. It was an ontological discovery of personhood that transforms conditions. It was a rediscovery of the purpose of the church in light of God's calling in the Old and New Testament. In the Old Testament, God sent Moses to Egypt, not to comfort Israel in oppression and tell them that "it's going to be all right," but to tell Pharaoh to let them go on a three-day journey from Egypt to worship Him in the wilderness. To this Pharaoh replied, "You must be crazy! How much sense does it make for me to disregard my balance sheet of economic progress, jeopardize my military defense posture, become embarrassed by other nations of my international prominence to allow you to go and worship an unknown who calls himself I AM? What divine arrogance! "I am that I am has sent thee!" The Eastern text reads "Ahiah Ashar High, which is translated to read, "I am the Living God; the God which always has been, the eternal God, the God of Abraham, Isaac, and Jacob."

Black Theology then begins from a perspective of the "Isness" and the purposefulness of a God that was, is, and shall be. The theology of Marx begins with a denial of God. Black Theologians move from a concept of a monolithic association with Marxism to a dialectical methodology that rejects any God or concept of God that is obedient to pharaohs of any day. It is the determinism in Black theological thought for freedom, equity and justice that gives birth to a theology of liberation because God has heard our cries. God has heard the cries of those who view themselves as His New Israel, his chosen people to bring forth light in the dark places of uncertainties in the earth. Whenever and wherever this is done, Black theology runs counter to the claims of Pharaoh, with faith, which shapes the religion of the comfortable pews of mainline churches. There is no effort on the part of Black Theology to destroy Pharaoh, but to sever Pharaoh from his claims so that his redemption can be made possible. To this end all Black theologians in America commit to Liberation Theology.

Writing in Black Theology: A Documented History 1966-1979, Cornel West says, "I shall claim that Black Theology and Marxist thought share three characteristics: (1) Both adhere to a similar methodology, the same way of approaching their respective subject matter and arriving at conclusions. (2) Both link some notion of liberation to the future socio-economic conditions of the downtrodden. (3) Most importantly, both attempt to put forward trenchant critiques of liberal capitalist America." There are several reasons for the renewed interest in Liberation Theology as practiced by the Black church. The very fact that it is Black theology says that it rejects White theology. It writes off Western theology and the God of the West as unworkable for Black people. Another reason Black theology is questioned today is that personal and institutional racism are so inextricably bound up in White capitalistic thought. It actually sends shock waves through the minds of some Blacks and most White Americans who would dare to think or act differently from the accepted order. This is particularly true when you think of the religious practice and theological thought of the West. Again, today's Black church has become so westernized or there is so much White thought in the Black church until many Black pastors have never discovered the meaning of their calling or their redeeming Lord. Pacification is now proclaimed from the same pulpits and in the same tradition that liberation used to call for. In many parts of the country Negro preachers are still determined to call Blacks together to celebrate the Emancipation Proclamation as if the struggle is behind us. Many Black people have such bitter memories of the past that they want every day, with its inherent and inextricable darkness, to be the day of the Lord now, or the day of – God's reign.

The question is how do we do liberation theology in the Black church today? How do we reverse hundreds of years of church practice without seriously jeopardizing our healing ministry? It is difficult enough for some pastors to change the annual revival meeting dates or any church work activity that has had as much as a three-year history. Aren't there some risks in changing the habits of people who are thoroughly satisfied with their religious lot and their religious conditioning that have been shaped unknowingly and vicariously by the White God of the West, White thought, and the practice and theology? Liberation theology does not take into account the cultural creature comforts and religious traditions of society. Jesus seems to say in the Sermon on the Mount that this business of the Kingdom of God is so serious that when your eyes come open, you are required to see what's before you and make some existential decisions that bring about dramatic change for the good of the Kingdom, (See Matthew 5:13-46 NET). How do you re-educate a front line congregation who want peace, tranquility and goodwill toward Pharaoh at any price? Is it possible for the Black church to do Liberation Theology in times when economic conditions are uncertain, the political pendulum is swinging to the unrighteous right, and the media "whites out or edits out" the cries and the concerns of Black people? How do you do Liberation Theology when even some Black folk agree that we have come too far to fast, and now it's time to "wait on the Lord?"

Doing Liberation Theology

Liberation Theology is not a new addition to the Black church. Before Karl Marx was born in 1818 in Trier, Rhineland, Liberation Theology was being practiced in America against chattel slavery, the most inhuman institution the world has ever known. The fact of racism will not permit Western theology to admit this is germane to the problem. Former President Reagan in speaking in 1981 to the oldest civil rights organization in America, the National Association for the Advancement of Colored People, said, "Let us not permit the misunderstanding of the past to keep us from working together in the future." Here our commander-in-chief, the color-blind leader of the free world, calls the most barbaric, deliberate destruction of more than a hundred million black people a "misunderstanding." That is just about all that Western theology, or the God of the West would permit the honorable President to admit to and he probably strained or blushed red to say that. This is the same President who on November 3, 1983 signed into law the bill that had been on the way for fifteen years marking the Martin Luther King, Jr. Holiday. He then gutted by executive order almost all of the social programs that Dr. King had proposed, lived and died for in his short lifetime and once made the statement that he was unaware of any race problem in America.

When Richard Allen founded the African Methodist Episcopal Church in 1816, it was the result of growing dissatisfaction with the inadequacy of White Christianity. This separation came about as the result of Liberation Theology, neither preached nor practiced in the White church. When the first African Baptist Church was organized in Petersburg, Virginia, in 1756 that was Liberation Theology at work. When Harriet Tubman organized the Underground Railroad with the Bible in one hand and a shotgun in the other, liberating captives from their captors, that was Liberation Theology at work. When the Rev. Nat Turner, Denmark Vesey and Gabriel Prosser led their revolts against the oppressive institution of slavery, they felt guided and led by the Hand of God to go to war against plantation pharaohs that they too might worship God in the wilderness as free men and women. Liberation Theology had not been conceived in Latin America at this time, and Karl Marx had not given the Black religious experience a thought. There was a time when Black Theology was at work between Sundays. Now that we have become so culturalized under the God of the West, and so afraid of our own shadows, that in many cases theology takes place at the beginning or at the conclusion of our sermons on Sunday mornings only if at all. The practice of Liberation Theology means, "doing the will of God" on a daily basis. It requires us to think beyond the social confines and cultural ceilings of our faith to an action that defies the odds. We have got to crawl, skip, hop or jump out of that "circle of sameness" or religious traditions and take a stand to represent Jesus, who is the Christ of Glory. We can be philosophical, sociological, psychological, but we must be theological in all that we do or say for the Christ of Glory demands it. We can no longer be afraid to embrace our brothers and sisters who are not of this fold, says Jesus. Anyone with an understanding of the Judeo-Christian faith must know that Jews, Muslims and Christians are all children by the seed of Abraham. We are all a part of the covenant with promise, and I am looking beyond narrow Christian traditions under the ceilings of a cultural faith that stops at the footstool of the God of the West. I feel most uncomfortable being what the earthly master wants me to be. I could never be satisfied at being a Black, powerless political pawn parading as one who has made it in the big house, and don't even have "out-house privileges." Neither could I live as a minister of the Gospel of Jesus Christ being ashamed and a scared sham, afraid of White or Black oppressors. There is no Justice Thomas in me, nor is there any Uncle Tom; I am called of God to proclaim His word, and to declare His way by both precept and example. That is what the Christ of Glory did.

A THEOLOGY OF LIBERATION

Every pastor needs to develop a theology of death and a theology of life. We need a theology of growth and a theology of grace, and it takes time and study to develop such. I can understand why some "safe" Black pastors cannot meet with the Honorable Louis Farrakhan, and the Reverend Sun Myung Moon. How do they deal with the passage of scripture wherein Jesus is praying and saying, "I am no longer in the world, but they are in the world and I am coming to you? Holy Father, keep them safe in your name that you have given me, so that they may be one just as we are one" (John 17: 11, NET). Are we as Baptists still under the impression that Jesus came only to save Baptists? At the last Virginia State Baptist Convention I attended, the President, who was a graduate of the Samuel Dewitt Proctor School of Religion at Virginia Union University, said, "I am a Baptist born, a Baptist bred, and when I am gone, I'll be a Baptist dead." This same Pastor gave me some unheard of excuses when Minister Farrakhan's Lieutenants were seeking a church in Norfolk, large enough to hold a thousand persons before the Million Man March in 1995. Here ten years later, they were looking for a congregation of the People of God, the called out, the Ekklesia, the community of faith, to hear a brother speak and inspire us regarding our deliverance from this "Ceiling Bondage."

The only church in the area that has invited the Minister to speak on a Sunday morning was the New Calvary Baptist Church, and I was the Minister then. Minister Farrakhan spoke that Sunday on "Jesus as Lord." I invited him to town on several other occasions and that seems to have disturbed the shaky peace of the community. While some Black pastors and clergy have done many good and worthwhile things such as developing a scholarship program for ministers, and supporting some candidates for public office, you wouldn't believe the strong objections the brethren and sisters had in refusing to endorse or support the Million Man March, an occasion on which I was one of the speakers in October of 1995. It was from the storefront church where we held worship services that we organized seven busloads to attend that March. I don't know why Black people, and especially some Black clergy, seem to be afraid of the Honorable Louis Farrakhan. He has done more in the cause of getting millions of Black people to rethink their apparent psychological bondage than any other man in America. He says what millions feel but they are afraid to say it or to read the Final Call in closed closet. We should never allow anyone except the Spirit of God to select our friends, our brothers and sisters for us. We are "Children of the King, the Christ of Glory." Minister Farrakhan has suggested that the Willie Lynch doctrine of control still has a lingering effect on us. I hope you know who Willie Lynch is. Just in case you don't, I will give you a brief explanation. Willie Lynch, according to reports, was an owner of three hundred slaves that he kept under subjection. He was invited to Virginia to explain to slave masters how to keep their slaves under control forever. The method he said that works was to keep them divided. Keep them fighting each other, and pulling each other down like crabs in a bucket if one tries to get either up or out. Keep them divided by color, by class, and treat the obedient ones kindly and punish the disobedient and the arrogant ones, and they will be your slaves for 300 years. Personally, I won't give Willie Lynch all that credit. When I read my Bible and open my eyes to the biblical history of man and the so-called Christian church, I think it is the spirit and the power of the devil that has most of us tongue-tied, glue-stuck, and sin-bound. I don't think any "white devil" nor "black devil" has ever been that smart. Paul said, "For our struggle is not against flesh and blood, but against the rulers, against the authorities, against the powers of this dark world and against the spiritual forces of evil in the heavenly realm" (Ephesians 6:12 NIV).

When folk ask me, "What kind of doctor are you?" I often tell them, knowing that they are still in the dark unless I explain. I give them the correct answer by saying; "My degree is in Liberation Theology!" Normally the response is, "what is that?" A good answer has been for me, "Doing the word of God, and not just learning or hearing it." When you do liberation theology you sometimes have to go against the world and abort yourself as a child of your culture to become a child of our once risen and ascended Lord of Glory. You see Jesus called on us "to be lights of the world and salt of the earth." But many of us have hidden our lights under the bushels of culture and, as Dr. Martin Luther King has so eloquently said, "we have become taillights rather than headlights." Our salt has lost both its taste and its usefulness when we are too afraid to practice "Liberation Theology." Jesus never called on us to invoke His blessings on this world, or to pronounce benedictions on this fallen age. Most of us know John 3:16. But the verse that follows says: "For God did not send his Son into the world to condemn the world, but that the world should be saved through him" (John 3:17 NET). This verse is equally as important as verse sixteen of the third chapter, but I have never preached it from the pulpit. I have tried to practice it in the world.

The Reverend Sun Myung Moon

I met disciples of or followers of the Rev Sun Myung Moon as members of the Unification Church in the spring of 1973. I had only heard of Rev. Moon and what I had heard was not positive. However there was something unique about him that made me want to know more about him. Allow me to say Reverend Moon has only been a help to me as I grew in more and more disdain for the God of the West and the non-relevancy of some Black churches in particular. The media have more often than not expressed negative concerns about Rev. Moon. They look at Moon's being banned from traveling to some countries and his prison terms as making him illegitimate. This is following the civil rights movement that jailed me a total of eleven times, including twice since I met Reverend Moon. I reasoned, here is a man who is being discriminated against just as I am. He believes in Jesus, and so do I. I wish you would read his sermon on Simon of Cyrene, the Black brother who helped Jesus to bear His cross. He refers to me as brother, and I refer to him as my brother. He believes that Jesus was God's Son; so do I. He has been seen as a cult leader, outside of the mainstream church, I say hallelujah, I am on the out side of the main stream, and I thank God for it. He took a position that the Jews were responsible for the death of Jesus. I agreed that not only the Jews; read the Bible, and you would find that Gentiles were also complicit in the death of Jesus as well. It has been said that Jews have objected to His doctrine that the Holocaust is a consequence for killing Jesus. I state this clearly and unequivocally that the cause of the Holocaust was the sin of man's inhumanity to man, not only in Germany but in the estimated 100,000,000 Africans that were killed during the vicious slave trade by White Christians who, apparently like the Reverend Pat Robertson, worship the God of the West for economic gain with millions of dollars pouring in and who speak disdainfully about the Reverend Sun Myung Moon. For more than 30 years I have been associated with Rev. Sun Myung Moon, and Minister Louis Farrakhan and I see them both as brothers in Christ. When I was going through the church/state battle at New Calvary Baptist Church, both Minister Farrakhan, and the Reverend Sun Myung Moon came to my rescue. Brother Farrakhan left Chicago and came to speak to my people while I was in jail and never charged me a dime. Reverend Moon sent ministers and staff persons from many parts of the country on a hot summer day when we had a demonstration marching from New Calvary Baptist Church to court. Members of the Tidewater Metro Baptist Ministers Conference did come in a body and prayed with me following their Monday's meeting. A former president of that conference, the late Dr. Spencer L Scott, a personal friend of mine, had recommended that the ministers would volunteer to spend a day each of my time in prison. When they arrived, I was happy for a "breakthrough" with the clergy. I asked the new president, Dr. Ronnie Joyner, how many of the brethren are going to stay? He very sheepishly said, "we didn't come to stay, we came to pray."

I was one of the main speakers during the common suffering meetings in Washington during Reverend Moon's imprisonment. Although many of my brothers forsook me, these two giants became my brothers during my struggle. Now if you want to believe what the media say about both of them, see if you can digest the history of media reports that have come down about Jesus, the Christ of Glory! Did He create a cult on the night He instituted the Lord's Supper? Did He create a cult in Caesarea Philippi when He asked for a declaration as to who He was? "When Jesus came to the area of Caesarea Philippi, He asked His disciples, who do people say that the Son of Man is? They answered, some say John the Baptist, others Elijah, and others Jeremiah or one of the prophets. He said to them but who do you say that I am? Simon Peter answered you are the Christ, the Son of the living God. And Jesus answered him. You are blessed, Simon son of Jonah, because flesh and blood did not reveal this to you but my Father in heaven! And I tell you that you are Peter, and on this rock I will build my church and the gates of Hades will not overpower it" (Matthew 16:13-18 NET). Even though Jesus prayed that we might be one, it is the desire of the God of the West for us to go our separate ways, even in heaven. It has been reported by believers in the God of the West that there will even be "a colored section," for the noisy crowd.

THE LORD'S DAY

I was brought up believing that Sunday was the day of worship and we should stop all labor that wasn't of an emergency nature to worship God through Jesus Christ. As I told you, I made my entrance on planet earth on Sunday January 26, 1930 at 3:00 P.M. I grew up in the country-side of Norfolk County and attended church in the Oak Grove Community of what became Chesapeake, Virginia, where worship services were held twice a month at the Little Zion Baptist Church, on the first and third Sundays and twice a month at the St. Luke's AME Church, on the second and fourth Sundays. If these were the Sundays on which we were to worship, what were we supposed to do on the other Sundays at each church? One of the things we did was to attend Sunday school every Sunday. We could also attend some programs on the "off" Sundays. Quartet singing was the place to go to be spiritually or emotionally fed on the off Sundays. The Reid's Family Four Quartet sang all over Tidewater on those days, filling in the gap on Sundays when there weren't any scheduled worship. At an early age I had some ideological suspicions about skipping Sundays on which we worshipped. When I was extended my first call to the pastorate, (New Hope Baptist Church of Chesapeake) where I met my first real deacon, Deacon Napoleon Smith, the call was for three Sundays in the month. They had "upped" it from two Sundays. I soon led the congregation into having worship every Sunday. In the Second Church I was privileged to serve, the Mount Olive Baptist Church in Virginia Beach, services were held on the second and fourth Sundays. I led them into having services each Sunday and into establishing a parsonage for the pastor and his family. We got as far as laying the foundation for the parsonage before I accepted a call to the First Baptist Church of Petersburg, where for years worship services had been conducted on every Sunday. I was in seminary (The Samuel Dewitt School of Religion) when I was called to the First Baptist Church of Petersburg. By the time I got there, some folk were calling it the Harrison Street Baptist Church. I learned that the First Baptist Church (white) made a deal with the deacons to change our name to Harrison Street, because there was a conflict with two First Baptist Churches in the same town. First Baptist Church (white) made a sizeable donation to the Harrison Street Baptist after the church suffered from a fire.

As I look back over those days, in Norfolk County we were not encouraged to attend other denominational worship services, even on the "off" Sundays. Yet we have gleaned from the scriptures that the day of worship was on the first day of the week because that was the day on which Jesus arose from the dead. When John said, "I was in the Spirit on the Lord's day" (Revelation 1:10 NET); we have associated that passage with being on Sunday. While I am in favor of worshipping on Sunday, I am more concerned about our lack of worship between Sundays. In some of our churches, our worship on Sundays has become a time for religious entertainment, with the God of the West playing a significant role. This kind of worship restricts us into believing that God is to be praised or worshipped on Sundays only, otherwise we just might bring ruinage to the economy.

We had a blue law in Virginia that restricted our purchases on Sundays, that was enacted in Jamestown in 1610. In 1961, the U.S. Supreme Court ruled that the blue laws were constitutional in that the law was civil and not religious. As a student of history and theology, I questioned then, what happened to the law in 1610 that said; "we should keep the Sabbath day holy?" At any rate, the General Assembly enacted 21 exemptions to the blue law, and it became so confusing that in 1988 the law was changed. The Virginia Supreme Court struck down the blue law. The ruling was handed down on Saturday, and many businesses were open on Sunday selling just about everything that was in stock. Now you can buy anything on Sundays that is for sale.

What we do "on" Sundays is just as much a concern of mine as to what we do between Sundays. The late Janet Mosby Wilkins, a deacon with Gideon's Riverside Fellowship, used to began every prayer and testimony with this quotation from Psalms 118:24, "This is the day that the Lord has made, let us rejoice and be glad in it." Janet was flamboyant and ninety-nine percent happy, always right and outgoing all the time. I called her aside one day and asked her in jest, "If this is the day that the Lord has made, who made yesterday?" What happened to it? What happened to my yesteryears, as I grow old? I want them back!" She said, "the Lord giveth and the Lord takes away, blessed"...I said 'blessed be the name of the Lord." My point here is that the God of the Ages calls us to worship everyday. God gave Moses our first directive on worship. "The Lord, the God of the Hebrews, has met with us. And now, let us go three days' journey into the wilderness, so that we may offer sacrifice to the Lord" (Exodus 3:18 NET). God was not calling Israel to worship then on a special day of the week. To offer sacrifice to the Lord means to worship. Worship begins with acknowledgement and sacrifice. Jesus said in essence to that woman at the well, you are drawing the wrong water from the wrong well. It is not the place where you worship that is significant. It is who you are and whom you worship. "...A time is coming and now is here- when the true worshipers will worship the Father in spirit and truth, for the Father seeks such people to be his worshipers. God is spirit, and the people who worship him must worship in spirit and in truth"(John 4:23-24 NET).

We may worship God on Sundays, but we should worship him every day of the week as well. In my house, we pray openly three times a day, and some times we pray all through the day. Remember, it is not the place that is important. It is who you worship and how you worship that is important. Some of us have come to the place where we worship robes and uniforms that we dedicate to the Lord. Where are these dedication ceremonies found in the New Testament? We worship the buildings, our stained glass windows and our carpeted floors. We worship our clergy when we are not crucifying them. We worship what we wear and the coordination of our dress, all on Sundays. What do we worship and whom do we worship between Sundays? Don't allow our witness to show up in the faulty stewardship chart. Let us use our church buildings to the glory of God all through the week. As bad a shape as we are in as a people, we need to sing out one more time with Annie S. Hawks; "I need thee every hour, Most gracious Lord. No tender voice like thine can peace afford. I need Thee every hour stay Thou near by, Temptations lose their power when Thou art nigh. I need Thee every hour in joy or pain. Come quickly and abide or life is vain. I need Thee, O I need Thee; Every hour I need Thee, O bless me now my Savior, I come to Thee." That is every day and not just on Sundays. Just to sing this hymn is an act of worship.

Pilgrimage of Prayer at The VA State Capitol.

CHAPTER IV

TODAY'S BLACK CHURCH

"Going to Church or Being the Church!"

All of my life I have been a part of the Black church. My father and my grandfather were all preachers in the Black church and they ministered to it as they felt the leading of God to do so. Why I became a dissident from the traditional beliefs and practices of the church is becoming clear but the awesomeness of the responsibility leaves me with an uncertainty of the outcome if the Black church fails to become a part of the Christ of Glory, our Liberating Lord. I am not alone in my thinking. Paul's letter to the church at Galatia is a case in point that tells me and testifies to the world that the Christian church has not separated itself from the law or the God of the West. It has not broken with the traditions and the thinking of the past to deal adequately with "Freedom in Christ" that His Redeeming Love brings to the world. If we had an understanding of Paul's "idealism" of the church as found even in Ephesians, there is no way that we could digest the "isness" of what we do every Sunday morning with the "oughtness" of what we do between Sundays. What some of us do doesn't mesh or make any holy sense. The first reality of the practice of the Black church dawned upon me in a church meeting at the Poole's Grove Baptist Church in Woodville, North Carolina, where my father was the pastor. I came in the meeting and sat in the rear of the church with my 82nd Airborne uniform on and the meeting was so "hot and heavy among the saints" that no one noticed my presence. I was on my way home on a weekend pass and I knew my father would be in church that night and would be there for services on that Sunday. I really wanted to greet him and keep on moving. I did not know what the heated discussion was about then, nor do I know now. I do know that it was really a "carrying on" between the two major families in the church; one on one side, and the other on the other side, with my humbled father standing in the midst, agreeing with both sides. As a chaplain's assistant in the army, I had taken correspondence Bible courses and a course in law from La Salle University in Chicago. I saw no connections that night between Jesus, Paul, and the practice of the church in the "oneness" of the Body of Jesus Christ. This was a local congregation in dispute in a meeting. After sitting there in the back of the sanctuary, I had no idea what the discussion was about.

The good people at Poole's Grove acted out their love and respected my father. They never felt that thirty dollars a month was sufficient salary for him, so they "pounded" him with fruits, meats, vegetables and other staples that he would bring home after that second Sunday weekend, once a month. If my father had to pull from his memory files his most effective sermon, it would have to be "You Must Be Born Again." Even today most folk have little understanding as to what that means. That is one of the most revolutionary statements in the New Testament, and Jesus said that to an inquiring member of the Sanhedrin court who came to see him by night. It is always some midnight experience in the life of anyone to really become born again because a new day dawns with the Christ of Glory, front and center. It is in this midnight experience that faith takes root and brings hope alive. It is in this midnight experience that the redeeming love of God floods one's soul – that eternal day is born. It is in this midnight experience that the redeeming love of God floods your soul with a perpetual stream from on high, and the things you formerly did, you don't do any more. You become what Paul called a "New Creation of God." And when that happens you get a new world's view, and you see both your neighbor and the world from the viewpoint of the Divine. That brings about an ecological balance and a reflection of what you think of the God you serve, and the fellow human beings with a sense of divine justice and love.

It was in 1957, two years before I met Dr. Martin Luther King, Jr., that I accepted the call to the historic First Baptist Church of Petersburg, Virginia, that had found misinterpreted solace in some of Paul's earlier writings. I was the first pastor since 1774 that the church had called when women in the church were privileged or permitted to vote. In many Baptist churches, the constitution and by-laws take precedence over the Bible and the Holy Spirit. First Baptist got its start in 1756 with 'new light slaves' who had won their freedom, but had not been accepted in society as free men and women. The socio-economic conditions of slavery soon ran this church underground, and it has had a continuous history since 1774, making it the oldest authentic Black Baptist church in America. After the Commonwealth of Virginia (the first state to enslave Africans) through its General Assembly passed laws that said, "No blacks could assemble without a white man being its immediate overseer," First Baptist experience the calling of five White pastors. None of them could deal with the contradictions of what the Bible said *vis-à-vis* what the practice of slave holding Christians was. This law became effective as the result of the Rev. Nat Turner's insurrection of 1831 that took place in Southampton County, Virginia. During my years at said First Baptist, Ms. Peggy E.C. Lee became the secretary to the pastor. Peggy was a great secretary. She helped me in writing my letters, my speeches, news releases, and was my grammatical lifesaver. I would give her my hand-written sermons or my half-typed sermons during church school. Sometimes she would get them to me just before I stood up to preach. Peggy has been helpful in gathering information for me for this book. She doesn't quite seem to get rid of me because I won't let her. After nine years however, I thought I had gained a rather productive education into the ministry of the Black church, and believe me, I was truly tested. The first agenda item thrown at me was the appointment of a constitution and by-law committee. Some of the brethren still could not deal with women voting and speaking in church, a matter that they misread and misunderstood, regarding Paul's writing on the subject. I got around to that committee's reports in the eighth year of my ministry and by that time the congregation had grown and we never looked back at women keeping quiet. I began my work in the civil rights movement officially while at First Baptist Church.

When I arrived at the New Calvary Baptist Church, not only was I wrapped up in the civil-rights movement, I had become involved with the social imperatives of the gospel. I was dissatisfied with the "isness" of the church and the promise of the "pie-in-the-sky-after-while" theological concept, and as usual, I was in a hurry. I wasn't so much concerned with golden streets in heaven when we didn't have concrete sidewalks in the here and now. I was always concerned with the outcast and the downtrodden. I got to know, under Dr. Martin Luther King, Jr., that "America was suffering from a high blood pressure of creeds and a low anemia of deeds." When this call came in 1966 from the New Calvary Baptist Church of Norfolk, I had been the organizer of the Virginia State Unit of the Southern Christian Leadership Conference that had led a pilgrimage of prayer to Prince Edward County, Virginia, a county that had closed its public schools rather to obey the Supreme Court's order of May 17, 1954, and subsequent orders to desegregate them. Several Norfolk, Virginia, public schools had also been closed. It was the presence of the military in Norfolk that forced these schools to reopen. The court order was like the tail wagging the dog. I had been jailed for civil disobedience in Petersburg, Danville, and Lynchburg, Virginia; as well as in Edenton, North Carolina, and Albany, Georgia. Little did I know then that I would be jailed in Norfolk for divine obedience some twenty years later. When I came to New Calvary, I had been "doing" theology in the Black church, with the support of the congregation. While attending the State Baptist Convention in Norfolk in May of 1966, I was notified by a trustee of New Calvary that I had been called. He didn't seem to be enthused about my selection nor did he offer any words of congratulations. He said, looking me straight in the eye, "I already have your license number." It was because of that statement that I exchanged my license number to a personalized tag so that there would no chance of any one's failing to recognize me wherever I parked. He died within two years without any further comment. What a sad way to leave this old world, as my chief remembrance of him was his saying to me, "I already have your license number." I had known of New Calvary Baptist Church and had preached there on several occasions when Elder Samuel A. Wilson was the pastor. He had recommended me to the church in Petersburg while I was serving the Mt. Olive Baptist Church in Virginia Beach. Mount Olive, and my first church, the New Hope Baptist Church in Chesapeake, was full of good people who were adjusting to the social conditions of a segregated society and had accepted western theologians' pseudo theological understandings for their practice. They would pick up (out of context) pieces of Paul's early writing about the practice of women in the church and settle with that. Had they kept on reading Paul, they would have discovered how faithful, believing women actively worked with him in his ministries. My ministry probably would not have been as effective had I not asked God for a wife who seemed to find a joy in giving me support and believing in my understanding of the awesome calling of God to higher purposes. When I ran for city council in Petersburg, Virginia, my life was threatened repeatedly. A picture of me, posted in a Black cleaning and pressing shop, was shot by someone through a window, and we received a phone call, which my wife answered, saying, "I would be the next if I didn't stay in my place." Like all other threats, my wife took it in stride and kept praying for me.

Before accepting the call to New Calvary I submitted a total of 41 questions to the clerk of the church to get information about New Calvary. They dealt with church administration, church mission and education, church programs, church finance, and of course, pastoral compensation. The late and sainted Mrs. Pearl Holloman answered twenty of the questions asked. The others were left unanswered and the church officers said they would discuss them with me. I met with the officers and leaders and to me they looked like a battalion of men who came to see and to question him whom the church had called. I was very upfront, candid and open with them. I tried to perceive my call into the ministry. And I made it clear made it clear that I was not a traditional pastor. They knew of my experience in jail and my work with Dr. Martin Luther King, Jr., and SCLC. I requested that the officers would call another meeting of the church and tell them what I had told them and if they wanted me, to call again. The second call was unanimous. I came in July of 1966, and presented my fourteen- page program to the church in a meeting in late August. It was after midnight when I finished reading and explaining, but the church adopted the program. It called for a new order of worship, commissions on finance, missions, social justice, education and evangelism. There would be no funerals on Sundays. Funerals could be held at night, any day during the week and on Saturdays. The church would adopt a unified treasury and we would work our way to a one-board church that would include women as well as men deacons. One agreement was that the church building would be used during the week for spiritual and educational purposes. The Church agreed. Dr. Martin Luther King, Jr., was one of the speakers on my service of installation on October 30, 1966, and I sang during the service, "When I've Done The Best I Can..." Dr. King spoke that morning from the sermon, "A Knock at Midnight." There wasn't even standing room left. The chairman of the board of deacons, Charlie Cooper, a venerable old man, stout and always well dressed, was to tell me later that he could neither read nor write. But he said, "Brother Pastor, I am with you. I am with you when you are right and I am with you when you are wrong. But I'm with you when you are wrong trying to get you right." Now that meant more to me than the silence of those who could read and write. I went to New Calvary committed to building a new church people in a new church building. So I treaded water for four years and labored to complete the interior of the building. We then paid off the mortgage of some $200,000.00, in four years. I then went to work on developing senior citizens home, which was finally funded fifteen years later when Calvary Towers, which I named, was constructed. I met with the HUD officials and elected officials, particularly Senator John Warner, who helped us to get it through. The Honorable Samuel Pierce was the Black Secretary of HUD. Ms. Margaret White of the Regional Office in Richmond presented me with a check from HUD. All of this was done without any support from the City of Norfolk. To get this project through was a slap in the face of the City that was determined to keep me in check and offered absolutely no help.

When the crisis at Calvary came about (see chapter 6), our board of directors agreed to resign and turn over the project to the dissident members of New Calvary who had fought the project vehemently during the two years before construction.

As pastor, I presented the Church with its first budget, with the support of the officers. Each year we listed the amount of funds that came in, what funds were spent for, and a projection for the next year's budget. I never handled the money at New Calvary, nor did I ever sign any checks, except those of the Minister's discretionary fund. I did require a copy of the weekly tellers' report and the expenditures in order to know what was going on with the gifts to the Lord. At New Calvary we collected and delivered tons of food and clothing in 1967 to the hungry children of Mississippi. We also collected tons of food, clothing and other necessities in 1972 for refugees and liberating forces in Southern Africa. New Calvary would be the headquarters for the Poor Peoples Campaign in Norfolk in 1968. Mayor Roy B. Martin and the City Council opposed these and other actions. Both fear and ignorance seemed to grasp many in the New Calvary congregation and other churches in Norfolk in the tug of war between the practice of theology and western reflections of theology that we learn from traditional mainline White seminary professors and White churches. When I enrolled in Boston University School of Theology to pursue a doctorate in Liberation Theology, I could not find any Black pastors who could appreciate what I was about. Suddenly I became a "him" to them – and a persona *non-gratis* to many. I became more and more selective about whom I would bring to the Church to speak to the people that I was trying to lead into the "Faith that was once delivered unto all the saints." After more than thirty-seven years in the pastorate, I found that the "Isness of the Black church, the *status quo*, is just as lost from the saving grace of Jesus Christ as those Galatians who had turned back to slavery under the law. Constructing buildings, burning mortgages, and enlarging "Isness" had become the dominant practice of the Black church. More than that, "emotional fervor" had become identified as the Holy Spirit, and not many of us had the courage to challenge that falsehood. My understanding of the Holy Spirit was not that it made you feel good, but it made you to be about doing good. The church became a place to look good and feel good on Sunday. Of course the pastor has to preach a good sermon and a little gravy would make it just right in many of our churches.

I took a different course when I became the pastor of New Calvary. I held an Easter Sunrise service on the steps of City Hall that was interracial and ecumenical. I even had the participation of the Unitarian pastor in Norfolk at that time, in the resurrection worship service. Like the prophet Amos, I saw our problems anchored in the seat of authority. So, in 1974, on April first, I purchased the Guide Publishing Company that produced the Journal & Guide Newspaper, the third oldest Black weekly in the nation. I challenged the power structure in Norfolk and its oppression of the poor. I openly argued with Mayor Roy Martin, who was about as insensitive to the aspiration of freedom and justice as Pontius Pilate when he washed his hands in the waters of delaying tactics, and wiped them dry in the towels of shifting responsibilities. The Council was adamant against Black representation in the running of the City. Many young aspiring students moved on to higher grounds elsewhere, away from Norfolk. Only a few would stay in Norfolk trying to make conditions better. Norfolk has a history of complacency and compliance among African-Americans. Most of us have accepted the historical God of the West and we tend to stay in our places. There were some exceptions, such as the late Mrs. Vivian Carter Mason, Dr. F.C. Carppage, Attorney Victor Ashe, Robert D. Robertson, Dr. William P. Robinson, Dr. J. B Henderson, and P.B. Young, and there were others. These I knew and "their works do follow them." After purchasing the Journal & Guide and using my home as collateral, I couldn't leave town if I had wanted to. Efforts by merchants tried to force me out of publishing by not advertising.

I called for boycotts or selective buying but I didn't get much support, even from the clergy who knew we were being oppressed. Like my father and his peers, they knew that God was going to 'fix it after a while.' As long as they were getting good anniversaries, and some getting half of the funds raised during revivals after the evangelist was paid, and getting the goodies from other church groups, why not feel content? Why bother the Man? I took an editorial stand against the resegregating of Norfolk Public Schools. I took an editorial stand against statewide elections favoring single-member districts in both the House and Senate and in the City Council elections. I editorially took a stand against what I called the black mafia, who exploited Black people with the blessings of White people for their own good. I broke ranks with the Democratic forces and the Golden Rod Ballot people, who selected candidates on what seemed to have been their ability to pay large sums of money, to draw poll workers, to attract advertising and to line their pockets. So when a few handpicked insiders at New Calvary demanded a special election to dismiss the pastor, I knew where they were coming from. I will always believe that it was the White man's idea to get rid of this non-conforming Black radical that did the City a "disservice," according to the late Mayor Roy Martin. And whenever some White folk speak, some Black folk tremble. I took issue with powerless Blacks being appointed and forgetting immediately that they were Black. That wasn't the case, however, with the late Judge Joe Jordan. A paraplegic and a World War II veteran, he was a lone voice on City Council and voted "no" on almost every issue. He was also a "hard" Judge. I personally don't know and have not heard of any decision he made from the bench that was influenced by mercy. No one could call him a pushover, despite the fact he was pushed much of the time in a wheel chair. All of my stands had foundations in the faith and the freedom that the Christ of Glory brought to us and which we had lost in obedience to the God of the West and the teachings of the White church. So I took issue with the courts interfering in the internal affairs of the church. So did about 300 members of New Calvary. Our problem was and still is we had the Bible that had been misinterpreted, and the Constitution that had been overlooked or disregarded. It plainly stated: "***Congress shall make no law respecting an establishment of religion or prohibiting the free exercise thereof; or abridging the freedom of speech or the press or the right of the people to assemble and to petition the government for a redress of grievance.***"

It was in the late summer of 1982 when Ms. Brenda H. Andrews joined New Calvary. A journalist in the U.S. Army, she became a Godsend, and immediately a member of the staff of the Journal & Guide as special assistant to the publisher. It was through her efforts that the Journal and Guide survived some of its darkest moments. While publisher, I had been invited to the White House under every president since 1973. I really did not have the time or the credentials necessary to stay full time with the Newspaper that had a business office staff that could not be trusted. My daughter, Maravia Anette Ebong, succeeded the late John Rover Jordan, as Executive Editor of the paper. She graduated from Virginia Union University in English grammar, and form Ohio State in journalism, both with honors. She married NSE Ebong, a Nigerian and went on to teach Mass Communication in Calabar, Cross River State in Nigeria. While an excellent writer, sensitive to the Black condition and the White problem in America, she had no experience in the business office.

Like me, she took the reports from the businesspersons in the office that we found later to be erroneous. Michelle Avella, my youngest daughter, became the advertising director. Her business acumen helped to save the Journal & Guide until help came through. Carlton B, Goodlette, M.D., Ph.D, and with his coming, all of us breathed a sign of relief. He owned several Black weekly newspapers on the West Coast, in Brooklyn, New York and Houston, Texas.

When Ms. Andrews came in she began to take a closer look at what was happening in the business office. We discovered a tax liability, and the business manager, a graduate of Hampton University, immediately resigned. The way he kept the books was incredible. During the entire time, he had not made one entry into the general ledger. He was inexperienced, but because of the respect I had for his late father, a lawyer and a substitute Judge, I erred in thinking that honesty was somehow an inherited quality. While the Journal & Guide was in shambles, from the standpoint of the business office, things were also falling apart at New Calvary. In 1985, Ms. Andrews, who had been in fact the CEO, accepted my offer to her to become the publisher. I turned it all over to her with my thanks and appreciations. She was given the responsibility for running the company. Dr. Goodlette, chairman of the board, supported this move for the good of the company and myself. It was my task then to get back with the church and try to get the gospel of love in the hearts of the people who had decided. Come hell or high water, they were going to get me out of Norfolk and the Journal & Guide. It was a disappointment that the City and dissidents would long regret.

It is not easy to do liberation theology among a people who never really left the slave dungeons constructed by western theologians and supported by elected officials. They had the support of judges with a racist and a paternalistic disregard for Black people, let alone their unfeigned faith in the God of the Ages. It is almost unbelievable that people whom you have taught, trained, given retreats, with outside professional consultants and speakers, on the purpose of the church and the meaning of our witness, given seminars and had listened to sound preaching for nineteen years, would react like heathens when the White power structure assured them that I would not be in their midst for long. It was not a matter of Christ and culture; it was a matter of Christ or culture. Obviously, they chose culture through the courts and I chose Christ for my part. And because I did, I can say today, along with others who have had similar experiences, Hallelujah Anyhow.

The Black Church today has come closer toward a vital witness in many cases. Many pastors are now elected officials throughout the Commonwealth of Virginia and across the nation. Tragically, some have been appointed and embraced by the limited goodwill of the power structure as good boys who know how to agree and not raise questions of oppression and justice or racial issues. They gladly come to functions of Black folk and hand out the key to the City or, in the case of Norfolk, the Mace, to esteemed and honored guests. But they will not raise their voices to a tremble when it cuts across the grain of the popular thought or thinking of oppression and injustice. Some of these leaders want to speak out but they find themselves in too deep to talk. They have no comment, abstain from voting, or just be absent. They can find love and support among their congregations because they have been anointed by the enemy of the poor and disinherited. They had to make the decision between "kicking down or kissing up." There are a few churches across the nation, along with their pastors, who know what it means to decide with the freedom that the Christ of Glory brings. Many would rather take a stand with the freedom that the power structure allows. Jesus would say that this is the kind church or pastor who keeps its light burning under bushels, and have trampled its salt under foot. This is the kind of church that is neither hot nor cold, and it makes God sick enough to spit them out of His system of redeeming Love and saving Grace.

The potential power of the Black church today is enormous. But seldom does that power supersede the commitment and the theological practice of the pastor. The late Dr. Wendell Somerville, Executive Secretary-treasurer of the Lott Carey Baptist Foreign Mission Convention, says that, "A little pastor (in theological practice) will bring a big church down to his size, or a big pastor (in theological practice) will bring a little church up to his size." In most instances, a pastor is always "safe" when the people have him at heart, and he is at the same time in the heart of the God of the West. When Jesus went into the synagogue to preach his first sermon, taking his text from the 61st chapter of deuteron Isaiah, according to Luke, the Gentile physician, he told a sweet story that had been heard time and time again. It had been read over and over across many years. The Living Bible says, "All who were there spoke well of him and were amazed by the beautiful words that fell from his lips. "How can this be they asked? Isn't this Joseph's son" (Luke 4:22 LASB)? Jesus had given the book back to the attendant and sat down. Jesus knew that they had heard Him but he also knew that they did not understand Him. He wasn't looking forward that day to "Reverend, you really gave us the word today or that was a beautiful presentation." Many times in the Black church we get caught up in the Word but we fail to point out the way. It leaves the congregation both impotent and powerless. So the potential power of the Black church often goes down the spiritual drywell of the soul and seeps out into the soil of forgetfulness.

Some of our preaching is so sweet, and is enjoyed so well, that half of the congregation cannot give you either the text or the subject if it was not included on the worship bulletin. When Jesus told Peter, "If you love me, feed the sheep; that means you must also watch the sheep." When Jesus saw all of those smiles of approval in the midst of sin, when he noted their joy in missing the mark, he had to get back up. He said, "The Spirit of the Lord is upon me." The Spirit of the Lord reveals little evidence in being upon some Black churches. Now there is a Spirit in the Black church, but we must learn to try the spirits by the Spirit. The Spirit brought Jesus back to his feet and engaged him into a hermeneutical exegesis of that sweet story that enraged the congregation, raised because a red flag in theological practice had been revealed. Jesus said, "These scriptures came true today." Now, just suppose they had listened to Him that day? Suppose they had heard Him! They heard His words, but they didn't hear Him. I don't know where I got this from, but for years, I would pause in my sermon and ask, "Are you listening?" The folk in the temple had made the Temple the center of their sins so long until they were satisfied. But when Jesus made it clear, they mobbed him and tried to push him off the cliff on which the city was built. Right in the midst of one's troubled dilemma while ministering to and in the Word of faith, God always makes a way. I think Luke included this story to tell us that, when we cooperate with the world through the Word, we'll always get congratulations from the church for the practice of "theological reflections," while by-passing theological practice.

The Black church has a calling of God to be "God's New Israel," many scholars of note have concluded. To a large extent, however, the Black church in many experiences is not heeding that call. The Black church today needs to become the drug czar in every community. We need to become the economic floor that undergirds the poor and the homeless. We have a need now as never before to support black businesses, and open up tutorial centers for intergenerational learning. We need to support the two hundred or more Black newspapers that tell our story. It is missing the mark when we have to close service so that we can get to see the games, whether it's baseball, football or basketball or any other kind of sports event for that matter. We should never elect Black officials and neglect them after they are in office. They must be held accountable. After all, Jesus said; "You are the light of the world." Preaching and teaching services should be held in every community, if not every church, every day or every night through the week. Our folk are never going to see the way from Sunday to Sunday when they stay at home and become engulfed in TV ministries that come and go in the style that we are so accustomed to seeing and hearing, particularly when it appears after those ministries go off the air, much of what they have said and sung was to the God of the West, and they might as well have been worshiping an idle of stone!

With more than 53% of the jail population Being black, with Black teenage pregnancies on the rise, with more Blacks dropping out of school than are graduating from school in the high noon of our technology, we must stop blaming and begging the "man." Isn't God our Father? Do we believe that God is real? Do we believe that He will supply all of our needs according to His riches in glory? Don't we know that there are personal sins and corporate sins in our midst? Are we not concerned about the demise in Black hospitals, banks, universities, and businesses? The answer is that we must begin to do theological practice in our churches through the God of the Ages and the Christ of Glory. We have got to put an end to those little sweet stories that make us glad on Sunday and we are just as "mad" on Monday as we were glad on Sunday. We have an awesome responsibility to go up against the neutralized and invincible ignorance in our churches today. We will never get away with "worshipping worship." We must began to worship the God of the Ages in "Spirit and in Truth." Some who hear must go away disturbed about the Word. It is a cutting Word and a revolutionary Word. It is a devastating Word, yet it is a promising Word and a redeeming Word to be put into practice. It is not a political party; it is not a social or a civic organization. It is not a fraternal organization or a secret lodge; it is the Word of God that we must honor and reverence. The Word will help us to find food for the hungry, and clothes for the naked. The Word will help us to find homes or build homes for the homeless and work for the unemployed and the underemployed. We will not win them all; neither Jesus nor the Apostles did that. But we ought to be winning some. We will win some that we thought we had already won, and win others who have never given us a thought before. Brothers and sisters called of God, let us "Do theology in the Black Church by preaching a "Liberating Word."

The Black church must become more involved in the political process that can help in the transformation from the "pie in the sky in the sweet by and by," to the practice of meeting the needs of people in the here and now. As a student of history, I was encouraged to learn that following slavery and during the period of the Reconstruction of a divided nation along the lines of Black and White, there were some Black men in Mississippi, Georgia, South Carolina, North Carolina, and even in Virginia who had the political guts and the fire of freedom and justice to run for political office. Many of them won. During Reconstruction a total of 17 Black men were elected to Congress, and two Senators from Mississippi, Hiram Revels and Blanche K. Bruce, were elected to the U.S. Senate. Senator Bruce was elected in 1874 and served a full term. He was born in Virginia and ended up in Mississippi. Senator Hiram Revels was the first African-American senator elected in 1870. He was an African Methodist Episcopal minister who served a church in Baltimore, Maryland. The Mississippi State legislature sent him to fill a vacancy in the U.S. Senate. He was born in North Carolina. When I learn where the decision makers were, and saw that we were absent, I began a political career that eluded a prophetic voice and view. In 1960, I was already stirring up the social and political sediments that had settled in Petersburg and Virginia. After discussing this matter with the officers of the Church, I threw my hat in the ring to run for the city council in Petersburg. One of my deacons and close friends, Joseph Owens, a strong member of the Democratic Party was my campaign manager. The campaign went well and Marguerite Bellefonte came to Petersburg upon my request and spoke at a banquet on my behalf. Other national speakers also came, such as The Reverend Dr. Walter Fauntroy, Pastor of the New Bethel Baptist Church and Congressman from the District of Columbia. Walter and I were classmates at Virginia Union and we graduated in 1955 with our Bachelors degree. Walter, experienced in the political process, came down to speak for me and to support me. When I first went to the National Baptist Bathhouse in Hot Springs, Arkansas, Walter Fauntroy went with me. I went across the street to a greasy spoon restaurant to get a late breakfast. There was this huge sister behind the counter plucking her fingers to the raving jukebox music. She was so into it she didn't notice that I was standing there waiting to be served. Before I could order she asked, are you going to the dance at the Baptist Bathhouse tomorrow night? I said very calmly, "I hadn't thought about it." She then said, "Are you married? (In that instant, the devil paid me a visit). I said, "Yes, but my old lady and me are separated." Her next question, "Are you staying at the Baptist Bathhouse?" I said, "Yes, I am." She said, "Do ya want to go with me to the dance?" I said, "I'll think about it." She said, "Give me your room number and your name." I gave her the room number. She said, "What is your name?" I said, "Walter Fauntroy." I came back to my room almost bursting with locked in laughter. I told Walter that there was a fine chick in the restaurant and she is going to call you to go to the dance with her. When that woman called with all of the broken English she could muster, Walter looked at me and I cannot print what he said. And he was a good preacher too! (I learned that from the late Dr. R.G. Williams). You may now better understand why my dear wife Marian had to pray specially for me. Neither of us went to the dance. Senator Clarence Mitchell from Baltimore came and added fuel to my political fires. I just didn't win! I unwittingly joined the booming crowd of the "I also ran group.

"In 1963, I also ran for a senatorial seat in the eighth senatorial district of Southside Virginia, against Senator Temple. He was also a Byrd machine Democrat who was thoroughly entrenched. He was one frightened White man. A janitor shared with me a letter that the incumbent senator had written to his constituents telling them what a threat I was to his campaign. He was appealing for funds and all the help he could get. I really thought I was going to win that one. During that election we ran into a voting fraud situation involving missing ballots and also the voting registrar's conveniently closed on the day in Dinwiddie County when Black citizens were supposed to register to vote. Any excuse they could think of was used. I didn't know it at the time, but the Lord was using me in the political process to see how critically corrupted it was, and I was to play a role in helping to get passed in Congress, the Voting Rights Bill of 1965. Here again I lost.

When I came to Norfolk in 1966, Dr. Martin Luther King, Jr., preached my sermon of installation. His wife, Coretta Scott King, later came to speak on my behalf as I was running for a seat on the Norfolk City Council in 1974. I had checked with Attorney Joe Jordan about running and he had given me thumbs up. I took that to mean that he was going to support me. A reporter called me and asked my opinion of a letter, a copy of which they had received, written by Attorney Joe Jordan to Mrs. King, asking her not to come to Norfolk on my behalf. I was shocked beyond belief. Even when he read the letter to me, I still couldn't believe it. I had worked with Joe in the Model Cities Programs of the Great Society and I thought we were on one accord. We had never had a disagreement. When he told Coretta that I had joined the power structure, I couldn't believe it and neither did she? It was the news of the day, but she came to me anyway, and her sister in law, Mrs. Farris, came with her. Coretta came and supported me. She said to one reporter that I know Milton, much better than I know the person who wrote me; he has worked side by side with my husband and me for several years. "I stand by him because I know what he stands for." I had experienced what the politicians and the political pendants did in Petersburg and Southside Virginia, but it had never occurred to me that such political travesty would be carried on in Norfolk, especially by Black people. Whatever they did to work against me, worked for them. This was almost ten years after the Voting Rights Bill had been signed and passed on into practice. The truth of the matter is, again I lost. I had the support of Norfolk stalwart citizens like Dr. J.B Henderson pastor of the historic Bank Street Memorial Baptist Church, Mrs. Vivian Carter Mason, Dr. I. Joseph Williams, pastor of the Antioch Baptist Church, Dr. Johnnie L. White, pastor of First Calvary Baptist Church, next door to New Calvary Baptist Church, and Councilman Curtis Harris of Hopewell, pastor of the Union Baptist Church of Hopewell, who had run for just about every office in every election until he won. When he won, he was so shocked he wanted a recount. Councilman Harris went on to become the first Black Mayor of Hopewell. Curtis had made the march for the Voting Rights Bill, and it worked for him. He got elected. I was to tell him that 'the most qualified folk never get elected.' That was my rationale for eating the "political sour grapes of losers." I had received support also from Councilman W. P. Clarke of Chesapeake and others. If everybody who supported me could have voted for me, I probably would have had a different story to tell. Yet I did play a role in paving the way and helping others to get elected.

Dr. Clyde Johnson, who succeeded me as pastor of First Baptist Church in Petersburg, did get elected to the city Council of Petersburg. In 1964, my friend, Deacon, Joseph A. Owens, who was my campaign manager, got elected to the City Council in Petersburg. I rubbed it in by telling him he had a better campaign manager since I, of course, was his campaign manager. While I never got elected to office here, I am still running the race to join that great Cloud of Witnesses there. Nobody can stop me from that election because I am already among the Elect of Glory, to reign with Him throughout the ages. I want to sing with Cleophas Robinson and Mahalia Jackson, "How I got Over...How I got over...my soul looks back and wondered, how I got over." My soul may look back but I know I got over by "Being the Church," in the here and now.

The Black Church today, in particular, and all churches are trying to find ways to adjust to the new reality of a changing. Many churches and pastors are finding out that the God of the West has led them in a path of divine deception. The church has to be the church today "outside the box" of tradition. Following the calls of culture rather than the call of Christ, we have been conforming to this world rather than being transformed by the Christ of Glory. The Spirit of the Lord must be upon us as it was on Jesus when He explained Isaiah 61:1-11, in Luke 4:14-19. We must take a serious look again at Romans 12:1-16. The church can no longer be seduced by culture and conform to the world; the church is called on to heal our brokenness and to be transformed by the Holy Spirit to bear witness for Jesus Christ. Many Virginia churches, community civil rights groups and individuals are uniting with the Southern Christian Leadership Action Council and forming Christian Actions Councils in churches and communities that are free enough to witness for Jesus in the non-violent love of Jesus Christ. Many of our Civil Rights groups are dealing more with egos rather than issues. It is safer to buy buildings funded by multi-million dollar corporations, than to build brothers. When we don't follow the Christ of Glory we tend to lose some of our creature comforts, but the Kingdom comes, the people are served, and God gets the glory. Churches today must not be operated by Roberts Rules of Order and by the directions of secular corporations, but by the Holy Spirit. When the people sense and feel the presence of the Holy Spirit, and their eyes come open and their needs are met in the world, they will fill the "house" as they did on the Day of Pentecost. This is the challenge of not only the Black Church in particular, but to all churches across denominational lines in a world ministry.

Dr. Reid & Dr. King

These Were The Busiest Of Times, Trying To Win Freedom!

CHAPTER V

THE PURPOSE OF THE CHURCH

This chapter is revised from the doctoral thesis submitted during my studies at Boston University, School of Theology in 1980.

The church has been defined in almost every church since Jesus founded it, and there are still questions as to what it is. Historically, the church has become what man has decided it to be, based on the captivity of his culture and his interpretations of the scripture that fit his social and religious situation. This in turn shaped his understanding of the Divine. The church has been vaguely defined and accepted as a social institution promoting moral values that serves as a custodian over the behavioral patterns of its members. Condemnation is often pronounced on the conduct of others whose behavior varies from what a church deems proper. In the early days of America, the church often sat in judgment of the behavior of its members. More recently it has sat in judgment of its ministers. For the most part, the "straight pulpit" and the "crooked pew" have become its "modus operandus," or method of operation. In the Black community, almost anyone can name a minister who has either been put out of a church for one reason or the other, but seldom can we find the record of a member who has been expelled for misconduct. The church has to do something. The White church tends to expel its ministers for taking a stand on some moral issue that runs counter to the social context of patriotism or social justice. The Black church, on the other hand, has often expelled ministers for taking positions on issues of personal morals and being caught or rumored in the act. But seldom do members of either church get expelled for either of these actions.

The church has been defined as a "body of baptized believers in Jesus Christ." The church has been defined as "God's redemptive mission to the world." When you look at the Biblical definition of the church, you find that it is a select group, a called out body, and a chosen people. "But you are a chosen race, a royal priesthood, a holy nation, and God's own people, that you may declare the wonderful deeds of him who called you out of the darkness into his marvelous light. Once you were no people but now you are God's people; once you had not received mercy but now you have received mercy." (2 Peter 2:9, 10 NIV). In other places the church has been defined as "the people of God," "the Body of Christ," "the temple of the Holy Spirit." It is the Laos, the authentic new life, the ecclesia, and the called out, the redeemed of the Lord, the Koinonia, or the fellowship of the redeemed, the blood-washed, the sanctified, the spotless, and the remnant. The church is possibly all of this, but it is even more. I believe that the church is the sign of God's liberating activity through Jesus Christ on behalf of the oppressed and the oppressor that demands new behavior as the instruments of both the reconciled and the reconciling activity of the Holy Spirit.

It is both the finished and the unfinished product of God's invasion in history on behalf of his fallen and alienated creation in a redeeming effort to make it new. This is what Paul meant when he was bold enough to assert that the church was the very body of Christ and "any man in Christ" is not a Christian, not a dues paying member of the local congregation, not even an office holder in the congregation of the righteous, but a "new creation of God." He is a disciple of the way. Christianity, then, is not a religion in the strictest sense of the word. It is a new way of life that seeks identity with cosmic reality, through Jesus Christ, by perfecting its witness to the world (Aion), this fallen age.

If we know what a church is, then we know its purpose. H. Richard Neibuhr says, "The purpose of the church is to increase love for God and neighbor. God's love of self, and neighbor, neighbor's love of God and self, self's love of God and neighbor are so closely interrelated that none of the relations exists without the other." The church is not that building standing there on the corner or in the middle of the block. Just before the Reverend Dr. Henry Lyons was ousted as president of the National Baptist Convention, he named a recording, "Lets Have Church." You cannot "have church" if you are talking about the body of Christ, but you can

"Be the church." The church is not necessarily that congregation sitting there on Sunday morning. Any religious assembly can form or come together on Sunday morning without being a church. To understand the purpose of the church there has to be a correlation between the "isness" and the "oughtness" of it as God's mission to the world. If it is the sign of God's liberating activity on behalf of the oppressed and the oppressor, that demands new behavior as the instrument of both the reconciled and the reconciling activity of the Holy Spirit, then it is engaged in its purpose. The church is not just a Sunday morning affair. It is not just a dressed-up occasion for the "do gooders." It is not just performing. It is not religious entertainment, with Christ being the main attraction. It is God's sign of His liberating activity that retreats from battle and celebrates a victory that has already been won in Jesus Christ, as the church "gathered" and bears witness to His redeeming love as the church "scattered."

Whenever we see the church behaving in a specified manner, its actions grow either out of its definition of what it is, or it lacks the will or the courage or the power to fulfill its purpose of a priestly custodial role that does little other than try to maintain the status quo. Some churches thrive on the balanced budget, the paid-off mortgage, its endowment funds and, sometimes, its investment in multinational corporations that are exploiting the poor of the Third World. Man-made churches are quite content with its history of non-involvement in the liberating activity of God's reconciling love. In other words, this is the church that celebrates "nothing," for it has nothing to celebrate. There is not victory in Jesus; it looks at and gives thanks for the victory of Jesus and suggests to the world that it is making a witness. As the priestly custodial religious club, it majors in the by-products of the faith. Its vision of the kingdom is the goodwill of their kindred, or at least their kind. Its minister is called to perform the priestly functions of worship and occasionally a prophetic call. Being a helper in the church and serving on a non-functioning committee, paying one's dues and, of course, attending occasionally, is about all you can expect from this concept of the church. Of course this church keeps its bills paid and provides a refuge for its members, its kind and its kindred on Sunday mornings. Occasionally we find the liberated church that accepts those in their membership who are not their kind or kindred, but who can fit into their patterns of theological reflections. This church has a mission program and sometimes a benevolent society because there is felt a need on the part of the members (at least some of them) that somebody should be concerned about missions.

On the other hand, a new look at the church reveals that the church is God's mission to the world, not to just their kind and their kindred. If the entire church is not about mission development, whether it is inner city mission development or missionary endeavors abroad, if the church is not concerned about people who are not of the Laos, then it fails to meet the standards of the kingdom or the criteria as the "sign of God's liberating activity." There is no separation between "being" and "doing" that is acceptable to the calling of God through Jesus Christ. Missionary Circles became necessary because the church had failed. For the church to be, it must do. It must do the will of God in this world of alienation and separation from His will and purpose. To be or not to be is still the question. For the church to be and not "do" is not only deceitful and hypocritical, it is damnable as well. The church as defined in this discovery is the "sign of the liberating activity of God on behalf of the oppressed and the oppressor through Jesus Christ and His redeeming love." It is set loose in the world to bring man into both a reconciled and a reconciling relationship with God. It is most clearly the church when it permits nothing – social systems, foreign or domestic policy, court edicts or legislation – "things present or things past" to separate it from the love of God which is in Christ Jesus." While it does that, it refuses at the same time to permit anything to deter it from this human, redemptive and divine dimension of its purpose. The church is not limited to denominational ties, racial or social classes. It is not geographical. It is not racially exclusive. It is not American Baptist or Southern Baptist. It is both redemptive and redeemable.

Cultural Corruption

To say that the church has been corrupted by culture is an understatement. The command of Jesus to the church was to "go into all the world and make disciples of all nations," not to inflict new disciplines that conflict with our faith and our culture. The church as God's mission to the world is to make learners prod the minds of men in order that they might open their hearts towards God, and by so doing be opened to the leading of His spirit. The writer of the book of Hebrews says, "Now without faith it is impossible to please Him, for the one that approaches God must believe that He exists and that He rewards those who seek Him" (Hebrews 11:6 NET). What has happened in Biblical history is not all history. The most important thing that has happened is "His" story, but the results of history are our story. The church was not stamped out during the first centuries of its persecution, but it was severely undermined when the world went into all of the church and made deceivers of men. Whenever the church majors in the comforts of its calling and minors in its calling in the Christ of Glory, worldly corruption creeps in unnoticed, and all that is unholy permeates its being. The results are found in this kind of church from the pulpit to the door. Prospective pastors will be looking for economic packages that benefit them, over and against the opportunities to proclaim the word of God in a prayerful posture that pleases God and brings deliverance to God's people.

Sin Defined

The first degree of corruption of the church is reflected in its definition of sin. Sin has been so loosely defined Biblically and theologically that it has filled the ideological bay of corrupted waters over which the church is half afloat; half afloat because the old Ship of Zion is not sailing, but failing. Many times the church equates the effort to catch up with progress as putting on a new roof, placing new carpet on the floor or furnishing the sanctuary with cushioned pews. Sin is what it has always been, but not what the captive church has always understood it to be. Sin is alienation and separation from the will and purpose of God. It has a personal dimension to be sure, and we are acquainted with that. The masters of our captive condition and the systems that superseded them made sure that we had a personal conviction of sin that always pointed to the moral shortcomings of the individual. As we look back on the influence of Christianity in support of the institution of slavery, the founding fathers and plantation masters developed an accepted interpretation of Christianity that, in fact, made Christianity sinful.

Some of the slaves were wise enough to laugh at their master's interpretation of Scriptures that made them victims, while it made the masters more rich and powerful.

Unfortunately, not enough of the slaves laughed, and too many became believers in the corruption of the faith that promised them a place somewhere in heaven, without any thought of their social existence on earth as free men and women. To the extent that Black people accepted the White man's version of the White Christ who was often pictured calm and gentle on some mountainside talking with White children in a field with White lambs, the Black church went into an exile of sinful religious service. Anyone who accepts Christianity today as it fits into the role of the institutional church without disturbing the system of the world, without dealing with the oppressed conditions under which men of color are forced to live, without dealing with the sins of a Christ less capitalistic system and godless imperialism, is accepting sin. It leaves the religious sinner in a state of blasphemy. He cannot distinguish between right and wrong, good and evil, sin and salvation. When we settle with a lifestyle that is in opposition to the will and purpose of God, that is sin. An illustration of this "setting" with a lifestyle in opposition to the will and purpose of God can be found in the February 2, 1980, mobilization march against the Ku Klux Klan in Greensboro, North Carolina. More than 7,000 demonstrators started chanting a song: "We are fired up, can't take no more, fired up, can't take no more, fired up, can't take no more, fired up, can't take no more." I started thinking about the Black church in that City. In November 1979, the Klan rode into the Black community of Greensboro and shot to death five members of the Communist Workers Party. One of those killed was Black. Since 1863, just after the Civil War, Black people have been the target of the Ku Klux Klan. The Klan has added Jews, Catholics and Communists to their list. The Black Pastors Conference in Greensboro, made up of some 46 churches, went on record not to support the march. Some even went on the radio and told their audiences not to get involved because the Lord would take care of the Klan. Several members of my congregation were in that march, as well as several members of First Baptist Church, Bute Street, in Norfolk, Virginia. The minister of First Baptist, Reverend LaVert Taylor, coordinated the march from Norfolk. He had received commitments from 14 churches in Norfolk to help underwrite the transportation expenses. More than $300 was contributed by New Calvary Church, and more than $200 by First Baptist Church, Bute Street. Other contributions, except one, were nil. One of the largest churches in the city contributed $25, and none of the ministers from other churches in Norfolk participated. I was concerned that labor unions, civic groups, fraternal orders and other community organizations, including student groups, could get fired up, while the church remained dormant. The church is in sinful exile and is accepting its sins as salvation. Congregations are waiting on the Lord, who came some 2,100 years ago.

Soon after the rally, I went to South America to talk with some of the church and community leaders about "liberation theology." I had the opportunity to talk with a Catholic priest, a missionary, a pre-med student, two University of Cartegena professors and the assistant chief of the Family Institute of Columbia. I talked with members of a Baptist church and was astounded to find out that the church in Cartegena had gone underground. There was interest on the part of the people who saw me as one who had come to bring them some degree of deliverance. I went to Squattersville, where 200 residents took over government property and made homes for themselves. In this village I learned that more than 70% of the population lived on less than $1000 a year. I preached one night for more than two hours. My greatest obstacle was from the White missionary, who was not only teaching English in the school system, but also was carrying a message of a "captive Christianity" to a land where people were starving to death. He was concerned that the theology of liberation did not take into account the sins of drinking, playing cards and dancing. In his opinion, it was too liberal to be useful. I inquired about what he felt was wrong with dancing. He responded that dancing created sexual desires, and sex is sinful. What's wrong with playing cards? He answered that playing cards leads to gambling, and gambling is a sin. I asked further what was wrong with drinking. He said that drinking leads to drunkardness and therefore is a sin. Upon closer examination and conversation, he admitted that he drank, but he did it discreetly. He admitted that when he and his wife visited America, they danced when they went out for an evening of relaxation. I inquired further as to other concerns he had as a missionary. He responded that people in the church were always bickering over the minister's salary, and that the church was just at a standstill. Further, he felt that there were pro-Russian groups, pro-Peking groups and other pro-groups in the church fighting each other, all in the name of justice. This resulted in a standstill. Then, like Paul on Mars Hill, I opened up to him Jesus, the "God of the oppressed." When I finished some two hours later (some of the tourists had by now joined us), they wanted me to come back to conduct some seminars on doing liberation theology. I think the missionary was almost persuaded to become a disciple of Jesus Christ.

On the way back to the U.S, I began to think about our own condition and the purpose of the Black church in exile. I began to think how meaningless the Black church in America had become because we have adopted the lifestyle of our captors. We have forgotten the impact that men like Richard Allen, Nat Turner, Denmark Vessey, Paul Cuffee and Samuel Ringgold made in doing liberation theology. Some of the early proclaimers of the Good News used moral persuasion to uproot the Black slave from his immoral planting on American soil that was confiscated from the Indians. Others felt led by any means possible, including violence. It was Marcus Garvey who felt that any people who did not have a culture, a faith and a land of their own would always be subjected to the people in the land where they lived. As a result, he started the back-to-Africa movement through the American Colonization Society. All he could see for Blacks in America was a continuing struggle in the sins of White Americans who had declared that Black people were not persons, but chattel property, that they had "no rights that a white man was bound to respect" (Dred Scott Decision of 1857).

To the legitimate Black church, sin had a different definition. Sin was being oppressed. Sin was being captive in a racist society. Sin was not getting enough to eat after working too hard all week. Sin was accepting the laws of man that kept Black folk in physical bondage prior to 1865 and in psychological bondage ever since. Sin was denying Blacks the opportunity to read and write yesterday and denying Blacks quality education today. Today sin is the act of Sears, one of the largest retail stores in America, challenging affirmative action for Blacks that, through blood, sweat and tears, became the economic backbone of this nation. Sin was denying one of his humanity under God, thereby rendering Black men to an ontological rejection. Sin was all that made White folk and the White church prosper while it demeaned Black folk and made them hewers of wood and drawers of water. Sin was segregating Blacks in the White church, denying Blacks admission to White hospitals and schools. The Black church has to deal with the new definition of sin. The nature of our exile is in the false concept of what we have been taught by the enemy about sin. Jesus said, "If you continue in my word, you are truly my disciples, and you will know the truth, and the truth will make you free. Truly I say to you, everyone who commits a sin is a slave to sin. The slave does not continue in the house forever; the son continues forever. So if the Son makes you free, you will be free indeed" (John 8:34-36 NIV). We have come to call the results of "sin," sin. It is sinful, but the result of sin is not the sin. Sin is missing the mark. It is separation and alienation from the Will and Purpose of God. When I eat more than is enough, I sin. When I fail to take proper care of my body, I sin. When I permit the social systems of society to bind me to this earthly hell with hopes of a heaven to come on earth, is sin. Not until we become born of the Spirit of God can we be united with Him. Not until we become united with Him can He save us from sin. When He saves us from sin, it is not just personal sin, but also the social sins of society. That's the difference between soul salvation and whole salvation. If, in our exiled condition, we could get this vision of salvation, we can begin the process of being liberated.

Satisfaction With Sin

The purpose and mission of the Black church has become distorted because we have become satisfied with our sinful existence. We have accepted existence without essence and music without melody. While banished to the Island of Patmos, John wrote letters to the churches of Asia Minor, none of which was White. It appears to me that the church in Laodicea was a paradigm of the Black church in exile today. Religion is the most meaningful experience in the life of Black folk. But we should never become adjusted to this hell that God sent His son to redeem us from. When we allow ourselves to become adjusted to the sameness of our society, the resulting condition will be corruption. Corruption appears when the church is built around the self-interest of the members or the community without the presence of the Holy Spirit. When we become proclaimers without being claimed, when we seek to become satisfied without sanctification, corruption seeps in and we become self-righteous. Consequently, the divine is diluted and the purpose of the church becomes perverted. When Constantine, the Roman emperor, decided that if you cannot beat them, join them and made Christianity the state religion, it ended persecution. It also ended the vital witness of the church, at least for a while. Whenever the church escapes persecution, suffering, humiliation, sorrow and death, it escapes life's meaning and purpose.

The church faced another degree of corruption in an analysis of Christianity itself. When the disciples were first called "Christians" at Antioch, it was a slur, a bad name. We have come full circle. If you are a serious, committed disciple today, and someone calls you a Christian that defaces your discipleship. Not only do I resist being called "Reverend," which I am not, I don't want to be called a Christian in today's normal understanding of the word. If by Christian we mean being obedient and servants to White people, if by Christian we mean affirming institutional racism by portraying a White racist Christ on our walls, in our literature, in the church school, in the artwork of stained-glass windows and on posters for vacation Bible schools, if by Christian we mean accepting without question the immorality of capitalism and condemning without question communism, if by Christian we mean acceptance of religious morality and denial of the social imperatives of the gospel . . .If by Christian we mean, as Dr. Martin Luther King, Jr., said, "taking the necessities from the teeming masses and giving luxury to the privileged classes," then it is clear once and for all that I am not a Christian. I am a disciple of Jesus Christ.

Jesus never asked us to be Christians. He invited us to be disciples; His disciples. And there is no discipleship without discipline. He invited us to be learners: "Come unto me all ye that labor and are heavy laden, and I will give you rest" (Matthew 11:28 NIV). He invited us to be disciplined disciples: "If any man would come after me, let him deny himself and take up his cross daily and follow me" (Luke 9:23). Some of the most barbaric, inhumane actions in all of history have been committed under the corruption of the so-called Christian banner. The religious wars, fistfights in church councils, the dehumanizing institution of slavery, the exploitation of imperialism and colonialism, the hunger and deprivation in America, where church-going Christians are paid not to produce food in a world where one billion of the estimated six billion people on the face of the earth are literally starving to death. If the purpose of the church is to come alive, then we must reject Christianity, as we know it. It should be rejected because it has become corrupted. It is understood that Biblical repentance entails conversion. Literally, the word means "turning around." The Greek word "metanola," as Luther insisted so vigorously, means "a total change of mind." It is not only a change of mind; it is also a change of heart. It makes us, as Paul says, new creatures.

As soon as the church drops the title "Christian" and thinks seriously about being God's mission, the more likely we are to deal creatively with the corruption of culture and focus on its purpose. To be Christians in a church that refuses to enter into dialogue with one another but does not hesitate to dialogue about one another . . . to be Christians in a church that skirts by on the basic issues like its purpose . . . like nuclear power, institutional and personal racism, a human world order, a just economic system, unemployment, sexism, inadequate housing, inflation, law and order without justice and energy, is to accept the corruption of the church and the perversion of the faith as the order of the day. Not to deal with these issues is to make a mockery out of the Lordship of Jesus Christ and accept the reality of the anti-Christ as Lord. What matters most about the purpose of the church is that it becomes the sign of God's liberating activity in His world as "change agents" or reconciling man to his Maker. In light of the apparent corruption existing in the church today, resulting from a distorted definition of sin and a satisfaction with the existence of sin, one is led to question the purpose of the Black church today. I contend that the Black church has some specific and definitive purposes that give it credibility in today's world. The Black church must provide a forum for the preaching of Black liberation in light of Jesus Christ. It must have as its purpose the arousing of the spirit of freedom among Black people. It must demonstrate through its actions that the soul of the Black community is inseparable from liberation and must always be based on Jesus Christ. It must have as its purpose the recognition of the theological character of the Black community, whose being is inextricably bound with liberation theology through Jesus Christ. As the Black church lives out its mission, it must accept the task of freeing the souls of Blacks from sin and the bodies from physical, political and social bondage, and setting the conditions of existence so they may achieve full humanity.

Finally, the purpose of the Black church is to make disciples of all men, and not our Western concept of Christianity. Its purpose is to glorify God by engaging in fellowship or koinonia with each other and celebrating its victory in the Christ of Glory. Important to this glorification and celebration is the role-played by Black preaching in the worship experience. The Black church is the sign of God's liberating activity through Jesus Christ as the reconciled and the reconciling activity of the Holy Spirit. That is its purpose, and its witness commits the real Black church to the development of the beloved community. There is a passage of scripture in the book of Revelation that we should consider as we look at the purpose of the church. "Then I saw a new heaven and a new earth, for the first heaven and earth had ceased to exist, and the sea existed no more. And I saw the holy city-the new Jerusalem-descending out of heaven from God, made ready like a bride adorned for her husband. And I heard a loud voice from the throne saying: Look! The residence of God is among men and women. He will live among them, and they will be his people, and God himself will be with them as their God" (Revelation 21:1-23 NET).

The Church that worships the God of the Ages, and the Christ of Glory, through the directions of the Holy Spirit, is at work getting us to "this place," where God will dwell with us, and wipe away all tears.

Dr. Reid with the 1968 Poor People's Campaign.

Dr. Reid's Bid for Norfolk City Council.

CHAPTER VI

CRISES AT CALVARY

The Black preacher, if not all preachers, is familiar with "Crises at Calvary," or he or she doesn't understand Calvary. At Calvary one finds both opportunity and danger, and we don't have to go to China for that assurance. Jesus talked "about bearing your own cross" and if you don't, "you are not worthy of following after me." We need to remember that it was "the crucifixion" that took place on Calvary; and not the Resurrection. Unless there is a crucifixion, there can be no resurrection in one's life. That hymn of the Church by George N. Allen, and Thomas Shepherd, that raises the question, "Must Jesus Bear the Cross Alone And all the world go free?" can be understood more clearly in this chapter. To get a better understanding of the ministry at New Calvary Baptist Church in Norfolk from July of 1966, to July of 1985, we need to have a historical perspective of both the church and the pastor during that period. There are three strong churches in Norfolk, two of which are next door to each other and the third about three miles away. All of them have Calvary in their names, First Calvary, Second Calvary, and New Calvary. There is something about the name *Calvary* that was obviously dear to the founders. Without question the experience of our Lord on "Calvary" some 2100 years ago has had some influence on their names. First Calvary Baptist Church was organized 1880, some seventeen years after the Emancipation Proclamation was issued, and fifteen years after the end of the Civil War. Second Calvary and New Calvary were organized subsequent to First Calvary.

The whole eventful story of America in the "terrible thirties", from the crashing blow of the collapse of the stock market to the day war was declared against Germany, must be taken into account in building a chronology of New Calvary Baptist Church. As prophetic as one might have been during the 1930's, it assuredly would have been difficult to convince the populace that they would be witnesses to the greatest financial panic in American history. The 1930's would also usher in what was to be historically recorded as the most prolonged and desperate economic crisis ever in the history of the nation. The Great Depression had hit America a terrible blow. As Peter F. Drucker has said, "Depression shows man as a senseless cog in a senselessly whirling machine which is beyond human understanding and has ceased to serve any purposes but its own."

America through the looking glass was a reflection of hunger, desperation, destitution, unemployment, and broken dreams for many. Yet there was a shadowed reflection of a people desperately clinging to the ideals and assumptions of a time that was swiftly slipping through their hands. This, after all, was White America, a land of opportunity at least for some. In contrast, Black America, having survived a constant storm of destitution, economic, social and political deprivation, was further pierced by the tornado winds of the Depression. Having no economic, social, or political banker to retreat to, it was no surprise that Black America found refuge in the sanctity of the church. For it was God that could cease the winds of the Depression, scatter the storm clouds, and send the rays of hope for a better life. The small band of people whose thirst for religious comforts led them to establish New Calvary Baptist Church, were no different from the masses of Black Americans of the 1930's. Living in Norfolk, Virginia, did not exempt them from the soup lines, the unemployment lines, or the lines of sheer destitution. Neither did living in Norfolk provide a haven from the pain and agony of the gradual deterioration of the economic and political structure of the nation.

Against this backdrop emerged the history of New Calvary Baptist Church. In the first month and on the 26th day of 1930, I was born. Those who would find out my ability to consume food would perhaps suggest that I might have had more effect on that decade than was thought at the time. After all I was a product of prayer and supplication and the first male child born unto my parents after seven girls. During the period of the Great Depression in America, New Calvary was organized, specifically on May 16, 1934, in a building that had been repossessed during the darkest days of the Depression. As a result of the financial crisis that existed in the nation, jobs and income were limited for all Americans in general and Black Americans in particular. Second Calvary Church was padlocked and the wheels of gospel expression came to a screeching halt when the membership was unable to fulfill the financial obligation of the mortgage. Determined to let nothing stop the movement of the gospel train, some members of the congregation sought and found a new location for Second Calvary. Others, who felt a kinship to the "sacred place on the corner", organized and embarked upon a direct faith-in-action campaign to have the doors reopened. The place on the corner was renamed New Calvary. Truly it was a new day and a new direction in the midst of the seemingly backward movement of the nation. The Church called Dr. D.Y. Campbell of Washington, D.C., as its first pastor. Dr. Campbell was an evangelist whose sermons were considered by many to be matchless and electrifying with fervor. If his grandson, Dr. D.Y. Campbell, who succeeded me as pastor of New Calvary, is any indication of the quality of an outstanding preacher with a delivery of sermons, and considering his kinship with his maternal grandfather, then those of us today may have an idea of what his grandfather was like. God has a way of bringing things around to suit his purpose; after all he is God. The late Dr. D. Y. Campbell worked to improve also the financial condition of the Church with the success of a growing membership at New Calvary. The mortgage was paid off in ten years. Prior to his death in 1942, Dr. Campbell's success rested in giving the newly formed congregation a sense of direction and a bit more financial security. Further direction was given the Church when Dr. Campbell arranged with the local Baptist Ministers Conference to have the Church recognized as a "Missionary Baptist Church."

The word *missionary* is derived from a Latin word meaning "sent ones." The designation of 'missionary' is one of at least twenty-seven designations in the Baptist Church, or, better stated, among Baptist churches. I have never researched it but a professor of the Southern Baptist Seminary in Louisville, Kentucky, said on a trip to the Soviet Union in 1985, that there are 54 different designations of *Baptist*. The designation of 'Missionary Baptist' gives an evangelistic flare to the cause of the Kingdom whose fire was always diminished by other interests. In some churches the missionary circle replaced the need for every member's being a part of the missionary zeal. It was a locked-in deal that needs to be dealt with today. In some churches a Commission on Missions or a Board of Missions has replaced the Missionary Circle. During this first decade of its existence, New Calvary was engrossed in the business of winning souls and reaching out to the needy and to those who had been locked in by the socio-economic conditions of the time. It was to this end that New Calvary was led to take a kind of leadership in providing a home for the elderly in the Diamond Spring section of Virginia Beach, Virginia. Reaching out to others seems to have been a part of its early home-mission efforts under Dr. D.Y. Campbell and it was continued under Elder Samuel A. Wilson. Elder Wilson, as he preferred to be called, became the second pastor of New Calvary in June 13th of 1943. He brought with him his own evangelistic style that professed itself in what could be identified as a "tent ministry" in pastoral circles. Receiving a stipend of a salary from the Church, he distinguished himself as the only Black licensed chiropractor in the Commonwealth of Virginia. He was a very "artful" chiropractor who was highly recommended in his profession. I should know about this because I had been under his chiropractic care for a number of years and it all started with the first treatment or adjustment. Following the direction set by Dr. D.Y. Campbell, he immediately set out to liquidate the debts of the congregation. Having completed this task, he turned his attention toward the construction of an edifice that would encompass more of the needs of the members and the community. His vision of a new building that included both a sanctuary and an educational complex was realized on April 16, 1961, when the present structure was dedicated. Elder Wilson's dreams had manifested themselves in a structure that in 1961 cost in excess of $600,000. It was during this pastorate that the church committed itself to community outreach through the purchase of a home for the elderly, known as New Calvary's OLE Folks Home.

This home, purchased at a cost of $45,000 in 1945, was located on an eleven-acre site in the Diamond Spring section of Virginia Beach. It included twenty-two private rooms and was operated by a central board of the church. An account of the dedication published in the Norfolk Journal & Guide on Saturday, August 2, 1972, stated:

> *"New Calvary's OLE Folks Home was like a new heaven to the seventeen guests who lived there. It is an idea translated into an Institution to serve people in their declining years when they need care and sympathy. The home houses eleven women and six men. Every effort is made to maintain the atmosphere and facilities of a comfortable home for guests."*

Records indicate that there was unanimous support of the membership of the Church for the project. Elder Wilson's administration of the home terminated with his death in 1965. His vision, administrative skill, and his energy kept the home alive. During his declining health much of the life of the home began to fall from view.

Again the congregation of New Calvary found itself without pastoral leadership. Desiring to continue their forward movement, much time and energy were utilized in selecting a new pastor. In order to give ample time to this task, the members worked together for one year before a selection was made. I was among those who were extended invitations to deliver sermons and to outline goals and aspirations for New Calvary. Again on May 23, 1966, I was officially notified that I had been unanimously elected pastor of New Calvary Baptist Church. I immediately requested a meeting with the officers of the church. They turned out deacons and trustees like a mighty army. I gathered some information about the church and my primary source was Mrs. Pearl Holloman, the clerk of the church, the church historian and a member of the pulpit committee. The officers had some questions for me. I felt just a little tension when I responded to some of their questions. I had gone through nine challenging years as pastor of the historic First Baptist Church of Petersburg, a church that stood in the staying shadows of the largest battlefield of the Civil War. While First Baptist had its origin in Prince George's County in 1756, it moved to Petersburg and has had a continuous history since 1774. I assumed the pastorate of

New Calvary after I requested the officers to report their findings of me back to the congregation and have them, if they wanted me, to extend the call again. They did and with much enthusiasm and anticipation, I accepted the call.

While the building was up and had been dedicated, it was not completed. This we set out to do and to burn the mortgage, which was done in four years. I presented to the church a fourteen-point program, which was adopted. This program called for the full use of the building for social programs during the week, along with religious education programs. There were some members who had some serious reservations about community groups – even a day care center – being in the Church because this might "mess up our church." We developed the largest day care center in Norfolk, and we also developed the Ruth Nelson Cook Academy, a private school with grades K-6. This private Black school became integrated on order of the Spirit. It turned out to be one of the most noised-about learning institutions of its kind. All students who graduated from the daycare center and the private school were promoted when they entered the public schools. Mrs. Barbara Alexander was the Director and Administrator. She did not cut corners or grade on the curb. She held all students and parents to a very high standard. We don't know of a child in the academy that did not go on to some university and complete academic degrees. Many of them completed terminal degrees! Thanks again to Mrs. Barbara Alexander.

We got approved and were funded to construct 112 units of housing for senior citizens. We had a jobs program, a hot meals program for the needy, a clothing bank, and secular church on Saturdays. We presented plans for the restoration of the Attucks Theater, a historic landmark in the City that was next door to New Calvary Baptist Church, which were completely ignored. It was also during this time when I was feeling a void from my civil-rights leadership in Petersburg, Southside Virginia, Danville, and through the South in particular, I felt led to purchase the Journal & Guide, the third oldest Black weekly in America. I don't know yet why I did it, but I thought I could make a continuing contribution to the struggle in America's race problems. I am not sure if I asked God about this venture or not. But I am a witness that for 14 turbulent years, God did hear from me. When I purchased the paper I had no concept of the difference between a by-line and a balance sheet. I was already at New Calvary and I signed up for a Secular Calvary that would have an effect on my doing Liberation Theology. I was walking in the same path of the previous two pastors with "helping others" as my considered understanding of the social imperatives of the gospel. The church at this point was engaged in support for the following:

1. The Interreligious Foundation for Community Organization
2. The Southern Christian Leadership Conference
3. The Black United Fund
4. The United Negro College Fund
5. Virginia Union University, and the School of Religion
6. State Baptist Conventions, and the General Baptist Convention of Virginia
7. Lott Carey Baptist Foreign Mission Convention
8. Progressive National Baptist Convention
9. American Baptist Convention Region of the South
10. National Black Pastor's Forum

Hot and foremost on my agenda was the Southern Christian Leadership Conference, founded by the late Dr. Martin Luther King, Jr. It had since its inception worked to achieve Liberation and Justice for the oppressed people of the world. New Calvary has not only supported this organization financially but members had actively participated in protest marches, boycotts, and other non-violent demonstrations. The Tidewater Black United Fund, local affiliate of the National Black United Fund, was started at New Calvary by a group of interested members and myself. This organization had worked to raise funds for the support of programs in the Black community who did not qualify for support through the local United Communities Fund. As I see it now, red flags began to rise. Some of the stable businessmen became alarmed at the announcement of the United Black Fund. I was cornered by Mr. Harry Price, of Prices TV, in his store, and questioned with regards to the Black United Fund. My having been installed in New Calvary by one of the most vocal and gifted civil-rights leaders of all time, raised some more flags, but with the hopes that it would not disturb the status quo. Flags were raised during the Poor People's Campaign, of which I served as coordinator in Virginia. Now as publisher of the Journal & Guide Newspaper, which was a threat to the White power structure, flags, flags, and more red flags began to fly. There were several caterers in New Calvary who made their living serving the White elite in their homes, clubs, or wherever they chose to gather. The word came to me by several members of the concern that was growing in the White community. A mayor of Norfolk, Mr. Roy Martin, now deceased, had the audacity to tell me that I was being a disservice to the City by having the Poor Peoples Campaign to come to Norfolk.

The late Dr. Carlton B. Goodlette was a blessing to my family, the community, the nation, the world, and me with his input into the operations of the Journal & Guide. He was a newspaper magnate on the West Coast. He became the controlling stockholder in the Guide Publishing Company and gave me invaluable help with making the paper what it never had been, an institution to be dealt with by the local power structure. When we speak of the editorial stance of the Journal & Guide as an "iron fist in a velvet glove," that was only on out-of-town racial concerns. The late P.B. Young was a genius in sending vicarious messages to downtown Norfolk, via North Carolina, South Carolina, Mississippi, and Alabama, but he always seemed to avoid a direct confrontation with the local power structure. It was not a rejection of me personally, or my stance on doing "Liberation Theology" that brought an end to our ministry, but it was the illegal intrusion of the State into the internal affairs of the Church that still should be challenged and one day it will be. Many members never did understand what happened in that so-called meeting of the Church set up by the Circuit Court to determine if I should be the pastor of the Church. To show its utter disregard and disrespect, the Court sent in an overseer who was of the Jewish faith, into a congregation of Black Baptists, with armed guards, to take over the meeting. Then they took the votes back to the Circuit Court and counted them privately with only one questionable member of New Calvary present, and announced the verdict to the press, i.e., that the members had voted me out as pastor. It had been a three-year fight and most of us were tired. We did not have adequate legal presentation on the local level, although our attorney kept accurate records of his professional time and expenses and actually suggested at one point that we concede.

Approximately three hundred members, including all of the officers and members of the social actions programs and the Kiddie Kollege and the Private School, left the church. The treasurer, the chairman of the fellowship of deacons, the chairperson of the commission on finance, the superintendent of church school, and 90% of the teachers all left the church, and formed Gideon's Riverside Fellowship. It had been a critical time during the months of turmoil actually carried on by forces outside of the church that wanted to control the church. There was no easy route and no legal way that institutional and personal racism could find its way in to curtail the ministry, so the powers that "be" went after the pastor. There was no church property involved, no church funds, and no immoral impropriety at all. I was a hard-hitting editorial writer penning a column in the Journal and Guide that had a heading called, 'The Publisher's Pen,' and a pen it was. The publisher not only took issue with City fathers, he also took issue with the inverted racism of black leaders. With a few dollars well placed, it wouldn't take much to buy an election in the City of Norfolk. The West Side of the City dominated the City Council for years. As a community organizer around the country, I could get much more done in communities outside of Norfolk than in Norfolk itself. This was a City by the sea that was determined to ignore the justice needs of its citizens of color. And when it came time to file a suit against the City to provide for a ward system whereby Blacks could elect Blacks of their choice to the City Council, naturally one of the plaintiffs was none other than the pastor of New Calvary Baptist Church, Milton A. Reid. The suit had to go all the way to the U.S. Supreme Court, but so far as our ministry of Liberation and Celebration was concerned, we were living in our victory that was won on the other side of Calvary more than 2000 years ago. We never stopped worshiping, baptizing, teaching, witnessing, feeding the poor, and building homes for first-time homebuyers. We ministered to the homeless, provided jobs, and did everything we were doing outside of our church-home building but now continuing our mission in structures that God faithfully provided.

While a building is comfortable, convenient, recognizable, awe inspiring (like Solomon's Temple), it is not necessary for the work of the church. Isn't it strange that Jesus never did have one? The church building in many instances is too confining for the crises at Calvary. When we left the building in 1985, we had laid the groundwork and had received funding for the development of Calvary Towers, a mid-rise for the elderly. While we continued our worship in hotels, public schools, clubs, a store front, and the Norfolk State University, we purchased approximately four acres of land in Chesapeake and this began a hard fight with that City's government as we attempted to develop a subdivision of housing for first-time home owners. I must say that Mayor William E. Ward and Dr. Cuffee, the City Manager, were strong supporters of our efforts. Those homes were built and sold long before we began building a house for the Lord and this evidenced the mature faith of our congregation. We purchased, with the help of the American Baptist Extension Corporation, a shopping center on Campostella Road in the City of Norfolk, to build our church home, another home for the elderly, the Martin Luther King, Jr., Family Life Institute, and a commercial district. This project was laughable to many Blacks in City Hall, while others thought we had a good idea, but it was a little "ambitious" for a small congregation. We received estimates as high as one hundred plus million dollars to develop the project, which would have been the only one of its kind in America, built by Black people. Some of the largest construction companies in the nation submitted bids, with "Turner Construction" being one of them. It was unreal as I look back on it. There was no way that the conservatism and the staunch racism in Norfolk was going to allow me to build anything of that magnitude in this City. We went back and forth to the City of Norfolk, and if we thought we had problems developing 13 housing units in a new subdivision in Chesapeake, we had not begun to run into the red tape in Norfolk. Perhaps, if we had not developed a site plan for the area and had not caused a feasibility study that was positive to be done, we might have been able to put up a little colored church. We could have added some classrooms that we could have converted to a family life institute during the week, but our plans were too massive. Some planners, Black and

White, would and could not see our vision.

While I was using most of my time trying to keep the property of the shopping center maintained, keep the mortgage payments up, getting this fixed and getting that fixed, other things were running behind in our storefront church. You may ask yourself, why weren't the trustee committee or some building committee doing what I was doing in this area? The truth is, we didn't have any who knew how or what to do. I even found myself as CEO of the flea market when we had to put out the first manager of some 42,000-sq. ft., for bad checks. I had an earned doctorate from Boston University and I had nothing in my background that qualified me for operating a flea market. At one point we had about twenty stores on the inside, with a restaurant, a meat market, shoe sales department, a floral shop, several jewelry shops, and a mixture of others. The vendors were Black and Korean. If you think race relations are bad between Black and White Americans, just wait until you find yourself having to deal with Blacks and Koreans when the Koreans think they are beyond White and you cannot speak the language. We have had some Koreans in our shopping center that could not speak English "at will" in the Black community unless they were selling. 85% of the vendors could be counted on being late with their monthly lease payment. I have discovered that, in the world, you will seldom miss a day without being reminded of your crisis at Calvary. Jesus is very clear about your behavior in the midst of crisis. Read again his Sermon on the Mount. Although enough funds were being generated, our anchor lessor did not feel so moved to pay his lease to our officers, and kept making excuses, or giving bad checks. Time after time we had to go to court, and by the time we got to court, he would come up with funds just before our case was called. It wasn't so much of 'Lord, how many times should we forgive this tenant, but how many times shall we put up with this business transaction that was about to devour us?' We took action against him and he sued us for damages. We finally got him out with his owing us some eighty-five thousand dollars. Less than three months later he was killed instantly in an automobile accident in Crystal City, Virginia.

The World Witness

While this was going with the witness at New Calvary, I continued a witness through IFCO, (the Interreligious Foundation for Community Organization) and Pastor's for Peace, its new direction mass action arm. Having had some twenty-two years of service behind me with IFCO, and being a personal friend of its founder, Dr. Lucius Walker, I became Vice President of Pastor's for Peace. We were taking humanitarian goods, food, and material aid to Nicaragua, El Salvador, Honduras, Guatemala and Cuba, through the church communities. When we had trouble at the borders and with the watchful conservative eyes of custom officials, I would write editorials about those experiences. I had the privilege and the compelling need to tell the truth about Latin America and especially the United States' relationship with Cuba. I can say on short order that it is not what the "White House" has been telling us. The American investment interest in Cuba was purely exploitation for capitalistic gain and imperialistic control. The same racial war that was going on in America existed in Cuba. Black entertainers had to come through the back door in hotels to entertain Cubans and American businessmen, who used that island nation for their own immoral exploits. When the Castro Revolutionaries won the battle against America through the Bay of Pigs invasion, they threw out the American industrial and business interests also. And every elected US president since the Cuban Revolution has held a hard line against Cuba because they needed the American business financial support to get elected. It is not because they are Communist 90 miles off our shores any more than we are Capitalists 90 miles off their shores. This is the kind of summation of writings that came from time to time from the Publisher's Pen of the Journal & Guide Newspaper.

In other words, I was not the kind of conforming pastor that Norfolk had expected or desired. And the fact that I was jailed twice in Norfolk for religious liberty, with the state invading the domain of our congregation, and that became alright, made me stand up, preach, and teach, that it was all wrong. My sermons were taped every Sunday and taken to the circuit court every Monday morning by an unlettered preacher in our congregation who had looked forward to getting me out so that he could bring real leadership to the people. That was in his mind and God struck him down while eating his breakfast one morning with a heart attack. While still at New Calvary I had to preach "that" funeral. Believe me, "You will be tried in the midst of "Crises at Calvary." While "Crises at Calvary" will not have any mercy on you, God will. While in the midst of my Crises at New Calvary Baptist Church, I never made any attempt to evade or avoid either criticism or controversy, nor conflict, and neither did I seek it. When you take a stand for righteousness in an unrighteous world, controversy, conflict and criticism will find you. That is what happened to Jesus and the Apostles. It happened to the church fathers and the disciples of Jesus throughout Christendom. This is what happened to Dr. Martin Luther King, Jr., Malcolm X, and to a large extent the Honorable Louis Farrakhan. You have to make a decision as to whether you will go with the flow or whether you are going to stem the tide and swim upstream as you bear witness of Jesus. I am reminded of the words of Jesus when He said, "Either you are for me, or you are against me." At Calvary, like Jesus, we will find ourselves where we are because of the decisions we made before we got to be whose we are. And when we make decisions, we cut off all other alternatives. We cannot have it both ways at the same time. This seems to be what many preachers/pastors/ prophets are in fact trying to do today.

It took at least two "safe black powerless political pawn pastors," coupled with the racist crew of the status quo, to lock arms for my demise. Just as the gospel writers did not see fit to call the names of those religious powerless pawns that testified against Jesus, I will not call the names of those who testified against me. That is not important. What they thought would be my demise, actually was my resurrection. I considered my end at New Calvary a new beginning. It gave me the opportunity to write my memoirs. If Jesus could say while in agony and pain from the cross as the Christ of Glory, "Father, forgive them for they know not what they do," I can say it too. We must remember what the Christ of Glory said to us. "For if you forgive others their sins, your heavenly Father will also forgive you. But if you do not forgive others, your Father will not forgive you your sins" (Matthew 6:14,15 NET). One of those retired safe pastors is really a darling in the City of Norfolk. He is no doubt loved and admired by White people because he not only speaks their language; he is committed to doing their will, which has become his will. He was appointed to the City Council after having served on the Norfolk School Board. According to him, the late Judge Joseph Jordan and the late Delegate Robinson urged him to fill a vacancy on the Council by appointment. I appeared before the Council in the early years of his being on Council to get the City on record as observing Martin Luther King, Jr.'s Birthday, along with an upcoming majority of the nation. Dr. King had gone on to glory and would have been one of the first to object to a holiday in his honor. Although all of the Council did not speak, those who did speak were in strong objection to it. Several of them looked to this honorable black councilman to voice his opinion. Being the safe councilman that he was, he suggested a compromise. He suggested to the Council "they (talking about us) could agree to celebrate Dr. King's birthday on NEW YEARS DAY. "People will already be off," he said, "and it wouldn't cost the City a thing." I don't recall the Council's doing anything about his suggestion or even responding to it. I went to another Negro councilman, a safe pastor in the City who is loved by the White community, with a site plan for some property on Park Avenue and Princess Anne Road. I wanted to purchase the land from the City, build a church, and develop some housing and a Family Life Center. He thought it was a good idea (he said to me). It has been almost twenty years since I presented him with the site plan for the development. I have seen him on several occasions since then and he has never said a word. Soon after I presented him with the site plan developed by Livas Architectures firm, a Black architect, the City developed housing on that parcel of land, and it looks like they may have used the plans I gave the councilman with some modifications.

I went to the hospital to see a former member of the City Council who is a friend of mine, the Honorable Herbert Collins, who was very sick. As a matter of fact he was so out of it until he did not recognize my wife or me. While on Council he supported everything I brought to the Council. We both were plaintiffs in the Ward Suit against the City of Norfolk. Now what really got to me is this: I knew I was right in most of my presentations but I wasn't politically savvy enough to get things done. I was too prophetic. I still had not grown strong enough in the Lord to "season my words with acceptable political grace when talking to oppressors of the Black and poor." Councilman Collins told me of a meeting that he was in with the City on some projects in the Black community and mine was the chief among them. These two black safe councilmen ripped me from stem to stern "in confidence" before City officials. Councilman Collins was disturbed at how they downgraded me. On top of that, what really got to the City was a letter I wrote to HUD asking for an investigation on how the City was spending Community Block Grant Funding. The City of Norfolk had received millions of dollars across several years and had never spent a dime on a project in the Black community. The Martin Luther King, Jr., Family Life Institute had a funding proposal before the City for three years and had been turned down each year. I was put in touch with a "movement sister" who worked for HUD in Philadelphia. I think she was about as upset with personal and institutional racism as I was. I never met her and have never seen or known her but she forced the City to fund minority projects or they would be subject to be cut off from CBGD funding. That is how I knew she was a "movement sister that would stand up against oppressors." The City of Norfolk funded our project and put it in the daily paper but it was conditional. One of the conditions was that we would never receive the actual money. They had it set up so that vouchers would be made to the City and approved by the City before a check would be prepared for the director and the program director of the Institute. Te funds that were approved by HUD for the Martin Luther King, Jr., Family Life Institute were never actually received by the Institute. The City approved of a couple that we had recommended as being the executive director and the program director. We had known them or thought we knew them for years. They put their son on the payroll. The City of Norfolk approved all this. When we found out how the money was erroneously being spent, with City approval, including some programs that never existed, I called a meeting with the City Manager and my good friend Councilman Herbert Collins. Councilman Collins was then the vice mayor of the City when he agreed to meet with our board. Councilman Collins told me privately at that meeting, "Reid, let me tell you something. If you let these folk go (The Executive Director and the Program Director whom we had treasured as friends), the City is going to withdraw the money from the Family Life Institute." I said to him, "let them keep the blank money" (you fill in the blank with your choice of adjectives; I promise you I'll yield). "No money is going to be misspent on items for which I am going to be called on to give in account for when I know it is being spent wrong." I was never so outdone as with this couple that tried to steal our name and even our tax-exempt number with the help of a black accountant who was also on our payroll at the Institute. They took many of our records down the street to a "safe" preacher's church and set up office. No one but the Christ of Glory, through the Holy Spirit, saw to it that it never worked. I still have a warning letter on file that I wrote him to warn him what was happening. He never responded. It wasn't long before he was voted out of his church for "other" reasons we need not discuss. We were wounded, but not mortally. Today we have gone national in the Martin Luther King, Jr., Family Life Institute. You ought to say, "Praise the Lord." The Martin Luther King, Jr., Family Life Institute has chapters now in Virginia, Washington, D.C., Maryland, Georgia, Virginia, Pennsylvania, New York, and we are working on chapters in several other states. So the ministry continues today through a Bible study group, and the Martin Luther King, Jr., Family Life Institute. Currently we are on the Internet and we have contacted every Governor in the United States, several Senators, Congressmen, and mayors of major cities for resolutions focusing on a New National Holiday for Families, called AMERICA FAMILY DAY. Congress has introduced a bill for global family day and we are petitioning both the president of the United States and the secretary-general of the United Nations for global support. We are trying to restore, revive, renew, and bring together families, to prepare them to for the family of God Eternal.

Civil Freedom versus Religious Freedom

At Calvary in the day of Jesus, it looked on the surface that civil freedom won. At New Calvary, it looked like civil freedom won. The resurrection took place at both Calvary's. The Supreme Court refused to even hear our case despite the urging and petitioning of some forty organizations representing one hundred twenty-five million (125,000,000) Americans. The U.S. Supreme Court's turning its back on this landmark case lent silent endorsement to the lower court's ruling. This said in essence that the issue of Religious Liberty is not important enough to merit the attention of the nation's highest justices. It shows a callous disregard and disrespect for the religious life of this country, which should have set off alarms in the minds of all real Christians in America. Unfortunately, we have such an abiding faith and belief in those with whom we entrust our freedom that, if the Supreme Court says its not important, many Americans are too willing to take their licking and keep on kicking. However, I am not surprised by this current threat to religious liberty. Some of us have known all along that American Religious Liberty, like many other Constitutional guarantees, is a kind of "Spiritual Schizophrenia" that sooner or later would have its authenticity challenged. The late C. Eric Lincoln has said that the stage was set when, in Ephesians 6:5 we read, "Slaves, be obedient to those who are your earthly masters with fear and trembling in singleness of heart as to Christ" (KJV). I am not going to be persuaded in this life that Paul said this. It may have been what the King James translators saw through the traditions of slavery that could have meant "bond servants," or those who sold themselves as servants, or in Greek, "doulos." To paraphrase Lincoln, we note that this is the strange dilemma, which today mocks our cultural pretensions, enervates our national purpose, and challenges the moral commitments implicit in our claim to be a nation under God. By biblical standards, and the calling of redemptive faith, I have concluded without fear of contradiction, that America's God is the God of the West that is at war with the Christ of Glory.

Pulpit Freedom In The Black Church

The Black church has been the center and soul of Black folk in their common struggle to be free for all of the years that this nation has existed. All of the freedom...every iota of freedom, every ounce of freedom that Black Americans know today has grown out of an abiding religious faith and belief in a God who said "From one man (Adam) he made every nation of the human race (mankind) to inhabit the entire earth, determining their set times, and fixed limits of the places where they would live" (Acts 17:26-27 NET). While not many Black churches would challenge the above passage of Scripture, they won't fear to challenge their pastor through what appeared to be a racist judge who sought to control me in what I did and said. It was the pulpits of Black churches from which emerged the most eloquent speakers for civil rights and human justice, from the Reverend Samuel Cornish to Dr. Martin Luther King, Jr. Since Martin, the Honorable Louis Farrakhan, the Reverend Jesse Jackson, Dr. Joseph Lowery, Congressman Walter E. Fauntroy, Dr. Wyatt Tee Walker, Dr. Curtis Harris, Attorney William Smith, a classmate of mind from Virginia Union University, and a civil rights attorney, and a host of controversial speakers, including governors, ambassadors from African nations, and refugees from Latin America have spoken from our pulpit and that is a matter of record. At New Calvary, dissident members who had contributed less than $200.00 to the church's annual budget that exceeded $300,000, and who in no way evidenced a commitment to the liberation mission of the Laos filed their initial suit against four deacons and myself. They presented one hundred and twenty five "fraudulent" names of members, and not one of them admitted that they had signed the list. There were names of people such as college students who were away from the area on the list, which also proved the list to be fraudulent. From this scanty information, the judge of the Circuit Court in Norfolk ruled in the following manner. He nullified our first amendments rights

- He nullified duly called meetings of the Church.
- He ordered the Church not to install duly elected officers or ordain deacons elected by the congregation.
- Ordered a White man of the Jewish faith to conduct and oversee the annual meeting of New Calvary Baptist Church.
- Ordered the pastor and four deacons to turn over the Church's membership list to this Mr. Mazelle, the Jewish overseer, so that he could determine who would be eligible to vote, even at the objection of the congregation, which voted on two occasions not to turn its list over to any secular authority.
- Levied a fine of $1,000 a day against the pastor and 25.00

a day against four deacons for not complying with the court's ruling to turn over the membership list which did not belong to the Court.

- Nullified church disciplinary actions against the dissident members who embarrassed the Church and filed suit after suit against the pastor and officers. Judge Alfred Whitehurst ruled against all Church actions to handle its own matters.
- He ordered the Church not to pay for the painting of the sanctuary out of Church funds. This case was appealed before the 4th Circuit Court of Appeals in Richmond and the United States Supreme Court.

I know that you find it hard to believe that the Court would agree to enter into the internal affairs of a Church when its leaders and members had broken no laws, nor misappropriated any church funds or property, and were not charged with either. Would the judge have agreed to hear this case if the pastor were not an outspoken and persistent social and political activist who for more than 45 years (up to that time) had challenged the moral conscience of America? The judge held me in contempt of the Court and jailed me but God will hold him in contempt of Glory in the High Court of Heaven. I am convinced that Jesus is my advocate and will bring him and the dissidents who lied to justice. Why did he do it to me in my ministry? I have concluded that the judge was a child of his racist culture and that he couldn't help himself. He is in the same boat with the former Secretary of Education, William Bennett, who declared that he wasn't a racist but suggested that, "If you want to decrease crime, abort every Black baby in America. This may sound morally indefensible, but crime would go down." They are in the same racist boat. I felt and I still feel comfortable with the Psalmist who said in Psalms 34:19 "Many are the afflictions of the righteous, but the Lord delivers him out of them all."

Attorney William Kuntsler, famed civil rights attorney, joined us on the case and had the case removed from the circuit court to the federal system. Although the federal judge admitted in open court that attorney Kuntsler probably knew more about constitutional matters of law than he did, he denied the motion and it was appealed to the Federal Court of Appeals to the Fourth Circuit in Richmond.

The dissidents had a black lawyer by the name of Edward Delk who I suppose was taught by White folks to lie, although he couldn't lie enough to keep from being disbarred for dishonesty later when the case was over. The judge had ruled that I was in truculent defiance of the dissident members. I still have to look that word up. Jesus said after you have gone to your brothers and they would not hear, take another witness and if they won't hear, take them to the church and if they still won't hear, he said, in what I concluded, you should be in truculent defiance and let them be as heathens. Attorney Delk had asked the Court, at the behest of the dissidents, that I be jailed for disobeying this Court. Obviously he believed that "your hornna," Judge Alfred D. Whitehurst, had made up his mind to put me in jail. He said from the bench, "It appears that the defendant is not afraid of judges," which I immediately interpreted as paternalistic, if not a racist statement. Why should I be afraid of judges? Why should anybody who escaped the Willie Lynch mindset be afraid of judges? The Judge quoted from a misinformed lie quoted in the Supreme Court's majority decision that "the adherents" (meaning the Church) were going to build a 12 million dollar Senior Citizens Home on Church-owned property and that the civil rights and the property rights of members were being violated. Now why I had not heard or read of this lie before, I do not know. HUD officials were arguing about 3.8 million to 4.1 million dollars for the 112 unit Senior Citizens home to be named Calvary Towers. It was not to be constructed on church-owned property at all. It was to be constructed on a site owned by the Norfolk Redevelopment & Housing Authority. As a matter of fact, in October of 1982, we broke ground on that site after being assured that we would be funded. Present were members of the church, the board of directors of Calvary Towers, Inc., and a host of well-wishers. A year later, in October of 1983, the area manager of the Richmond office of HUD brought us a mock check in the amount of 3.9 million dollars for the project.

While I was in jail my Marian brought me palace specialties for dinner each evening, and I had enough goodies to carry me over for breakfast. I was given the Chaplain's office for my cell, and the chief jailer, Mr. David Mapp, Norfolk's first Black sheriff, made me the assistant to the Chaplain. I had computers, printers, VCR's, a telephone and my friends, like Attorney William Smith, a classmate from Virginia Union, Dr. Don Sills, and many others who "came unto me when I was in prison." Unlike Paul, I was not in an inner chamber of a jail downstairs; I was "living it up" in affluence in an office upstairs. Whether up or down, God will take care of you. Gideon's Missionary Fellowship continues now under authentic pastoral leadership. I am a member along with my wife. We had plans to redevelop the land, that we lost and build a church and family life Institute on it. But God had something else in mind. I remember the Psalmist saying, "The Lord delivers and vindicates me! I fear no one! The Lord protects my life! I am afraid of no one! When evil men attack me to devour my flesh, when my adversaries and enemies attack me, they stumble and fall. Even when an army is deployed against me, I do not fear. Even when war is imminent, I remain confident. I have asked the Lord for one thing – this is what I desire! I want to live in the Lord's house all the days of my life, so I can gaze at the splendor of the Lord and contemplate in His temple. He will surely give me shelter in the day of danger, He will hide me in His home, and he will place me on an inaccessible rocky summit. Now I will triumph over my enemies who surrounded me! I will offer sacrifices in His dwelling place and shout for joy" (Psalm 27:1-6 NET).

A 1968 Rally at City Hall with Dr. Reid and Mayor Roy Martin.

CHAPTER VII

THE FOREVERNESS OF JESUS

You stumble day and night, and the false prophets stumble with you; you have destroyed your own people! You have destroyed my people by failing to acknowledge me!

Hosea 4:5,6 NET

Jesus Christ is the same yesterday and today and forever!

Hebrews 13:8 NET

My youngest son, Milton, Jr., opted out of the traditional church in the mid-eighties during the Church/State battle at New Calvary Baptist Church and the Circuit Court of Norfolk. He could never understand why church folk could act so nasty, mean and ugly. A graduate of Norfolk State University, he was a brilliant student and an awesome debater on almost any subject. Milton Jr., became ill and was hospitalized some twenty years later. Just as a father would do, Marian, his mother and I lifted Milton, Jr., up in prayer at least three times a day. We visited him in the hospital on a regular basis. Maravia, our oldest daughter, took charge to see that Milton, Jr., was almost never alone. She insisted that some one from the family be with him everyday. She even curtailed her activities between her two jobs to be with Milton, Jr. Eyo Ebong, Maravia's stepson and a friend of Milton, Jr., was also faithful in his care and attention to his extended uncle. As a matter of fact, Eyo was in Milton, Jr.'s home when he was very sick and refused my suggestion of coming home with us or going to the hospital. It was Eyo who actually and in fact took Milton, Jr., to the emergency room where he was admitted. After days of agony and without food Milton's doctors shared with him their findings. Milton called us in to share with us. Knowing Milton had nothing to do with the traditional church, when I asked in the hospital "shall we pray?" he turned over toward me and grabbed my hand and Eyo's hand. The family, his mother and sister, joined in prayer for Milton, Jr. Prior to prayer, I said, "Milton, I am writing my memoirs. Let me tell you the title that I have chosen, THE GOD OF THE WEST VERSUS THE CHRIST OF GLORY. "A Liberating and Exhilarating Journey of Faith," is the subtitle. I said to Milton, Jr., I understand your frustrations with the church because the traditional church appears to be worshipping the God of the West. In shocking response he said, "I know that." His revolt from the traditional church was understandable. As I recall it, when Martin Luther, a priest in the Catholic Church, revolted, and nailed 95 theses on the door of the church at Wittenberg it wasn't his intention to rebel or to revolt against the church but to reform it. After 2,100 years of church history, and now living in the dispensation of grace, or the church age, I have committed my life to reforming the church to become relevant to the call of God and the needs of the people and to the full acceptance of its Redeemer and Lord who is forever. There are Milton, Jr.'s all over our nation and the world that have rejected this God of the West that many Christians seem to adore. For a long time my darling daughters no longer had traditional church membership, but they both not only support the church, they worship with Marian and me whenever possible. However they always believed in the God of the Ages and the Christ of Glory.

My Conversion Experiences

My experience with the Christ of Glory makes me want to testify of his "foreverness." I have been blessed since I met the Jesus who put it in my spirit that life in Him brings about a change, not only in me, but also in the fallen world around me where other of his children are standing and believing and holding onto Him. Though I got up from the mourners' bench in August of 1940, and shook hands, I really didn't feel any change. I was threatened by my sisters to get up after sitting there for a week, waiting and watching. After all I had come from a religious family. My father was a deacon then and was one of the "shouters" over the mourners. My mother was singing in the choir at the Pleasant Grove Baptist Church then in Princess Anne County, where her father, the Reverend George Odom, was the founding pastor. My grandmother, Mrs. Laura

Odom, who lived with us at the time, was a staunch member of Pleasant Grove long after her husband went home to meet his Lord. All of my sisters that had preceded me were members of the Church, either at Pleasant Grove or the Little Zion Baptist Church of Chesapeake and "satisfied with Jesus." I really went out behind our house one Friday night and prayed for salvation. I only told my father about my new religious experience and he was really happy about it. He told my mother and she told the children, who were all skeptical. The Lord put into my spirit His Holy Spirit of which I was to grieve across many years of my upbringing and maturing in the faith.

Due largely to the way I was treated from birth by what I call my 'jealous sisters, my being the first boy in the family, I didn't have very much to do with girls even after I was saved. I have felt being saved from the time I felt the indwelling of the Lord's Spirit within me behind our house in Chesapeake – the house that my father had built. I did have a few erotic flings at girls during high school because of the teasing I received from my peers. I felt it necessary to prove my masculinity. In high school I joined the NFA (New Farmers of America) because I had to, although I never wanted to be a farmer. We formed a quartette consisting of Norman Dozier, Cornelius Dozier and myself. We sang everywhere and won prizes and awards because of our blended harmony. I will always remember the trip we made to sing at Bowie State College in Maryland. While there I met a cute little thing by the name of Mary Frances Carter. We lost track before getting real serious. I was called a preacher's kid, or the preacher's son during those days and I rejected all of them, although I never rejected the Christ or felt any need to do so. I never wanted as a child to be a preacher. Although my father was well received by the two churches that called him, the Pleasant Grove Baptist Church of Virginia Beach, Virginia, and the Poole's Grove Baptist Church of Woodville, North Carolina, I just could not see myself as pastor of a one-Sunday-a-month church as my father did in North Carolina, and a two-Sunday-a-month church as he did in what is now Virginia Beach. I knew every day was the Lord's Day and every Sunday since the resurrection folk had worshipped the Lord on the first day of the week. My question was, "What were these undernourished Christians supposed to do through the week?" I didn't see myself in that kind of predicament.

When I volunteered to go into the United States Army in August of 1948, I wasn't there long before I felt a call to preach. Every payday we were confronted with the activities of gambling, horsing around, playing cards, drinking (and at that time I had never taken or touched an alcoholic drink.) I would later become a bartender on the post at Fort Bragg, after I was discharged in June of 1952. For the first time I tasted one or two just for the heck of it. During my early days in the military I would hold soldiers' money (at their request) to keep them from gambling it away. At times they wanted it back and I would not give it back to them. I held it until the fifteenth of the month as they had asked me to do in the first place. The soldiers began to put trust in me. They started calling me "preacher." I was stationed at what was then Fort Dix, New Jersey. Several of my high school buddies were also stationed there. George Godfrey, who lived in Butts Station, was my closest childhood friend. He would go into the army also but stayed in until he retired. While we weren't stationed together we stayed in touch and have remained in touch until this day.

It wasn't long before I went to see the chaplain about my call to the ministry. He was Lt. Colonel Beasley, a tall, well-educated minister who had nothing except pity and maybe empathy for me. After giving him my spill and my testimony he asked me "How much education do you have?" I told him that I had finished high school. He softened the blow when he told me that I needed much more than a high school education to be a well-prepared minister of the gospel. He said, "You have to do studies in the Bible, the Old and the New Testaments. You need to know something about homiletics, hermeneutics, the psychology of pastoral care, church history, counseling," and he listed about every subject taught in seminary in that day. He ended by telling me that I had time; I was a young man, and my whole life was ahead of me. I left him feeling dejected, but not rejected. I went away feeling down in my spirit but not for long. I gave the chaplain one of my Norfolk County testimonies of Jesus and His Love and I went on back to the barracks feeling the Spirit of God dwelling in my innermost being, that I was called to "testify of Jesus and His love."

I went about my duties in basic training as a soldier in the army.

I found myself on bivouac, learning how to kill men that Christ came to save. I was wrestling with the problem of shooting live ammunition with a bayonet at the end of my M-1 rifle rather than getting a deeper understanding about Jesus and the Sermon on the Mount. We had to crawl on the ground under actual live fire for several yards. I thought of other creatures that also crawled on the ground. I was always afraid of snakes. I was just about to give up when the sergeant called for a cease-fire and he called my name to report to him immediately. I was shaking in my boots wondering if he had heard me thinking or if I had been thinking out loud. He told me to report to the chaplain at once. To get off the rifle range and report to the chaplain was unbelief but I acted like I believed it. I had no idea what the chaplain wanted since he told me that I wasn't prepared to answer the call to preach. He talked to me about things in general for a few minutes and while he was talking he became tearful. Then he said, I have been thinking about you. You have been on my mind since we talked the last time. I need an assistant. I want you to work with me as my assistant. I am sure you can be of a great help to me around the chapel. Uncontrollably I said, "thank you, Jesus." In my spare time I began to work on my first sermon. "I Have Opened My Mouth to the Lord." I got in touch with Dr. W.A. Baker through my father, who arranged for me to preach my trial sermon at the Little Zion Baptist Church in Chesapeake, where I was a member. This was in December of 1948, and I really never looked back. I'll admit that I have had some ups and some downs. I have had some faults and failures and I have also had some disappointed hopes, but I never looked back.

The only way that I can explain the next few years in my life is to use the words of Ezekiel, "The hand of the Lord was upon me." I was transferred to Camp Gordon, Georgia, where I enrolled in the South Eastern Signal School. I graduated as a high-speed radio operator. While there I worshipped at the Macedonia Baptist Church in Augusta, Georgia. That is where I met Mama Annie Allen and her family. I was adopted as a son in the family and there was a daughter who became my sparring sister as we fought over everything from who was going to wash the dishes or who was going to drive the car, a black and white 1941 Buick. Juanita was married and she had a lovely daughter named Charlesnette. Her husband, Jimmy, was a warrant officer in the army and he was a helicopter pilot. Jimmy and I grew very close and we are friends even today. Mama Allen had a son whose name was also Jimmy. He was married to a beautiful woman who was a nurse. Her name was Doris. Mama Allen was a living "saint" if there ever was one. She dominated my life as a young Christian preacher of the Gospel and she insisted on protecting me from all that was sinful and evil. I don't know how I met Sadie Mack but Mama Allen didn't approve the relationship. Now Sadie was a beauty if I had ever seen one. Mama Allen had me playing the piano and singing every weekend, as I spent most of my free time in her home or supporting her schedules.

When I completed my schooling at Fort Gordon I volunteered to go to "Jump" School" at Fort Benning, Georgia. It paid a little more money. After jump school, and being made tough as a paratrooper, I was assigned to the Eighty-Second Airborne Division at Fort Bragg, North Carolina. I am not sure now how I got assigned to be the chaplain's assistant there, unless I was just hanging around the chapel, playing the organ with the one chord that I remembered, but that is where I became interested in religious education and law. I enrolled in correspondence courses at La Salle University in Chicago. I made straight "A's" but an opportunity opened up for me to attend Fayetteville State Teachers College during the morning hours and I would work in the afternoon and night in the chapel to make up for the time I spent in School. While at Fayetteville my status as a paratrooper with the 82nd Airborne Division got me on the football team called the Fayetteville Broncos. I remember one outstanding play with that team. We played Winston-Salem at their home field and I remember well catching the ball as a left end and running the wrong way. I heard the crowd roaring, and I was "flying on my feet." I had borrowed a dime to make a call to the president, Dr. James Ward Seabrook, to ask him if I could register for school and I would pay my tuition on payday. He agreed. When he saw that play or heard of it I am sure he had regretted hearing of me. I learned a lot at Fayetteville from professors such as the late Dr. John Parker, in English literature, Dr. George Scott, in geography, Miss Mary Terry in music, and Miss Walcott in music appreciation.

The Preacher Falls in Love

While waiting for Dr. Scott to get to his class and unlock the door I was waiting in the hall with the rest of the class when "LO and BEHOLD" I met the prettiest little thing that my eyes had ever seen in all of my days. I fell harder than any parachute jump that I had ever made. She had Asian slant eyes with bangs across the forehead and hair down to her shoulders. I didn't dare look down at that point because if I had, I don't think I would have recovered. The first thing I did was to tell Mama Allen about her and got her approval, sight unseen. I soon shipped out to go on "Operation Long Horn," a maneuver in Texas. At that time I was the organizer and director of the Division Artillery Chorus of the 82nd Airborne Division. I knew as much about music as a monkey knew about flying a jet; it had to be that the Lord was with me. I knew one chord of music and it has stayed with me all of my life. I arranged a concert upon my return at the Mt. Sinai Baptist Church on Murchison Road in Fayetteville, right across from Fayetteville State Teachers College. Marian would be my guest. You talk about somebody "throwing down" that night. I think the Division Artillery Chorus helped me to win what would be my wife for more than fifty-five plus years. I mean she has been more than a "jewel" and an everlasting love to me and for me. As a young minister I didn't want to lose her because I found out a star member of the football team had seen her first. I knew she was mine and Mama Allen had already approved of her. When I told my mother about her she also was filled with praise and she asked me had I told my Papa?

By this time my father was a pastor of two churches. He had quit his job at Smith/Douglass fertilizer plant and was trusting in the Lord to provide. He used to say quite often, "the cattle upon the ten thousand hills belong to my God, more than that the hills are his also." Say what you will I believe that my father believed in the God of the Ages. But on this occasion I trembled to tell him about my new jewel. When I did he said, "Thank God, my prayers have been answered." I knew then as well as I know now some fifty-five plus years later that God had His Hand in this selection. Not once has she urged me not to do something, no matter how dangerous or risky, when she felt the leading of the Holy Spirit was with me.

A news flash came over the TV regarding police who deserted their position as hurricane Katrina approached New Orleans. There was one officer who had been on the force for eighteen years who felt it was his first duty and obligation to protect and care for his wife and family. I asked my Marian, what did she think I would have done, and what would she approve of my doing? She said without thinking, "You have been called of God. And you should do what He tells you to do. He'll take care of us." This was her response during the turbulent years of the civil-rights movement. She knew I was at risk and the entire family was at risk. But the God of the Ages and the Christ of Glory have made some covenants and promises to us. "But you will receive power when the Holy Spirit has come upon you, and you will be my witnesses in Jerusalem, and in all Judea and Samaria, and to the farthest parts of the earth" (Acts 1:8 NET). He also said following his resurrection when He met the disciples in Galilee, "Therefore go and make disciples of all nations, baptizing them in the name of the Father, and the Son and the Holy Spirit. Teaching them to obey everything I have commanded you. And remember, I am with you always, to the end of the age" (Matthew 28:19-20 NET).

The Presence of Jesus

So far I had never been in a position like Job, to ask of the Lord, "Where art Thou?" There have been times when I have had to cover my head in shame but I have never been in a state of being where I had questioned the presence of God. I believe God has been with me in a very personal way all of my life. As a boy I had a paper route where I distributed the "Ledger Dispatch," the local evening's paper. While riding my bicycle delivering papers one afternoon I collided with a car that I didn't see coming or he collided with me without seeing me. I was hit and thrown from my bicycle and had a fall on my head. Some of my friends (like the friends of Job) declared that my "brains" had been shaken up. Maybe so because I have been known to do a lot of strange things that didn't make sense, although I have never conceded to "going crazy." And how many "crazy people" have conceded to being crazy? I refuse to concede even now as the evening shades are being gradually pulled. Right now my eyes are growing dim in my twilight years. My hair is turning white with the snowfalls of many winters. Spinal stenosis has settled in, apparently to stay. It has left me in a position that I cannot stand over a long period of time unless I am preaching. I can stand preaching and it doesn't bother me. I developed tendonitis in my ankles but therapy has restored that and I can walk now without pain or discomfort in them most of the time. I have gone to the Lord many times regarding this pain in my lower back that some doctor told me was "spinal stenosis" and he removed the second and fourth lumbar in by back to relieve the pressure on the nerve. It didn't help much. As a matter of fact I think I am in worse shape now than before. I have prayed for healing and I seem to get the answer that Paul received regarding his "thorn in the flesh," "My Grace is sufficient, or my grace is enough for you, for my power is made perfect in weakness" (2 Cor. 12:9 NET).

When I think back over what I have been through and have seen the tragedies of what has happened to others I am persuaded of the redeeming presence of Christ in my life. In my years of not knowing what was wrong with my back I have spent thousands of dollars trying to bring healing to it. While working with IFCO/Pastors for Peace, I went to a clinic in Western Cuba, Santa Diego, and de los Banes and received treatment for my back twice. These healing waters came from the hills and mountains of Western Cuba where President Castro, who brought the revolution to Cuba, originated. I felt that if there was any place in the land that could have brought me healing it was this place and in that land. I really felt good and relieved from the pain with the healing waters and massagers but it wasn't healing. In 1970, Marian and I took a tour around the world en route to the Baptist World Alliance that met in Tokyo, Japan. That trip had me calling Japanese Masseurs in to work on my back pain. I was rather huge in size and the masseur, who was female, was an expert. She pounded away on my spine and then crawled on my back and with her knees she "popped" every joint it seems in my spine from my neck down. Don't get upset; my Marian was sitting right there watching and praying. Boy, did I feel better? I have been back to Japan a couple of times since then alone but I never found nor did I seek that treatment again as I was relieved, but not healed.

On that trip around the world we visited China where we really dressed up in Hong Kong with tailor-made outfits and white boots. We visited Bangkok, Thailand, where we shopped by riverboat travel and I purchased for her a real wedding ring. We went to India where the entire plane had to be fumigated upon arrival. On subsequent trips we traveled to West Africa where, in Brewerville, Liberia, I was elected pastor- at- large in 1964, of the Salem Baptist Church. We traveled to Nigeria on several occasions for our daughter Maravia had met and married NSE Ebong in 1982. Marian attended the World Baptist Alliance in Europe in 1980, and left me behind. I got homesick for my Marian. I looked at her travel itinerary and I asked my secretary, Mrs. Heddy Sykes, a very understanding and compassionate person to get me a ticket to Paris, France. Heddy was one of the best secretaries with whom I have ever worked I think she knew me better than I knew myself. Heddy worked with me as financial consultant with the Journal & Guide. She kept my banking records and she knew I wanted to see my Marian. The crazy credit card company issued me the ticket and I packed a bag and got on board, but I had to see my Marian. Upon arriving in Paris I took a brief flight to Brussels where I met my dear wife coming out of her hotel with friends, "going shopping." Now the Lord had to arrange that. He knew how I had missed her and wanted to see her. I saw her and she saw me but she did not recognize me until I called her by name. She didn't go shopping that day.

The Lord had sent her "a gift that he had purchased" and she was in shock. I think she knew that I loved her but not enough to fly some 3000 miles to have dinner with her on a "liberation" budget. I managed to squeeze in with her that night and take the tour bus with her and the other delegates into Paris the next day. I was the envy of every preacher on board that tour bus, even those who had his or her companion with them. I hadn't thought about it but that was pressure on them! You see, "I knew the Lord was my Shepherd, but I had what I wanted," and right then it was my Marian. During the eight years of our daughter's marriage, we traveled to Nigeria, with the exception of the years when Maravia came home. It was in 1989 when Marian went to Nigeria alone to visit with Maravia. After two weeks of that visitation Marian contracted malaria. She was running a high fever and could not travel. We were in revival and Dr. Marcellus Harris of Newport News, Virginia, was the evangelist. During that service I announced Marian's illness and requested the "prayers of the church." Reverend John Boyd, a member of the church, volunteered to pray. He asked all of who would pray to point toward Africa. We did and I called Nigeria that night. It was around 11:00 when I placed the call. Have you ever tried getting a call through to Nigeria? Back then it was a real problem. Nigerian time was about seven hours ahead of us. But when the fever broke it was the same time when we were in prayer. I made plans then to go to Nigeria to get my Marian. When I arrived my daughter met me in the airport. My first question was, how is Marian? We had to leave Lagos and travel to Calibar, Cross River State. I was anxious to get there. As we walked along the corridors Maravia said, "Daddy, wait just a minute, I have someone I want you to meet." I said, "No, Maravia, I have to get to Calabar." She insisted that I would go with her to meet "whomever." When I saw whom she wanted me to meet it was someone who resembled Marian. Her face had lost all of its color and she was "white as a sheet." It was my Marian. The first thing she said in a weak voice was "Milton, I just prayed to God that I could see you one more time." I was in tears. We stayed in Lagos for about a week at the Sheraton Hotel until Marian was strong enough to travel. We came back and Marian wanted to go back teaching, and even tried to do so, but the malaria had a deteriorating effect and demanded that she would retire. I thanked God that the deteriorating effect wasn't a deadening reality. I often tease Michelle, our youngest daughter who started off in college at Virginia Commonwealth University, a predominantly White school, about the irony of her saying that she was going to major in "Black Gospel music". Michelle, who loves gospel music as well as other music, has always been daring. She decided to go to Nigeria to visit Maravia and I think she went to find that mosquito that bit her mother. "Michelle will get you". She has never taken any mess. When she was about four years old and our housekeeper, Mrs. Oretta Hines, threatened to leave her in the house if she didn't behave, that little "tot" started singing "Hit the road, Jack, and don't you come back no more, no more no more; Hit the road, Jack, and don't you come back no more." It may have been at VCU where she learned her computer skills. In that field she is a wizard. She heads a staff in the Virginia State Health

Department that keeps her running from hospital to hospital all over the State. She lives in Richmond but she never forgets home with calls each week, emails, gifts or physical visits, especially on holidays and special occasions.

A Test of Will

When Milton, Jr., seemed to have been ignored in the hospital it was Michelle and Maravia who worked as a team to get things turned around. When you come to the hospital on a Friday night through the emergency room in Norfolk without a doctor's order, you just have to wait your turn. But by Saturday evening those sisters, working together, were "livid," and they demanded and got action. All of us have had hospital experiences, especially the times when I was in as a patient. They made sure that Daddy and Mama were taken care of when hospitalized. You see they were guardian angels sent by the Lord Jesus Christ to look after their parents and especially me who had made so many White folk upset because of personal and institutional racism. They ran interference and I do appreciate them. They together coordinated and planned my fiftieth preaching anniversary, our fiftieth wedding anniversary and my retirement celebration. They worked with their mother also on the occasion of her retirement from Public School Education, where for 31 years she was an educator starting with her own school at First Baptist Church Petersburg. Maravia had been born in October and would have had to wait a whole year to begin school in 1957. But Marian was a pioneer pastor's wife and an educator. We have a picture of her now with the 21 children she taught in their pre-school years.

The Pastor's Wife

I had a head-on collision with Sister Helen B. Giles, a church activist and program director at First Baptist Church Harrison Street, while serving as pastor. Marian in her quiet way sought to resolve the issue. Let me show you how the presence of the Lord with me worked through her. Marian set down and had a long talk with me and she couldn't get any Spirit of reconciliation out of me for I was determined to be Rev. Right rather than Rev. Reid. I am not sure if she had talked to Helen or not but what I do know is that she invited Helen to dinner. Anyone who knew Marian would never refuse her invitation to dinner, especially Dr. Martin L. King, Jr., who had dinner in our home on several occasions. When dinner was served and it was time to go Marian said, "both of you sit down here and work out your differences." We did and Helen from that day forward was a tremendous help to my ministry at First Baptist. The Lord was with me in that experience directed by my loving wife. It was while I served as pastor at the New Calvary Baptist Church of Norfolk that I was given a roast in an appreciation service where activist and comedian Dick Gregory was the speaker. It was during this service, sponsored by "Friends of Milton", that the late Reverend Charles Bonds, whom I recommended to succeed me as pastor at the New Hope Baptist Church in Chesapeake, renamed by wife, "Marian the Marvelous."

I became ill while serving in my final days as pastor of Gideon's Riverside Fellowship. I was preaching one Sunday during regular morning worship when I began to lose my voice and my wind. I was struggling to keep going but my Marian came to the pulpit and told me to sit down. I was both grateful and obedient. I will perhaps never know what was wrong with me. I know I was under pressure trying to rebuild a neglected portion of the City of Norfolk and was getting nowhere fast. I brought on Reverend Emmanuel Lipscomb of Washington, DC, to help me with the fund raising for the project of the Martin Luther King, Jr., Family Life Institute. He worked hard against many, many odds, without success. He almost lost his life during 9/11 in what would become Ground Zero, while picking up a consultant who was going to help negotiate a loan for our project development. My blood pressure was on the high side and my cholesterol was bordering a dangerous level. My spinal stenosis had settled in and for a while I had lost the use of my left side. I could no longer put on my shoes and socks. I couldn't go to the bathroom without her help. No doctor could find a cause or diagnosis for whatever was troubling me. Marian kept praying and assuring me that we were going to get through it. I didn't know at the moment that she had been praying for a fiftieth wedding celebration, an occasion that needed my living presence. She was just a year away. Many years prior I had told her, "Without me, you can do nothing." I thought for a while she was going to prove otherwise. Marian really revived me by her faithful and enduring love. She knew that there were some things I had wanted to do badly and I believe God extended my life because of her prayers.

Deacon Ruth Lewis, Deaconess Ruth Lewis (she had served in both capacities), my devoted friend and prayer partner for many years, came by with her nursing skills and taught me how to get up out of bed. She demonstrated how a pregnant woman had to get up. She looked at my stomach and said, "You have got to get up the same way." I didn't know what was wrong with me but I did know I wasn't pregnant. She massaged my low back and my joints to enable me to walk again. Deaconess Odessa Anderson and Deaconess Rosa Stephen (both retired nurses), took turns, and sometimes together massaged my back and legs. I concluded that I had suffered a mild stroke. Several of the "saints" held me up in prayer and I recovered, with my lower back being the exception. During the civil-rights movement of the fifties and the sixties almost everything was done to discredit activists like myself. One night when I came out of a strategy session at First Baptist Church I found a pair of earrings on the front seat of my unlocked car, I wondered whose earrings they were and who put them there. I had to get home but I felt led to get rid of the earrings because I couldn't explain them. Now I just concluded some body was messing not only with my integrity but they were messing with me. I stayed away so much and I returned home so late talking with Dr. R.G. Williams, then the pastor of Zion Baptist Church of Petersburg, and Dr. Wyatt Tee Walker, then the pastor of Gilfield Baptist Church. We would be having fellowship with one another and laughing and talking about many things and issues. I knew all of those late night sessions would put some questions in my Marian's mind but she had never raised them and I didn't want her to start now. So as I drove into the garage and saw a shovel hanging on the wall, I got an idea. I would bury the earrings where they would never rise to shame me in this world and I would never have to explain them to my Marian. So I did. About a week later Marian asked me, "Milton, have you seen my earrings in your car?" There you go. I had to explain anyway. She paid no attention to my agony over the earrings but demanded that I go and dig them up because they were expensive and choice. She meant business. I had to dig up half the yard but I found them!

My Times in Cuba

Dr. Lucius Walker, a long time friend in the struggle for liberation and justice, both in America and around the world and who was one of my "field instructors while I was working to complete my doctorate in Ministry at Boston University School of Theology (I proudly mention that Miss Lillian Brinkley was the other field instructor), persuaded me to go back to Cuba during their fifteenth Friendshipment Caravan. I agreed to meet the Caravanistas in Mexico. With my walking stick and a half-aching back I joined them in Tampico, Mexico, and headed for Cuba. This was probably my fifth trip to that struggling nation under boycott from America, who apparently desires to make her a colony. It will never happen. Our nation's dishonesty in world affairs just might invade Cuba following the death of President Fidel Castro. I think and I hope they will meet with another defeat messing over the people of God in Cuba. God has sustained Cuba during all of the years of the boycott and brought her help from other nations of the world. I might have said this before but through the efforts of IFCO/Pastor's for Peace there are more than a hundred Black and poor students from America who are now in the medical schools in Cuba on a free educational scholarship studying to become doctors. All they have to do to pay for this is to sign a pledge to come back and serve three years in a deprived area in the United States. I am happy to have been a part of those Friendshipment Caravans. I personally met President Castro with Dr. Lucius Walker and we were invited to the Cuban White House one night after Dr. Walker and President Castro spoke before a crowd of thousands of Cubans. Now I am not much good now after 11:00 o'clock but back then I could stay awake until about 11:10.

We were in the Cuban White House until about 3 am in the morning and somebody had to gently wake me up several times. You see had they awakened me in English I might have sat up tall. But I couldn't even interpret a "Spanish shake" at that hour in the morning. Yet while I was asleep the presence of Jesus was with me. Even Jesus went to sleep on a short trip across Lake Gennesrat in the midst of a storm. When I really awakened I was standing in the pulpit of the Ebenezer Baptist Church in Havana. I was well received by their wonderful pastor, Reverend Rauel Swardis, his wife and the congregation. I preached there on several occasion and spoke on Dr. Martin L. King's Birthday at the King Center that his church supports. I spoke in several churches in Cuba and found a warm and a loving people who were glad to receive another word about the ever presence of Jesus in spite of the blockade by the "lawlessness" of our government.

On one of the Caravans I drove a yellow school bus from Minnesota to Laredo, Texas, right on the Mexican border, picking up whatever folk had to contribute to the churches, hospitals, and schools of Cuba. Little did I know or envision that I would be in Laredo marooned on a little yellow school bus in a 21-day fast. The weather there was 110 degrees every day and we were on a fast. After nineteen days I had to get back home on some urgent business but I was assigned the task of contacting the State Department to arrange a meeting to discuss the release of the computers and other equipment seized by U.S. Customs at the border. You can see how confused the enemy is. They permitted 92% of our collected cargo to pass on through to Cuba but they denied a little yellow school bus with several computers on it. At other times Custom officials waved us through with no searching or stopping, knowing that we had a shipment of goods of a non-military nature for Cuba. After much negotiation and pressure from Congress, and particularly the Black Caucus, headed at that time by Congressman Charlie Rangel of New York, we were permitted to continue. I, along with 12 other carvanistas, received the Cuban Friends Awards, the highest award that their government gave.

A Witness In Libya

Through the efforts of Dr. Carlton B. Goodlette, I met the Ambassador of Libya at the United Nations and I published some articles for him in the Journal & Guide. Some times later, in 1984, I was invited to Tripoli to the celebration of Libya's 15th Revolution Anniversary. After arriving and coming through customs an official asked me if I wanted him to stamp my passport? I thought it was his duty. I found out later that it was against US Law for its citizens to travel to Libya. I had never heard of that restriction but at any rate I was already there. I was looking for the driver who was to pick me up and a taxi drive looked at me and said what I thought he said, "Dr. Reid"? I forgot he wasn't speaking my tongue but I was happy to see a smiling face that looked like he had been sent for me. That "Dude" took me way out in the country somewhere to what looked like a "red light" house. He set my bags out and I went in. I wasn't expecting this. The man behind the counter looked at me and couldn't speak a word of English. Soon someone came from out of the kitchen that understood a little English. I kept calling the name of Ambassador Treikia. I understood him to say that he was going back in town after he got off and he would take me. I went outside and said, "Lord, as I looked up and saw a bright shiny moon, you know how I got here, please take me to where I am supposed to be." Around midnight this person in the kitchen came out and told me to get in the car that had just driven up. I got in the car and we drove back toward town. He was speaking in his tongue to the driver all the way. They came to a small community just outside of town where they stopped and there they embraced passionately. I had only seen something like this once and that was when I was catching a ride to Norfolk from Fort Bragg, NC. Its after midnight and I was lost! And I could not ask for my Government's help.

After the kissing was over this non-English speaking driver took me directly to the hotel where I was scheduled to stay. After getting in the lobby and checking in I saw Ambassador Treikia getting on the elevator. He was happy to see me and he doesn't know it yet, but he wasn't half as happy to see me as I was in seeing him. I praised God all the way to my room where fruit and water awaited me. I said Lord; the next time I get a chance to speak I am going to tell everybody about you. To my surprise, after a few days in Tripoli, I was asked to speak on the occasion of their 15th Revolution. I still have my notes on that speech. I talked about the Revolution that took place on American soil. I spoke to 121 nations of the world through electronic translations. I double-checked my awkward humor as to whether they were listening. They were and then I told them about Jesus. I had been close to Libya before but had lost my geographical sense of directions. I had been to Syria on the Northeast and Trans Jordan in Amman on the East, and to Egypt on the South. As a matter of fact I have preached by the mercy of God, the Eleeo of God, on five of the seven Continents of the world.

I was given a driver and a car and a free ticket to anything I wanted to eat or drink plus free lodging. That was more than I was ever offered while running revivals in traditional churches that I now see had "ceiling faith" reaching out for the God of the Ages, while serving the God of the West.

The presence of the Lord has been with me all of my life and I only knew it after I discovered Him behind our house in Chesapeake and received His indwelling. I am blessed today because He "slowed" me when He could have "stopped me." I am happy today to report that I am still moving in the blessed Name of Jesus, the Christ of Glory. I know that I didn't come here to stay. This world, this fallen age, this sphere of aliveness, this world – none is my home. The Choir sings some times, "Soon and very soon, I am going to see the King. Soon and very soon, I am going to see the King. Soon and very soon I am going to see the King. Hallelujah, Hallelujah, I 'm going to see the King.

Dr. Reid greets VP Humphrey.

Dr. Milton Reid with Mrs. Coretta King.

CHAPTER VIII

FROM HOLOCAUST TO HOLIDAY (IT'S FAMILY TIME)

Then Esther sent this reply to Mordecia: Go assemble all the Jews who are found in Susa and fast in my behalf. Don't eat and don't drink for three days, night or day. My female attendants and I will also fast in the same way. Afterwards I will go to the king, even though it violates the law. If I perish, I perish.

Esther 4:15-16 NET

I am the door. If any one enters through me, he will be saved, and will come in and go out and find pasture. The thief comes only to steal and kill and destroy; I have come so that they may have life, and may have it abundantly.

John 10:9,10

Introduction: As part of the apparent disintegration of our national will we are today hearing the cries for the restoring and the rebuilding of families as never before. Our foreparents did not have a lot of formal education but they had something that is lacking in many families today, i.e., the moral and spiritual stamina that the Lord requires. They knew that there were some principles, some standards, a mode of ethical behavior based on the love ethic of Jesus to which families had to adhere. We cannot put all of the blame on Dr. Benjamin Spock's liberalization of child rearing. Letting the child decide on his own punishment...letting the child decide on his breakfast, lunch and dinner...letting the child decide on what he or she should wear...letting the child decide on his or her curfew... letting the child decide on "what's in" and "what's out"..."what's hip and what's old fashioned and out of date." A whole lot of us are guilty and look what we have on our hands...trying to be the nice guy, with mother being our best friend. We need to thank God for our journey of faith, repent, and believe again on the Lord Jesus Christ and we shall be saved.

There is an Old Testament story that you perhaps have read and studied or at least heard of it that deals with the family that is appropriate for us today. I hope to end with a New Testament challenge that the Old Testament story didn't know about. This story is one of the great movements of woman's liberation in the Bible that most of us just might miss. King Zeroes (Xeroxes), who ruled over 127 provinces stretching from India to the Upper Nile region, threw one of the great parties in the Bible. The party lasted 180 days, which was the prelude to a great banquet lasting seven days. Wine was served in goblets of gold, each different from the other, and the royal wine was abundant. In keeping with the king's liberality, on the seventh day when the King was "high" in spirits... he wanted to display his queen and all he wanted was her crown upon her head so that all of the men could gaze upon her beauty.

Now you know the king had to be drunk or had become a full-fledged fool, or both. Look at this. Susa or shun Shan was the capital of his empire. It was located in Iran near the Persian Gulf. He wanted his wife to show her self...to unveil herself, not just her face before the drunken crew that her husband had assembled. The feast for the nobility lasted six months and the feast in the palace for the servants and officials lasted a week. Vashti, in moral outrage, said my family upbringing would not permit this. More than that I have my dignity. I am no belly dancer...I am no stripper... I am the King's wife but he is pushing it too far. I am about sick of this macho man. I am not going to do it...the hell with him!

So the King had to get himself another queen. A man by the name of Mordecia, who had been taken into captivity after King Nebuchadnezzar destroyed Jerusalem, had a beautiful and lovely young cousin. Her name was Ha das sah, called Esther, her slave name, whose mother and father were dead. Her father was Mordecai's uncle, which made Esther his cousin in the extended family. Mordecai felt responsible for her. Hegai, who was in charge of the harem, selected her. Mordecai told Esther not to tell anyone that she was a Jew. Before the king saw Esther she had been given six months of beauty treatments with oil of volay & Revlon, I mean myrrh, followed by six months of special perfumes and ointments... poison, red, Obsession and opium.

Different from our laws, our customs and traditions, when the head eunuch in charge of the harem selects you, you belong to the king. She was his wife. But the king had to make a choice out of his wives as to who was to be his queen. Now, my brethren, that was somewhere around 465 B.C.; it didn't work then and it won't work now. Esther was the king's choice. She pleased him. Mordecia went up every day by the king's harem's house to check on Esther. One sign of a stable family is when we check in on each other. I am glad Graham invented the telephone, (I don't know who attached a telephone bill to it) but if I hadn't checked by phone with my wife and children when I was marching all over America with Dr. Martin Luther King, Jr., I don't know whether I would have a family today or not.

The family is in serious trouble today and as Christians we ought to be checking up on each other. Not nosing in each other's business but checking to see if everything is going all right. We carry around a lot of burdens that we don't need to bear. There ought to be somebody in the family with whom we should be able to talk. When you check on family members for their own good you are bearing witness...you are putting your own faith in the practice of ministry. More than that, you will find yourself put to the test of your redemption in Christ. Here is an Old Testament book where God's name is not mentioned. Yet you can see the move of God on every page, if not in every sentence. God reveals Himself through the ties of the family. And the Book of Esther tells us today that it is Family Time both in our nation and in our world. We are dying daily and needlessly. It is high time that we do something creative about our holocaust since Jesus came that we might have "Life to the Full!"

I. COME FIRST AND SEE THAT IT'S HOLOCAUST TIME WHEN THE CRISIS OF DEATH THREATENS THE LIFE OF THE RACE BECAUSE OF AN EVIL DESIGN

Mordecia was always hanging around the gate in the company of the elders. He had to know what was happening. Because of his abiding interest in the family, although the Bible doesn't say it,

Mordecia was concerned about the people of God, the family of God in bondage. He no doubt would have watched CNN, read the N.Y Times, the Washington Post, the New Journal and Guide and the Black press every week. He had to know what was happening. He wasn't the kind to sit around home and say what will happen, will happen. He would never say, "my vote will not count," (Of course he had never lived in Florida or Ohio). Mordecia wasn't one to say, "You can't beat city hall." He situated himself to help make things happen for the good. You never know how God will use you if you allow yourself to be used by Him to make a difference. In our world today somebody needs to make a difference.

If Mordecia read the papers today... if he looked at the national news or read any major news source he would know that families are disintegrating. If he would review the brokenness in families, the absence of fathers, and sometimes mothers...the absence of families during worship, or Bible study, and especially during prayer time... he would know that something is terribly wrong in the life of our national will. He would be concerned about the "hip hop" gangs who have seen "so much violence" that they have a new mindset to destroy human life and give each other credit! Mordecia would be concerned that a whole generation of Black boys will do more destroying of each other than the Klan and the institution of slavery ever did. I am sure he would note that the enemy is really not external to us but much of the enemy lies within us. In other words, as the comic strip Peanuts would say, "The enemy is us." Mordecia would be appalled at babies having babies with no knowledge as to how to take care of themselves or the babies to which they are giving birth. He would be struck and baffled at the burgeoning prison cells with more than 52% of the prison population in the nation being Black while we are only about 13% of the national population.

He would be shocked at what we are calling good news that is in fact bad news. These booming radios and music boxes will have most of today's young people wearing hearing aids before they reach prime time 35 years of age. He didn't have a church in exile but we do and we talk about "having church", rather than being the church. I was persuaded to go hear an evangelist who was scheduled to conduct a tent revival in a dilapidated section of

Norfolk. He said in a sermon leading up to the revival, "I didn't come here to deal with social issues. I did not come to deal with current events...I didn't come to deal with political corruption, I came to talk about Jesus" and it was obvious that he didn't know Jesus. The Jesus I know said, "The Spirit of the Lord God is upon me for he has anointed me to preach good news to the poor. He has sent me to proclaim freedom for the prisoners and recovery of sight for the blind, to release the oppressed, to proclaim the year of the Lord's favor." The Jesus I know said, "You are the light of the world, and the salt of the earth...Let your light so shine before men that they may see your good works and glorify your father which is in heaven." We blessedly something that Mordecia didn't because he had not heard Jesus say, "And you shall receive power after the Holy Spirit has come upon you and you shall be my witnesses...you shall testify of me in Jerusalem, and in all Judea and Samaria, and to the ends of the earth." The Martin L. King, Jr., Family Life Institute is calling on America for a National Family Day Celebration for the evil design of death is upon us.

This appeal has been expanded in Congress to include a call for a Global Family Day Celebration Day.

II. COME FINALLY AND SEE THAT IT'S FAMILY TIME WHENEVER YOU FIND THE CREATIVE COURAGE TO BEAR WITNESS EVEN IF MEANS YOUR DEATH

There was a man in the king 's court by the name of Haman, who because Mordecia would not bow down to him, had the king to sign an order that all of the Jews would be killed. Mordecia had to get the word to Esther. He told her that she had to get the word to the king. Esther said, "I know that I am beautiful but I also know that it means death if I go to the king and the king has not sent for me. I know something about this place. I know the rules and the regulations. I went to beauty school to learn how to get here and how to stay here. Once you leave the streets there is no desire to go back across the tracks. Tell Uncle Mordecia, `I likes this place. ` I have maidens and servants. I have more money than I have ever heard of...wait a minute. Take him this unlimited gold card...good in all 127 Provinces. While thumbing through the catalog she said to order the king a three-piece Heart Chaffner and Marx. While you are out shopping for him get him a Brooks Brothers doubled breasted suit and go by Victoria's secret and get him some silk Roman underwear, and tell him everything is going to be all right."

Mordecia refused the offers. He said go tell Esther, "This isn't about material goods and the latest style, Baby. This is about life and your life is included. You are not safe. You see the decree that all Jews are to be put to death and it is all because of an evil design; not a disease, not a calamity, not even some erupting Tsunami. The man who ordered it doesn't know what I know...don't forget I know who you are! I promised your mother and your father that I would look out for you." Now let us come upon the text found in the Living Bible. "Do you think you will escape there in the palace when all other Jews are killed? If you keep quiet at a time like this God will deliver the Jews from some other source, but you and your relatives will die. What more can be said but that God has brought you into the palace for just such a time as this?"

Esther got the message. I don't know if she had to sleep on it or not. But the very next verse says, "Tell Mordecia to go and gather all the Jews of Shu shan, the capital in Iran, and fast for me; do not eat or drink for three days and nights and I and my maids will do the same; and then though it is strictly forbidden, I will go in to see the king; and if I perish, I perish." Most of the translations never mention God's name in the book of Esther but the Living Bible does. God is so obviously present that I don't understand how any translator could miss it. God was active in Mordecia's life and in Esther's ascendancy to the throne. God was evident in Mordecia's adopting her. The devil puts all sorts of stuff in children's heads today, such as, "I found out that I was adopted and I want to find out who my real mother and father are." I'll tell you who your real mother is and who your real father is. It's Mother God and Father God. Somebody said He's my Mother...He's my Father... He's my sister and my brother, He's everything to me." When that sperm hits that egg just right and the life of chromosomes converge on each other in the genetic content of life, it is made possible by Mother God and Father God, and God has used a vessel of human instrumentality that He also made to make it happen. Like my mother and father, your mother and father will pass away but Father God and Mother God will walk with you throughout this life and will dispatch two little boys, the name of one being Eternal Goodness and the other being named Eternal Mercy, who shall follow you all the days of your life so that when the proper time comes, you might dwell in the house of the Lord forever.

CONCLUSION: God is very much present throughout this book. You don't have to call him GOD, King James... You don't have to call him GOD, Jerusalem Bible...You don't have to call him God, New International Version, but He's still God! God, who scooped out the valleys and bulged up the mountainsides, GOD: who spat out the seven seas and filled the rivers with tears of joy. GOD...who bedecked the twilight twinkles of the evening and cast them in the silver sockets of the universe and men called them stars. GOD, who is Omnipresent, meaning everywhere at the same time. Omnipotent, all-powerful, Omniscient all knowing...God is all through the book of Esther. Let us look at what happened to that king who was drunk with power and wine and a runaway ego. I don't know if I told you he wasn't too bright. You know just about all of us have some, had some, or probably will have some drunks in our families, but don't get upset and don't cast the drunk aside when he or she shows up. God didn't. There is a difference between getting drunk and staying drunk. If you let a drunk alone and just keep his drink out of his reach he'll eventually sober up. God has a Divine sobering-up process already in place. He doesn't need a cold shower or any hot coffee just leave him alone. All you need to do is to stand on your family's dignity while the sobering up process takes place.

When the king saw that beautiful woman standing there desiring to have a word...When he saw the quintessence of beauty and the epitome of femininity in palace purple and royal rubies ...when he saw this woman who had impacted his life beyond rhyme or reason he said, "Come on in, Baby, and tell Daddy what you want." You see Esther had called the family into prayer, ... she had turned her plate down for three days and three nights when her staff, her maidens and her servants turned their plates down for the same period... God fixed the heart and the mind of the king. How do I know? When Esther broke all the rules and she came in to see the king unannounced, looking the way that she could look with an added divine halo over her head...the king forgot about royal precedence. He forgot about palace protocol...when he saw that fine woman standing there as if she wanted something... (Now before you get upset, this is what the Bible says he said)."Now what is your petition? I'll tell you right now that whatever you want, it is yours, even up to half of my kingdom. Esther couldn't say this, but I want to say it for her. RIDE ON KING JESUS, RIDE ON CONQUERING KING, RIDE ON KING JESUS, I WANT TO GO TO HEAVEN IN THE MORNING. Allow me to fix it. Darling, tell me what you want. She said I want you and the Honorable Secretary of State to have dinner with me tomorrow night. Now Haman was the secretary of state and he drew up the edict that would have killed all of the Jews. At dinner the king said, what is it, darling? She said, "If I have won your favor, O' king, and if it pleases your majesty, save my life and the lives of my people. My people and I have been sold to those who will destroy us. We are doomed to destruction and slaughter. If we were only to be sold as slaves, perhaps I could remain quiet, though even then there would be incalculable damage to the king that no amount of money could begin to recover." "What are you talking about, darling? Who would dare touch you?" This wicked secretary of state Haman is our enemy." Haman grew pale with fright. The king jumped to his feet and went to the palace garden. Haman, realizing that he had "torn it", went to Esther to beg for his life. She was reclining on a sofa. When the king came back in Haman was falling on the couch where the king's wife had been reclining. The king asked, "Will he rape or molest my wife while I am in the house with her?" As soon as the king raised this question a cover was put over Haman's head. The gallows Haman had made for Mordecia were used for Haman instead, by order of the King.

You know what happened to Esther and Mordecai. They escaped the holocaust. They were given a holiday in which to celebrate life. That is what the Martin Luther King, Jr., Family Life Institute is still working on. We are calling together the family of God for a holiday that we can all celebrate, a renewed and a revived family life. We have to set some motions in action for family renewal and family reunions. We need to go back and dig the old family wells that have been cluttered with misgivings, mistrust, miscommunications, and the lack of real redeeming Love that Jesus makes possible through the grace and the mercy of God. We don't need to try to take our streets and communities back. Let us start by bringing our families back under the power of the cross. It was at the cross, "at the Cross, where I first saw the light and the burdens of my heart were rolled away. It was there by faith I received my sight and now, I am happy all the day." We have got to bring the family together. No matter what they have done or what they have not done, bring them together in the Spirit of Jesus Christ. Like Esther, we may have to turn our plates down. Like Esther, we may have to call our nation back to powerful praying grounds. Like Esther, we must go to our congressmen and women, our senators, our governors, and to the leaders of our nation and point out the enemy that would destroy us. We must not be afraid for the Giver of life, The One who was in the beginning with God, The One who taught us to pray "Our Father," The One who said, "I have come that you might have life, and have it more abundantly," was Himself raised as part of a family. And, "If when you give, the best of your service. Telling the world, that the Savior has come. Be not dismayed when men don't believe you. He'll understand and say well done. If when you try and fail in your trying, hands sore and scarred from the work you've begun...take up your cross, run quickly to meet him, He'll understand and say, well done." We can do it because IT'S FAMILY TIME. And you know what happened? The holiday came and those who were scheduled to be annihilated, those who were to be destroyed, were put in charge of the holiday! It is family time when we move from holocaust to holiday.

The Poor People's Campaign Headquarters, Norfolk, VA.

CHAPTER IX

THE GORY AND THE GLORY OF THE CROSS

First delivered at Union Theological Seminary In New York

November 17, 2003

It is a well-known fact that the event of the Christ was not the matrix of the cross in history. Long before the story of the nativity in Bethlehem the cross was used as capital punishment in the Roman Empire, especially for the slaves. It was a cruel and unusual punishment that served not only to put one to death but it was a warning or a supposed deterrent to other slaves who dared to think about their freedom or violating their masters' rules that kept them in bondage. It was only by the seal of Roman authority that this form of punishment could be used. This Jesus of Nazareth, a Disrupter of the status quo and a Light of Divine, origin came shining in the darkness and the darkness has never understood it or welcomed it. According to John, the only one of these disciples that lived to a "ripe" old age, (and a relative of Jesus), "He came to that which was his own, but his own did not receive him. Yet to all who received him, to those who believed in his name, he gave the right to become children of God – children born not of natural descent, nor of human decision or a husband's will, but born of God" (John 1:11-13). He came into the world, (Aion, a godless world) to bring man into redemptive relationship with God in the New Heaven and the New Earth.

The Cross or in Greek, the Stauros, "denotes primarily, an upright pale or stake on which malefactors were nailed for execution. Both the noun and the verb (stauros in Greek) mean to fasten to a stake or pale, or originally to be distinguished from the ecclesiastical form of a two beamed cross. The shape of the latter had its origin in ancient Chalde, and was used as the symbol of the god Tammuz (being in the shape of the mystic Tau, the initial of his name) in that country and in adjacent lands, including Egypt." There is little argument that the cross had its matrix in gory, a bloody-minded and murderous beginning. It was most inhuman and homicidal and was seen as a way to deal with the worst criminals. To those in spiritual darkness Jesus was destined for the cross as a most likely candidate for Calvary. It was tailor-made for him. Man's inhumanity to man had its matrix in the Cross. It was thus befitting to show the world a way of dealing with insurrection and revolt against established authority. Jesus did not come to establish a new religion; He came to proclaim the Kingdom of God, which amounted to a New World Order under the domain of God. Jesus called it the Kingdom of God. He taught His disciples to pray: "Thy Kingdom come, thy will be done on earth as it is in Heaven" (Matthew 6:10 NIV). The significance in the coming of Jesus demands that change must come in the world (Aion) as we know it. The Kingdom of God is no easy sell. If you believe it is try discarding the creature comforts of our society and try selling it in this technological age and in our computerized culture. The fact is we have been selling a watered down ideology of the cross to the extent that we have found it more profitable to "wear" the cross around our necks than to "bear" the cross in our hearts. We have been marching under a false banner that we have called Christian, yet we have diluted the word of God with interpretations that never were intended. The same thing has happened to the Constitution of our nation through the various contradictions of our courts, especially when it comes to the separation of church and state.

We create biased and unjust laws and then watch a questionable court interpret them in the best interests of powerful forces loose in the country. This nation has never recovered from the decision rendered by the Warren Court on May 17, 1954, that ruled unconstitutional the "separate but equal doctrine, as it applied to education, and that children could not be segregated based on their race nor the color of their skin." This unanimous ruling shocked certain segregationists in the executive and legislative branches of our government. Earl Warren had been the man in California who interred Japanese in concentration camps during the Second World

War and three Southerners sat on the Supreme Court. After that decision the late George Wallace, Governor of Alabama, said in his January, 1963, inaugural address, "I draw the line in the dust and toss the gauntlet before the feet of tyranny and I say segregation now, segregation tomorrow, and segregation forever." The 1954 decision, led by lawyers of the NAACP, laid the groundwork for the actions of Rosa Parks, the birth of the Montgomery Improvement Association, and the coming into being of Dr. Martin Luther King, Jr., who forced America to rethink her role under the cross as a Christian nation. Since the Fifties we have witnessed the transition from segregationist to the Moral Majority, from the Moral Majority to the Religious Right, and from the Religious Right to the neo-conservatives who have become the evangelicals who want strict conservatives on the high court and not anyone who will purportedly `legislate from the bench. ` If you ever need a lawyer and you find one that doesn't know the law or the Lord, find out how much he knows about the judge. Sometimes that works. If he doesn't know the law or the Lord and doesn't know the judge, you need to find yourself another lawyer. Thank God we had some legal minds that represented Black folk in particular and who knew the Lord and the law.

Paul, who was a brilliant lawyer, never surrendered his Roman citizenship. As a matter of fact it saved him on several occasions. He tells the church at Philippi, "Dear friends, pattern your lives after mine, and learn from those who follow our example. For I have told you often before, and I say it again with tears in my eyes, that there are many whose conduct shows they are really enemies of the Cross of Christ. Their future is eternal destruction. Their god is their appetite; they brag about shameful things, and all they think about is this life here on earth. But we are citizens of heaven, where the Lord Jesus Christ lives. And we are eagerly waiting for him to return as our Savior. He will take these weak mortal bodies of ours and change them into glorious bodies like his own, using the same mighty power that he will use to conquer everything, everywhere" (Philippians 3:17-21 LAB). Paul wrote more about the cross of Christ perhaps than any other New Testament writer. He saw it as being essential to our faith. Let's look at the cross in history from the perspectives of "Gory and Glory."

THE GORY IN THE CROSS

The cross, from its matrix in history, has been steeped in gory from the standpoint of wasteful blood letting. Sometimes in the name of Jesus men have used the cross as their symbol of fighting and killing. History records the so-called vision of Constantine the Great, the Roman Emperor who through the Edict of Milan in 313 made Christianity a recognized religion in the Empire, and soon thereafter, made it the state religion. At the same time this called for a cease and desist of the persecutions of Christians. In his vision and co-called "conversion," he saw the cross and a sword that told him, "By this sign conquer." He perhaps had never read what Jesus had to say about the sword. In John 18:11 Jesus said, "Put your sword away, Peter! Shall I not drink the cup the Father has given me?" Constantine also embraced varying pagan religions and tolerated them. This rules out any possibility of a genuine conversion experience. Conversion includes repentance, or Metanoeo, which means, "to perceive afterward." Evidence of his actions following his purported conversion experience tells us that this just didn't happen. It was through his assimilation of other religions into the faith that Christianity legally and historically became what the Greeks called Apistos, or untrustworthy or faithless. It lost its power, its fervor, its convictions and its directions.

The Christian church has never been the same since its birth on Pentecost when Peter preached that earth-shaking sermon that led to the expansion of the embryonic and ecclesiastical community that we call the church or the Ekklesia, the called out, the sanctified, and the soon to be glorified. We can see the effects of its decline through the period from Constantine to the Christian crusades of the Middle Ages. Constantine was the first in the history of the church to envision the cross for his own political and social benefits. Under the goriness of the cross White Christians were to build a new nation from Black slave labor making them "hewers of wood and drawers of water" in America. They would come to include "In God We Trust" on our capitalistic coins and bills. It is also inscribed on the walls of the Supreme Court, the highest court in the land. Are we trusting in the God of the West or the God of the Ages? They are not the same. This action sends out the message that you could do whatever was profitable to you under the imperial aegis of the cross. It was after his vision and so-called conversion experience that Constantine killed his son over a rumor that he was having an affair with his wife and later boiled her to death strapped in a palace bathtub. He thus created the basis for a Euro-theological perspective that the church in the West is built upon. Godless humanism is always without the cross. It was the church that stamped its approval of slavery and snatched our foreparents from Africa and brought them to America on a ship named Christian. Black men were rendered to an ontological rejection and were legally not persons but were defined as chattel property.

There have been almost endless discussions on Christian warfare and the issue of war all through the days of biblical writings until now. God has been called a "Battle Ax" in the time of trouble. We have given the cross a place in our lives and on the battlefields of the world. Paul tells us, as he told the church at Ephesus, "We are not fighting against people made of flesh and blood, but against the evil rulers and authorities of the unseen world. Against those mighty powers of darkness who rule this world, (Aion) and against wicked spirits in the heavenly realms" (Ephesians 6:12 LAB). We must be careful about the mistake we make sometimes with the literal interpretation of Scriptures. It appears to me that Paul was saying that our problems are deeper than race, although some of us might see them as racial. The principalities and powers in high places do have racial manifestation but evil is a force that is beyond race and most racists don't know it, especially those who have not embraced the decisions of the Cross.

More closely in our day the gory of the Cross is seen in the activity of the Ku Klux Klan, a band of white Southern Christians organized in 1865, following the Civil War. They became prominent during the period of Reconstruction to slow down and bring to a halt the idea of freedom for freed slaves. This was a group in hooded sheets with crosses embroidered on their robes, front and back, and a burning cross that lighted up their gathering to intimidate Black Americans. Later they included Jews and Catholics to their growing hate list. In many instances Black Americans responded out of fear and trepidation to this group. They were discovered to be councilmen, chiefs of police, policemen, bankers, judges, governors, and members of the Christian church, primarily Southerners. It was the Southern Baptists who pulled away from what is now the American Baptist over the issue of slavery. This fraudulent practice of the faith that was delivered unto the saints made a mockery of the cross (Greek Hagios). It was the Ku Klux Klan that bombed the 16th Street Baptist Church in what we in the civil rights movement called "Bombing ham," Alabama, that is Birmingham, Alabama, that killed four little Black girls in Sunday school.

It took several decades to bring the guilty to justice because of the all-white jury in Alabama that could not bring themselves to "Love mercy, do justly and to walk humbly with God." It was the same with Medgar Evers, the field secretary of the NAACP, who was shot and killed by Byron de La Beckwith, a White Christian Klansman, and it took some forty years to bring him to justice. There are scores of others murdered by racist White Christians. It was a strange sight to see a handful of Black people in a sea of religious, right-winged White conservatives at the Capitol in Texas petitioning for the Ten Commandments to be placed on the State Capitol. They want God to be acknowledged in stone even after Jesus said that God was Spirit and they who worship him, must "worship Him in Spirit and in Truth." I stood with Dr. Martin Luther King, Jr., and hundreds of ministers and civil right activists at the state Capitol in Montgomery demanding our right to vote in a voting rights bill that was before Congress. I wonder where these cross-wearing Christians were when we were demonstrating for freedom and justice? Where were they when we marched from the sleeping town of Selma, Alabama, to the methodical city of Montgomery? Where were they when we demonstrated in Mississippi, South Carolina, Georgia, North Carolina and Virginia, for justice and freedom? John, who wrote the Fourth Gospel, the three Epistles, and the Book of Revelation said, "If anyone says, I love God yet hates his brother, he is a liar. For anyone who does not love his brother whom he has seen cannot love God whom he has not seen. And he has given us this command: Whoever loves God must also love his brother (1 John 4:20-21 NIV). You cannot love your brother under the goriness of the cross. It requires redeeming Love to even know who your brothers and sisters are.

THE GLORY IN THE CROSS

The Glory of the Cross speaks to the bright side of God's redeeming love, His mercy and His grace. The glory in the cross means one's decision to follow Jesus by cutting off all other alternatives. The synoptic gospels record Jesus saying, "If anyone would come after me, he must deny himself and take up his cross daily and follow me." If we are going to take away the cross or diminish it in any way we may as well take away Jesus, and I am in no position to even consider either one of these pseudo prospects. There is a recent philosophical thought that says "If the Jews had received Jesus when He came to His own, He could have bridged the chasm between man and God by becoming the Pontifex Maximun, a bridge builder, a title that Constantine held for himself, and He would not have found any need to die on Calvary. That is purely suppositional. It is non-biblical and is certainly not theological. The Cross is not only your decision to believe, it is your decision to know and to do the Will of God. It is not that two-beamed symbol that we hang or wear but it is our decision to follow Jesus and to submit our will to the Will of God. John says, "For God so loved the world, (Aion) that he gave his one and only Son, that whoever believes in him shall not perish but have eternal life" (John 3:16 NIV). By the same token we could become speculative regarding the first man, Adam. Had he been obedient there is a good chance that Jesus, the second man Adam, would not have needed to come at all. But Adam was disobedient and, according to John Milton, "Fell nine times the space that measures day and night." I don't know how far that is but it appears to me that it is the state of fallen man without the hope of the Cross of Christ. When God created man he was endowed with the power of contrary choice. The late Dr. Vernon Johns said of God's creation that, "Man could ascend as high as angels in heaven or fall as low as devils in hell," and man still has that choice."

It is not that I have a closed mind to other theological interpretations and dogma, but for me there are some things that are settled. They are just as settled as Christ is Himself, being the Son of God. The Cross or the Stauros, is a non-erasable fact in history and it has a dark side and a bright side, so much so until it cannot be delimited by any humanistic ideology or the burden of time. The Resurrection speaks to the bright side of the cross. I think Protestant theologians were right when they exchanged the crucifix for the bold face cross that speaks in inaudible silence saying, "He is not on the cross." John heard him say, "The reason my Fathers loves (Agape) me is that I lay down my life-only to take it up again. No one takes it from me, but I lay it down of my own accord. I have authority to lay it down and authority (Greek Exousia) or power to take it up again" (John 10:17, 18 NIV). The theological notion of diminishing the historical fact of the Cross in Christian theology is nothing short of being apocryphal, unscriptural, non-canonical and untrustworthy or "Apistos" in Greek). I can and I have dealt with the gory of the Cross from the perspective of Constantine the Great. As a Son of God's redemption (Apolutrosis in Greek) and the positions on Love between Peter and Jesus, I learn something new about love. I understand that Jesus asked Peter three times, "Peter, do you love me more than these do?" Peter said, "Yes, Lord, I love you or I Phileo you." Jesus thought even that was useful so he said to Peter that with this Love you can "feed my sheep." He asked Peter a second time, "Simon, son of John, do you love or do you (Agape) me?" Peter said, "Yes, Lord, you know I love you." Jesus told him, "Shepherd my sheep." Jesus said to him the third time, "Simon, son of John, do you love (Agape) me?" Peter was distressed that Jesus asked him a third time, "Do you love me?" and said, "Lord you know everything. You know that I love you." Jesus replied, "Feed my sheep" (John 21:15-17 NET).

So with as much of God's love as I can muster I have learned to agape the Klan, even in their corruption of the Cross. If I can love the Klan with God's Love I can love those who seek to "delimit" the Cross and not keep it central to our faith. Without the Cross there is no resurrection. Without the cross there is no redemption for us, for there is no one to pay the price for our sins. In addressing the luncheon of the M&M Board of the American Baptist Convention in Richmond, Virginia, Dr. William J. Shaw, President of the National Baptist Convention, said this. "...I am pleading for a willingness on the part of religious communities in this country to take the cross seriously and make it not just some abstract spiritual presence that would be effective when we die, but make it a way of life that is powerful as we live. If we live in the power of the cross, God will take care of the matter of our dying." Paul, who identified himself as a "Hebrew of the Hebrews," wasn't just any lawyer but he was an astute one. The only lawyer that represented him in his many trials was his Chief Advocate in the person of Jesus and the angel who stood by him. Paul was a member of the Sanhedrin and a student of Gamaliel. He was fluent in several languages. He traveled all through Asia Minor and finally made it to the City on the Seven Hills, just off the Appian Way. He was a debater with the Greek philosophers on Mars Hill and a founder of churches. He wrote about half of the books in the New Testament so he was a prolific writer. Paul said in his letter to the Galatians as he was dealing with the matter of circumcision, "As for me, God forbid that I should boast about any thing except the cross of our Lord Jesus Christ. Because of that cross, my interest in this world died long ago, and the world's interest in me is also long dead " (Galatians 6:14 LAB). Paul tells the church at Corinth, "For the message about the cross is foolishness to those who are perishing, but to us who are being saved it is the power of God" (1 Corinthians 1:18 NET). I'll hold hands with George Bennard, who wrote one of my favorite hymns about the cross in 1913, and with that veteran Apostle Paul, and sing, "So I'll cherish the Old Rugged Cross. Till my trophies at last I lay down; I will cling to the old rugged cross, and exchange it someday for a crown."

We need to revisit the cross, not to limit it or neutralize it as an outdated symbol of our faith, but to research the depth of its meaning. We must make those kinds of decisions that would restore us by the mercy and grace of God in His Divine favor, so that the Holy Spirit would shape us, make us and mold us again into "His Image and in His likeness" through our glorified and resurrected Savior, Jesus our Lord.

Wyatt T. Walker with Dr. Reid in Petersburg, VA.

CHAPTER X

THE FOOLISHNESS OF PREACHING

(Preached on the occasion of the 33rd anniversary of Dr. Johnnie L. White, pastor of First Calvary Baptist, Norfolk, Virginia)

"For the message about the cross is foolishness to those who are perishing, but to us who are being saved it is the power of God"

1 Corinthians 1:18 NET

Introduction: Most of us who are called to preach the gospel of Jesus Christ feel both our unworthiness and a high sense of obligation to this divine and noble task that much of the world sees as foolishness. When I think of preaching and reflect upon the gravity that it entails, what it is supposed to ignite, and what it was meant to do. And to then when I am reminded God has no other alternative to get done what He wants done, my mind often goes back to Edwin Charles Dargan, in his volume, "A History of Preaching." In this book he calls the roll of great and eminent preachers from the apostolic fathers of the first century to the great reformers of the sixteenth century. Dargan says, "The life and progress of nations, the rise and fall of governments have often been closely connected with preaching." He makes reference to preachers like the Apostle Paul, John Chrysostom, Augustine, the heroic Black Bishop of Hippo, Ambrose, Leo Gregory, Savonarola, the golden-tongued orator, Luther, Calvin and Knox of England, Whitfield and Wesley, and the list goes on. Now he didn't call the name of your pastor or mine. You see he died in 1907, and some of us (I can't speak for all of us) but some of us had not been born.

I haven't seen the revised edition. It is really not important that "you" even call our names as being great preachers. I just want the Lord to call me by my name when life is over and say to me, "Well Done." The world said you were foolish but I say you were faithful or Pistis, persuaded unto action.

In the beginning God only had one Son and He ended up preaching. He was a Builder and an Architect; John said, "He created everything and that nothing exists that He didn't make"... but He ended up preaching. He was a great teacher. When the authorities went to arrest Him they themselves were arrested by His matchless words of divine wisdom and came back saying, "Never a man spoke like Him, for He speaks not as one of the Scribes and Pharisees but as one who has "Ex-ousia (authority) or dunamis," from which we get our English word 'dynamite.' When He spoke...the deaf heard...the blind received their sight. When He spoke...disease became at ease, death, whom no man has seen grew ears, and life stood up over what it had claimed. The late Clara Ward sang, "When He spoke...I recognized His voice...When He spoke, it was the day I made my choice...O...when He spoke, that man, that man, that man from Galilee..." but He ended up preaching.

He had a hand in healing. Luke, the Gentile physician, said He healed all manner of diseases...even diseases for which there were no cures. I heard David say one day, "Bless the Lord O my soul and forget not all of His benefits, who heals all thine diseases, who redeems thy life from destruction, who crowns thee with loving kindness and tender mercies." He could have made it in any medical center in the world. He even had healing in the hem of His garment but He ended up preaching. The preacher is just about the only professional out here that still deals with the total person. The preacher ministers to the whole person and he often asks, along with Jesus, DO YOU WANT TO BE MADE WHOLE? That's why somebody said, "the preacher of the gospel is the most indispensable person in the world." Someone has said, "God needs the preacher, the world needs the preacher and the preacher needs the preacher." But God cannot and God will not use any preacher that He anoints to preach until he surrenders. The story of our text talks about a situation in the church in Corinth that reminds me so much of the people in the churches with whom I have come in contact. They either loved the preacher or hated him and thereby sometimes missed their mission or calling as disciples of Christ's Kingdom. Of course there is a new crowd today who aren't with anybody.

They are in the church but they refuse to allow the church to be in them. Listen to their typical complaints. "I belong to Paul or I belong to Apollos, or I belong to Cephas, or I belong to Christ." They were not nearly as concerned about the message of the man as they were about the man of the message. When Paul was informed of this division he told them that the preacher was important only to the extent that his message was one of divine redemption. This message of redemption's story was and still is a stumbling block to some and foolishness to others. Come let us see why preaching is foolishness to many people today in and out of the Church.

I. COME FIRST AND SEE THAT PREACHING IS FOOLISH TO SOME FOLK BECAUSE IT IS STRANGE OR FOREIGN TO OUR CULTURE.

We are living in a day of advanced medical technology and scientific know how that has challenged the very fibers of our faith. This is the day not only of miracle drugs, laser surgery, transplants, computerized and robotic medical technology, but a day of the specialist. We are running out of family practice physicians. Should they should be called "physician coordinators? You have to get the right doctor now for everything and for the right price you can get done now what you don't have to pray to get done (sometimes). When I was growing up the late Dr. J.Q.A. Webb was our family physician and he treated any ailment that you had. It is difficult to find a doctor who treats the whole person today. We are living in a different day, a day of medical specialists. Medical science is still pondering the miracle of humankind and of life itself. We need specialists today for better health care. The preacher however, treats body and soul, mind and spirit. He follows Jesus in a holistic ministry that was practiced in the early church.

We live in a day of accelerated pleasures in the here-and-now and no one wants to be tied down to an old, outdated life in religion in this hip-hop generation. We live in a day when progress and breakthrough are coming in so fast that we hardly know what to call this age. Is it really the inter-planetary age or is it the age of guided missiles and misguided men? Is it the age of the new world order or is it the age of His second coming? Preaching in a day like this is rather foreign to the mandates of culture in our affluent society.

Jesus ran into this kind of a society when he came preaching about the Kingdom of Heaven. This was a day when the religious leaders were having a mundane picnic. The high priest had complete control over man's means and his mind. And this man Jesus comes to town. This untutored Son of a Nazarene carpenter came preaching about the Kingdom of God. He had made headlines in the *Morning Herald* of Palestine for about two years when a one-time rich ruler and a member of the Sanhedrin came to Him by night and wanted to question Him about the Kingdom. Nicodemus was not interested in the new birth. He didn't know anything about it. He wanted to know about the Kingdom of which Jesus preached. Jesus told Nicodemus that when He talked He used illustrations. He told him that He could illustrate and show him the Kingdom but that he couldn't see it. For a man has to be born again before he can even see the Kingdom or understand anything about it. I suppose that is one of the reasons that revivals are so unpopular. That's why evening services went out like a blackout some forty or fifty year ago. The church has become a maternity ward with pregnant potentials. All of us do not show signs of faith that come along with the new birth. Preaching tells me that a whole lot of us are in the church but so many cannot find the church in us. It is not a matter of "having church," the call is upon us that requires us to be the church and we will never be the church as long as we serve the God of the West.

This matter of preaching is foreign to you if you have not been born again. A man doesn't know what the Love of God is until he responds to God's Love through the new birth. This preaching tells us to love our enemies. Isn't that strange? It tells us to pray for them that persecute you. Isn't that strange? It tells us to do "good for evil" and that when you do good men will speak evil of you, even when your heart is broken. It tells us that vengeance belongs to God, God will repay. "Amen, somebody." Preaching tells us to bring the tithes and offering into my storehouse and try Me, says the Lord, and see if I won't open the windows of heaven and pour you out a blessing that you will not have room enough to receive it." You see I really don't care what happens to the economy, just keep tithing and you will not have room enough to receive it. David said, "I was young and now I am old and I've never seen the righteous forsaken or his seed begging bread." Mahalia told me before she left the other day, "He's got the whole world in His Hands." But that is foolishness even to some church folk. The Christ of Glory has sent us to teach and to preach for the Kingdom of God is at hand.

II. COME NEXT AND SEE THAT PREACHING IS FOOLISH BECAUSE IT DEALS WITH AN INDESCRIBALE COMMODITY CALLED THE SOUL.

Someone has said that preaching is an easy job but don't you believe it. They reason that all you have to do is to stand up and talk about the Lord about thirty minutes once a week and most folk want you to cut that to the size of their shrinking attention span. They may have gotten spiritual exhortation confused with the Divine proclamation of God's word. You try to show someone something that is invisible. Convince him or her that it can mean eternal life or eternal damnation when at the same time you can't describe it, locate it or even prove that it is there., Now you can get an idea of what's involved in preaching. Preaching speaks the language of Love. John centered his preaching on repentance. Jesus centered his preaching on faith. Paul would say after you hear and heed preaching, "Present your bodies as a living sacrifice; holy and acceptable unto God which is your spiritual worship." Preaching speaks the language of Love. At the core or the center of preaching stands a God of redeeming Love, not church folk liking or not liking one another. Preaching speaks of redemption, regeneration, the soul of man as the spiritual regulator for activities of the physical and the metaphysical.

The late Dr. M.M. Peace of the Monumental Baptist Church in Philadelphia once said, "If some one would ask the average preacher what is the soul of man, he or she would probably give you an answer that is just as foreign as the one you have." The soul has been defined as the breath of life. Well, what is that? It has been defined as a spark of the Divine. Well, what is that? The center of man's being or the heart of man, well, what is that? Well, preacher, if what it is bothers you, tell me where it is! If you can't define it then locate it. If we dissect the human body in a laboratory the anatomy would reveal all parts by name. The heart, the lungs, the stomach, the brain, the arteries, the liver, the intestines, the spleen, the glands, every bone, every bristle, but nothing called the soul. Take one more step in the preacher's defense and put this same body in test tubes. You will find that man is 65% oxygen, 3% nitrogen, 10% hydrogen, 1% phosphorus, or enough to make 2,200 matches. He is 18% carbon, or enough to make 9,000 black led pencils. He has about 12 1/2 gallons of water in him and enough fat to make seven bars of soap, and (when you get my size, you could make 14). He has sugar and iron, 3 1/2 lbs of calcium and other substances but nothing in the test tube labeled the soul. So to many, preaching is foolish because we are trying to save that which we cannot describe, we cannot locate, and as far as many folk are concerned, it does not exist.

I think it is well that we took this unfruitful physical search. The soul of man is not a physical substance but a spiritual quality. Frederick C. Grant in his book, "Introduction to New Testament Thought," says, "The soul is this quality in man which is the divine image in him, not his physical form. The soul is the vital principle life. It is the seat of conscious, the reflection of personality." The soul is the growing image of God that has no form or likeness. It is the spirit of righteousness that has a kinship with the eternal. The soul is like the pilot on a stove. It burns low, yet it burns. It will keep on burning, all things being equal, until a greater power turns it off. Yet you cannot do much cooking on the pilot. You cannot keep warm in cold weather with "only" the pilot burning. The stove must be turned to the "ON" position. You cannot turn unless you respond to preaching; the thing men call foolish. The trouble with the church is that too many Christians are trying to cook and keep warm with just the pilot burning. Some have big ideas but little hearts; big living but little giving. They want big office with no official standings. These "mad" Christians, these hostile Christians, these indifferent Christians, these "ain't got time" Christians can stay aloof from the Lord and ignore the pleadings of the Holy Spirit because we are trying to save what isn't lost and it doesn't exist because we can neither prove it, describe it, or locate it.

III. COME FINALLY AND SEE THAT PREACHING IS FOOLISH TO MAN BECAUSE IT DEALS WITH A FACT IN TIME TO ASSURE ONE OF THE FELLOWSHIP OF ETERNITY.

All preaching since the first century has dealt with the fact of the cross. This fact of time changed the course of man's downstream drift from God and paved the way for his back up-hill journey. It was at Calvary where all of the nobodies in history became somebody's in His story. The fact of the cross gives us the theme of preaching that was born in the days of the apostolic reign, i.e., JESUS CHRIST IS LORD. To the hearers in and around the church in Corinth this did not make sense. Preaching deals with both a fact and a fellowship, something that our pastor calls the Koinonia. Until you have experienced the fact, you cannot enjoy the fellowship for the way of the cross leads home.

Preaching then points to a place and leads to a place where the preacher himself has not been. It always ends with a challenge toward heaven or it ends in heaven itself. Yet all preaching has a message of redemption through the cross. Many folk would say that it is foolishness because one cannot lead you where he has not been. The story has been told of a student at Yale who once asked Dwight Moody, "where is heaven?" Had he been living today he could have said, "We have scanned the universe with the most powerful telescope known to mankind. The Hobble has sent back pictures of stars and other planets but nothing called heaven. The Russians have just been rescued from the bottom of the sea and there are no reports of heaven." Moody said, "I'll tell you where heaven is, turn right and keep walking straight." As true as this may be you cannot turn and you will not turn until you have become imbued with the power at Calvary. You don't have the power to turn. You are too weak, too mundane, too frail and too sinful to turn. How many times have you pleaded with the Lord saying, if you just get me through this experience? If you just let me get on my feet, one more time…and everything remained the same?

Many have tried to turn from alcoholism, drug addiction, moral laxity and even grudge-holding, we've tried to forgive and forget but every time we are reminded of our shortcomings when something whelms up on the inside and whispers, "you ain't there yet!" We have tried to turn from hatred, bitterness and jealousy but you cannot turn by yourself. The premise is false to believe you can turn on your own. If you have the power to turn one way you also will have the power and the option to turn back where you were. I know what I'm talking about because I've been there. It takes a miracle from the Christ of Glory make the turn. At Calvary, ...Where Agape (Love) is stronger than Eros or Phileos. At CALVARY...Where love overpowers hate and good overcomes evil. AT CALVARY ...where right overpowers wrong and forgiveness is offered for torture. AT CALVARY ...where time becomes eternity and sin becomes salvation... AT CALVARY ...where the dust of night becomes the dawn of a new day and clouds of despair give way to the sunshine of hope. AT CALVARY ...where dying thieves can be forgiven and turned from the road of ruin to the promise of paradise. AT CALVARY ...where a crown of thorns becomes an array of glory' ...where Death loses its grip on life and the sting of death becomes null and void; where the sacrifice of the Lamb becomes the salvation of the world. And how do I know? It was at the cross "...at the cross, where I first saw the Light and the burdens of my heart rolled away. It was there by faith, I received my sight, and now I am happy all the day." It is there where you will find the power to turn and lose the desire to turn back. It is there that a fact in time opens to the fellowship of eternity.

CONCLUSION: This is the message of preaching. It is foolish to non-believers, but unto us who are saved, it is the power of God unto salvation. Preaching is not foolish to the trusting soul. Preaching is not foolish to the believing heart. It is not foolish for it tells me something. It tells me that if we would believe the preaching of the Gospel our Sunday Schools would not be empty of teenagers at a time when it is unconstitutional to praise God or pray in public school. It is not foolish when drive-by shootings have become as common as coffee. Preaching tells me that our boys and girls would not be filling up the jails and detention homes in this city, state and across the nation if "we" were listening to and heeding the preaching of the word that saves from traditions, culture or the secular socialization of society. Preaching tells me it wouldn't take a hurricane, a plane falling out of the sky, or an earthquake to get close to one another or to have compassion for one another if "we" would listen to preaching and heed its cry.

God is saying you may not listen to preaching but you will be still and know that I am God. I don't know about you but preaching tells me something. It tells me that in spite of my sins God still loves me. It tells me that when I fall God gives me the grace to get up again. I couldn't hear this if I didn't hear preaching. Science won't tell me this. Elected officials won't tell me this. When my soul is burdened and my afflictions are upon me preaching tells me that, "Many are the afflictions of the righteous, but the Lord will deliver him from all of them." It tells me that it matters not how my enemies come upon me, "Greater is He that is in me than he that is in the world." I couldn't hear this unless I heard preaching. Preaching tells me about a Boy Child of destiny who came down through forty and two generations, 'born', as Jesse Jackson has said, 'not in a palace looking down, but in a manger looking up.' It tells me that He laid down His royal diadem in glory, put on human flesh, left the celestial and came to the terrestrial, went around doing good and said, "One day all that the Father gives Me shall come unto Me, and he that comes unto Me, I will in no wise cast out." Preaching tells me that He'll take from us a heart of stone and put in us a heart of flesh, pour His spirit in us and cause us to walk in His path. "I love to tell the story of unseen things above, of Jesus and His glory, of Jesus and His love. I love to tell the story because I know it's true. It satisfies my longing, as nothing else can do." That's why I came to Jesus, my living Lord. I came to Jesus, the Christ of Glory, just as I was, weary, worn and sad; I found in him a resting place and he has made me glad.

Stops along the way
Dr. Milton Reid
2409
EVERY BELIEVER IN THIS WORLD MUST BE A SPARK of LIGHT
1st State Officers of VA SCLC 1960
Dr. Reid & MLK, Jr.
Coordinator, Poor People's Campaign
Sing for Freedom
Martin, Coretta, & Reid
Dr.Reid Receives Medal of Friendship from Fidel Castro in Cuba
Abernathy, King, Reid & Dot Cotton
ILTON A. REID
STATE SENATOR
Dr King's Press Conference
Rally-Elect Dr. Reid!
In Petersburg with Wyatt T. Walker

CHAPTER XI

WITHOUT SCARS AND THE CHRIST OF GLORY

(Inspired by Dr. Gardner C. Taylor, retired American Baptist Pastor; Written by the author)

"From now on let no one cause me trouble, for I bear the marks of Jesus on my body."

Galatians 6:17 NET

I am coming to the end of my sojourn on planet earth. I have spent most of my years dealing with my own fall and the fall of mankind in this Aonic sphere or in this fallen age that God loved so much that he sent his Son to deliver us. I often talk to my Marian about my departure for it seems that after all I have done and after all that has been done to me, it is almost like I was never blessed with birth and opportunity. I am not above or beyond getting a little depressed when I see how little impact Christianity has made on the sinfulness of mankind despite the coming of Moses and the prophets, Luke and the disciples, Paul and the Apostles. It is almost unbelievable that many of our youth today know nothing about Dr. Martin Luther King, Jr., outside of his "I Have a Dream Speech," and the holiday that was forced upon this nation some 15 years after his assassination. Congressman John Conyers, Democrat from Michigan, submitted legislation for the commemorative four days after King was assassinated. It seems to me that nothing has actually changed in the "soul" of America, that is, if America, a so-called "Christian nation," has a soul.

My grandson Eyo Ebong arranged for a birthday dinner for my son, Milton, Jr., who had recently been discharged from the hospital. The dinner was set for 6:30 at a relatively new restaurant named "Smokey Bones." I felt a slight discomfort in the name. But at 6:30, we were seated. It was about 6:54 when we placed an order for appetizers. We sent for the manager who came to the table after we had eaten around 9:00. I had sent for her but I was unable to speak to her when she came. My grandson did handle the situation masterfully. It was nearly 8:00 when we were served. You see I had just read that afternoon an article in the *Greenville News* of a Greenville Technical College official who twice referred to New Orleans evacuees in Greenville as "yard apes" and she was forced to resign. She, the vice president of the college for student services with a staff of some 40 employees, said she was "shocked and numb" at being forced to resign. The other thing about this story is that Paul Guy, president of the NAACP"S local chapter, said 15 black workers attended the meeting and heard her say that about our brothers and sisters and none of them said a word. I had also read an article by Dr. Cornel West entitled, "Exiles From a City and From a Nation," wherein he spoke honestly about the racism in New Orleans, FEMA and the White House. He said, "From slave ships to the Superdome was not that big a journey." I tell you I was emotionally full at that dinner to the point that I lost my appetite and I just could not take it anymore. I had to go on the outside and let some cool refreshing air come upon my burning soul. I thought about my many struggles, e.g., being jailed 11 times in the civil-rights movement, being scarred by the City of Norfolk, Virginia, that took control of a meeting called by our congregation, sent in a White non-Messianic Jewish overseer to act as moderator and a Black deputy sheriff with a gun on his side, and called the meeting to order to put me out as pastor. I may have mentioned this elsewhere but they took the ballots down town and counted them and published in the daily paper that I had been voted out by the congregation. You see I had exposed the City's handling of the Block Grant Community Funds, where for years they had not funded any organization in the Black community and there was a threat to cut off the funds. I became *persona non-grata* to the City of Norfolk.

Like Paul, I know I bear in my body the marks of the Lord Jesus Christ and I hope to meet Him with my marks very soon. But just before the verse of benediction, found in the last chapter of the letter of Paul to the Galatians, Paul sums up all that he had said in the preceding six chapters. Paul was dealing not only with his credibility as an apostle born out of due season but he was dealing with the Jewish influence that had made inroads into the church under the pretense of Hebrew legalism. It was their argument that Christians coming into the church had to be circumcised. They had to become Jews first and then embrace the Christian faith. In other words they opined that `you have to get like us before you can become like Him.` That's a mistake that the Black church made centuries ago. White masters taught their slaves how to be good slaves in accord with the King James Version of the Bible that admonishes slaves to obey their masters and to be kind and subservient to them. This also follows the teachings of Willie Lynch, who came to Virginia in 1712 to teach slave masters how to make their slaves obey. But the devil was here before Willie Lynch. Who do you think taught Willie Lynch and the slave masters and the so-called mainline Christian Church in America, a church that supported the institution of slavery and thereby rendered children of God to an ontological rejection. We had gone downhill from "being" to "non-being" but Jesus called on us "to be" in his Sermon on the Mount.

Paul said, "Anyone in Christ is a new creation of God, the old has passed and the new has come." He urged us "to have the mind of Christ in us, and be not conformed to this world but to be transformed by the renewing of our minds." That is why the Jews were so upset with Paul and why our nation was so upset with Dr. Martin L. King, Jr. Paul, however, in the text for this message is saying, `I have an authenticity, I have an authorization of credibility, I have an inextricable witness of God against all of your arguments for I bear in my body the marks of the Lord Jesus. Scars of any kind are indications of conflict and battles. Scars have given rise to the cosmetology of one's countenance. No one wants scars. Scars are reminders of what happened and whatever happened demands a whole lot of explanation. I suppose that is one of the reasons I am writing my memoirs. I am trying to explain my witness of the glorified Christ. Paul's scars and marks were the evidences of the things he suffered for Christ. These were evidence of his brand as a slave for Jesus Christ. In Bunyan's "Pilgrim's Progress" he has Mr. Valiant for Truth saying, "My marks and scars I carry with me to be my witness to him who will now be my rewarder."

What Paul is laboring to set forth to the Galatians is the fact of suffering in Christ and the suffering with Christ. The calling of our cultured church that blindly worships the God of the West, the false god of our times, is against that. We only believe in suffering when we can't help it and we have a lame line in some of our prayers, preaching and testimonies that "everything will be alright." I learned as a novice on the use of computers that when some things go wrong they don't necessarily or automatically get right. Some times you have to call in a technician or go to your Internet provider and server to help you to get right what has gone wrong. Jesus, our Lord and Master, is to the church more than its Internet provider and server; He is its Founder and Kurios, or Lord. We expend much of our toil and labors not only trying to avoid scars and bruises but to cover them. In comparing or contrasting with a political or a business cover up the church does not fare much better, whether from the standpoint of Bible study to the preaching of the Word and witnessing to the world like a mislead church. It is not enough for churches to give thousands of dollars to the Red Cross during the turbulent times of the "Katrina's" and the "Poveritina," as Dr. Cornel West has called it, when they have empty school rooms through the week that could be used for evacuees and unused church kitchens. One church in the Gulfport region of the storms was set up to take in 250 evacuees but ended up taking in 650. That is a church that is on the witness stand in the Kingdom of God, making the Kingdoms of this world the Kingdoms of our Lord and of His Christ. We tend to cover our scars with cosmetic surgery because the reality of our wounds is too awesome. Paul said to the church at Corinth, "But we have this treasure in clay jars, so that the extraordinary power belongs to God and does not come from us. We are experiencing trouble on every side, but are not crushed; we are perplexed, but not abandoned, we are knocked down, but not destroyed, always carrying around in our body the death of Jesus, so that the life of Jesus may also be made visible in our body. For we who are alive are constantly being handed over to death for Jesus' sake so that the life of Jesus may also be made visible in our mortal body" (2 Corinthians 4:10 NET).

Even with my admittedly or less than perfect understanding of God's Grace, I cannot see anybody's making it in the presence of

God's glory without scars of suffering. This message of Paul tells me in no uncertain terms that he who makes it to the end of life without scars comes to his end without Christ. As I look at Paul's one-line testimony there are two things I would like to say about scars that I think are worth mentioning.

The first is that Paul's scars were evidence of his love for Jesus Christ. As I see it there is no way that anyone can love Jesus Christ without the mark or the scar of Love in evidence. To follow Jesus means to go against the grain of everything you know in order to redeem it in the love of Jesus Christ. To follow Christ is to love Him and to serve Him and to obey Him, meaning that you have to get out of the circle of sameness. You must move beyond that which is expected. You must go beyond that which is socially acceptable. In other words, Divine purpose must exceed man's traditions and social consciousness shaped by culture and the God of the West. Our witness must never be shaped by whatever we are presently doing without the divine purpose of God's revelation in Christ. Whatever it is, if the redemptive love of Christ is not in it then we are not being the children of His redemption. The love of Jesus Christ, as Paul would say, is so essential, so necessary, so redeeming, so rewarding, and so purposeful that your scars will remain the visible marks of the intent, the motive and the outcome.

Paul knew that it would be possible to have all kinds of scars. We could undergo all kinds of adversities and come out of them, not with the marks of Jesus but with the stamp of Satan, if God's Love were lacking. In speaking of his scars, Paul says, "Five times I received from the Jews forty lashes less one. Three times I was beaten with a rod. Once I received a stoning. Three times I suffered shipwreck. A night and a day I spent adrift in the open sea. I have been on journeys many times in dangers from robbers, in dangers in the wilderness, in dangers at sea, in dangers from false brothers, in hard work and toil, through many sleepless nights, in hunger and thirst, many times without food, in cold and without enough clothing. Apart from other things, there is the daily pressure on me of my anxious concerns for all the churches" (2 Corinthians 11:24-28 NET). If I must boast, if I must glory, I will not glory in my linguistic ability. I will not glory in my travels. I will not glory in my Hebrew history as being a Hebrew of the Hebrews. I will not glory in my ability to understand the law. If I glory, I will glory in my marks or in my scars. I will glory in my infirmities, for these are the marks. These are my dog tags of identification, these are my certificates of the One to whom I belong."

If we are in love with Jesus our love must be an action love. It cannot be a Sunday kind of so called Christian-liking love. It cannot be a cultural kind of cosmetic love. It cannot be a fair weather love. It cannot be a "because of" love. It has to be stronger than Eros, a kind of self-love, more than the way I look, the way I feel or the way I perceive it. It has to be stronger than Phaleos, a brotherly kind of love, a community kind of love, a love of kindred, a love of ethnic identification that can find pseudo biblical justification for racial separation. Love for Jesus Christ has to be stronger than that. It has to be Agape. It has to be an in-spite-of love. It has to be a love that says in the midst of persecution, in the midst of trials and tribulation, in the midst of persecution, it has to be a kind of love that says "Father, forgive them, for they don't know what they are doing" (Luke 23:34 NET). It has to be a love that testifies, "While we were yet sinners, while we were yet guilty as charged, while we were reprobates from redemption's pleadings, Christ died for the ungodly. "As he died to make men holy, we must live to set them free, as truth goes marching on."

Paul's scars were also the natural outcome of his calling to be faithful or as the Greeks would say, Pistis, meaning persuasive belief unto action. We can be faithless or Apistos and escape a lot of wrath of this present world. All we have to do is to find out what the thinking of the masses is and "go with the flow." All we have to do is to go to bed with "isness" and completely ignore "oughtness" and we can escape scars, wounds and embarrassment. The problem with this is that you can have "ceiling faith" in the church as it is and be consumed by it without being faithful to the call of Jesus Christ at all. Like Paul I have discovered that "being faithful to Christ" will not make you popular in this world of fallen men. It could make you get names like "being an odd ball," being strong-willed, being determined to do it, whether it is a different or an unusual way. I have always tried to do whatever I did as a disciple of Jesus Christ to the glory of God no matter what the cost of that deed was. I was in search for healing of my lower back (spinal stenosis) and was on my way to Cuba by way of Montego Bay, Jamaica, from Miami, Florida. I missed my flight to Cuba and had to stay in Jamaica for two days. At that time flights to Cuba were three times a week. While waiting in Jamaica I met a cab driver by the name of Paul Grimes who took me to The Big Apple Hotel near the airport. When he noted that I could not walk very far or very fast I had to explain to him my physical condition. He assured me that I did not have to go to Cuba for help. He told me about a prayer chapel up on the mountain (which turned out to be a high hill) where a healing prophetess could anoint me and heal me. He convinced me so until I didn't feel that I needed to pray about it. I did pray however but to thank the Lord for the good news. The next day he took me way out somewhere to the foot of a nameless mountain. It was near his home. He called his son to guide me up the hill (it seemed like a mountain to me) to the healing chapel. I had a knap sack strapped on my back with my walking stick and I was on my way up the hill. I don't remember climbing a mountain before and I was to wish I hadn't seen that mountain.

After about an hour of trying to get up that meandering trail of grown over footprints among the weeds and the rocky stones, I was too tired to go on. My guide, who could not speak English, kept going. I finally called out to him, "Hey, I need to rest." He looked at me strangely and I sat down and began to pray. He finally came back and waited. We traveled on for another fifteen to twenty minutes and I had a serious fall. I fell some 25-30 feet down the mountainside and my upper left shoulder hit a huge boulder. My stick went one way, my glasses another and my backpack held fast, otherwise I would have been a goner. I thought I was in pain before the fall but with this additional pain I wondered if I would survive. We came to a little village where I was offered a seat, as I remember it on something less than a chair. There was an old woman in that house who looked with pity upon me and offered to take me to the chapel on her back. She had to tell me several times before I could believe what she was saying. The aged old woman looked as if she had not had a good meal over the last few years. She possibly weighed between ninety-five to a hundred pounds. My weight at that time exceeded three hundred pounds and she offered to take me further up the mountain in all of my pain. I politely declined the offer. She seemed a little offended. After resting and praying to the Jesus that I know who was still with me despite the fall, my guide took me further up the mountain to the prayer chapel. When I got to the crude looking three-room building called the prayer chapel the healer wasn't there. I had to wait for her about forty-five minutes. I was hurting all the time. I also was dreading going all the way back down that mountain trail that appeared to have been by-passed by travelers for ages.

When the healer arrived it wasn't long before I discovered that she didn't speak English. She had to make the medicine by which she was to heal me. They had to make a fire and pour something from one bottle to another and heat it. I said to myself, well if it takes all of this to get healed why should I even think complaint? After about an hour of her preparation I was directed by my guide to come in the chapel. The healer did know a part of the 23rd Psalm. "De Lorde is my Yepperd". She repeated it and chanted it. She signaled for me to remove my clothes. I pointed to my shirt and she pointed also to my pants. I said, now Lord, I know I have done some things in life that were displeasing in your sight. I know I have fallen short but please get me out of this fix. If you do I will praise your holy name forever as never before. She poured that "stuff" over my head and over my body. I was both embarrassed and frightened. I said, Lord Jesus, please get me out of this fix and I am going to double my love...hey...triple my love for You. The sun was beginning to go down. And I looked up and whom did I see other than the cab driver, who was grinning and I am sure waiting to collect. I asked him how much did I owe her. When he told me I almost doubled it in American money. She didn't want it. She wanted Jamaican. He was there to explain to her how much it was in Jamaican money. I discovered that she was his aunt. Then I knew I had been had but I knew the Lord Jesus had me first and was holding me, otherwise I would have fallen all the way down that mountain. I got back down the mountain without incident just before dark. But if it were my foolishness that took me up, it was my faith that kept me and brought me down. I was hurting so bad in my new pain that I gave up going to Cuba. I called my Marian and I returned home. I discovered I had a rotator cuff tear in my left shoulder and that scar will take me to my grave. It has left me with a weakened muscle in that arm and shoulder but I thank God not for my arm alone, but for my life.

Up to the time of his testimony in this chapter Paul had answered three calls and each of the calls had to do with his faith. He was scarred that day out on the Damascus road where I would be blessed to travel with my good friend, the late Reverend Elmer Williams, of the Sixth Mount Zion Baptist Church in Pittsburgh in 1964. It was our departure from the "Spiritual Safari" led by Dr. Wendell Somerville of the Lott Carey Baptist Foreign Mission Convention. Jesus turned Paul around that day. Paul was scarred by blindness that later opened the eyes of this good man who had been going against the grain and his higher calling. He was so scarred that scales formed on his eyes that Ananias had to anoint and take off so that he would really see. He was scarred again when he turned around from his mission to persecute and became the Jewish missionary to the Gentiles. He then had to go bound to Jerusalem, not knowing what was going to befall him other than troubles and tribulations that were waiting on every hand. He was scarred. Now here he is a founder of churches, a writer of letters that would be canonized in today's Bible, an Episcopas, an Angelos, and a Perfecter of the faith who is now being called "false." Here he is now being called a non-true Apostle and is being troubled by church folk. He was troubled by his troubling of sin and by preachers who failed to see his struggle to be faithful in tribulations. They didn't see his being in perils or dangers. They didn't see his being in trouble among false brethren, often in hunger, often in wanting. They didn't see his constant fight with the Judaizers, his shipwreck, his anguish, and they were blind to his scars of faithfulness.

There was another chapter in Paul's life, yet to come to the surface, when he wrote these words. I have been to Rome on three different occasions. Each time I had the privilege of visiting in the inner chamber of that Roman jail off the Appian Way where he wrote perhaps his last letter to his son, Timothy. The first time I was there I was excited. It was just good to be where Paul had been so I could tell somebody that I was there. When I told it nobody was excited except me and my excitement soon faded. The second time I was there it had a little different meaning to me. It was here that Paul wrote, "For I am already being poured out as an offering, and the time for me to depart is at hand. I have completed well, I have finished the race, and I have kept the faith! Finally the crown of righteousness is reserved for me. The Lord the righteous Judge, will award it to me in that day-and not to me only, but also to all who have set their affection on his appearing" (2 Timothy 4:6-8 NET). The third time I was there, just a few years ago, I wrote with Paul, "... I know whom I have believed and am convinced that he is able to guard what I have entrusted to him for that day" (2 Timothy 1:12 NIV). In my paraphrasing of that passage I said, "I have finished fifty years in the pastorate and am completing fifty-nine years in the ministry. My eyesight is growing dim with the twilight of old age, my hair is turning white by the snowfalls of many winters, my hearing is faulty, and I don't move with agility any more, but thank God I am still moving up to now. I have completed my three-score and ten and am on my way to fourscore years. I attended the Million More March on October 15, 2005. As I look back I have had my ups and downs but I have kept the faith." There may be some more scars awaiting me. Can I go all the way? Reason, sometimes called common sense, says no, you have paid your dues. Can I pull in here? Reason says no! You have a family that you have sometimes neglected trying to make the kingdoms of the world the kingdoms or our Lord and of His Christ. You have done enough. Should I quit now? Reason says be kind to yourself. You need to rest yourself but Jesus speaks through John on Patmos saying, "Remain Pistis, or faithful even to the point of death and I will give you the crown that is life itself" (Revelation 2:10 NET). I hear another voice singing and saying, "Be not dismayed what-e'er betide, God will take care of you. Beneath His wings of love abide, God will take care of you. No matter what may be the test, God will take care of you; Lean weary one, upon His breast, God will take care of you."

I take courage every time I read that beautiful story written by Dr. Luke in Acts. "Now Stephen, a man full of God's Grace and Power, did great wonders and miraculous signs among the people. Opposition arose, however, from members of the Synagogue of the Freedmen (as it was called) – Jews of Cyrene and Alexandria, as well as the provinces of Cilicia and Asia. These men began to argue with Stephen...but they could not stand up against his wisdom or the Spirit by whom he spoke" (Acts 6:8-10 NIV). Do you remember where Jesus preached his first sermon? It was in the synagogue in his hometown in Nazareth. Do you know where Paul went preaching on his missionary journeys? It was primarily in the synagogues. The synagogue was a place of worship in the New Testament time of Jesus. It is still a place of worship even today. Most Protestants worship in churches or cathedrals. Isn't it strange that many people of God (the Laos) claim God to be Omniscient, all knowing and Omnipresent everywhere at the same time? But when you push them just a little in their faith they know nothing more than what they heard or what was spoken of in tradition. Like the folk who stoned Stephen too many folk are worshipping the God of the West in blind ignorance and this only makes for an adversarial relationship with the Christ of Glory. In his dying hour, as Stephen was being scarred to death, Luke says that Stephen looked up and saw Jesus who had already arisen from his seat at the Right Hand of God, "standing up in Glory." Stephen was a man of faith who died in love in the midst of ignorance from church folk. And Paul of all people, stood there holding some coats as Stephen was being stoned. But look what the love of God did that day by his faithfulness. Stephen's spirit followed Paul in his conscious and in his spirit on the Damascus road where Jesus arrested him, rescued and saved him. I don't claim to be a Paul or a Stephen but I can testify that He not only loved me and died for me, He saved me and He keeps me. I haven't found this in the Scriptures but I don't think it is possible to go home to God without scars. I get troubled every time I view a body that has been cosmetically erased of its scars. Some "sane" living folk put glasses and hats on dead folk that they may look like living folk as if what they look like is any way reflective of what they have been like. I led my congregations into not viewing bodies after the eulogy of worship ever since folk started falling out and trying to get in the casket at one of the first churches I was honored to serve as pastor. So for many, many years they agreed with me to view the body before the eulogy of worship because they were convinced along with me that "what was is not what is." What was is "corruptible" but what is is "incorruptible." What was is "mortal", what is, is "immortal." What was, is "earthly", what is, is "heavenly." What was, Immanuel Kant called the "phenomena," but what is, he called the "numinous." I just don't like the idea of covering up what was with what is. "What was," has "docked," but "what is," has been "launched". You cannot get home to God with what was. Isaiah said even Jesus the Christ of Glory could not do that.

The Psalmist said as he was leaving Calvary, the antiphonal choirs came together to sing, "Lift up your heads O you gates be lifted up, you ancient doors, that the King of glory may come in. Who is this King of glory? The Lord strong and mighty, the Lord mighty in battle. Lift up your heads O you gates; lift them up, you ancient doors that the King of glory may come in. Who is this King of glory? The Lord Almighty- he is the King of glory." Call him "King," David, but I call him the Christ of Glory and we are talking about the same person. I sing with R.H Cornelius, the hymn writer, "O, I want to see Him, to look upon his face, There to sing for ever of His saving grace; On the streets of Glory let me lift my voice; Cares all past, home at last, ever to rejoice."

By faith I see Him now through my eyes of faith, the eyes of the prophets, the disciples, and the apostles and in the faith of Stephen. Isaiah points Him out to me. There He is, "Coming from Edom with dye garments on from Bozrah, treading the wine press alone." There he is, bearing our griefs and carrying our sorrows; yet we esteemed Him stricken, smitten by God and afflicted. There he is, "wounded for our transgressions, bruised for our iniquities; upon Him was the chastisement that made us whole, and with His stripes we are healed. John, the disciple who lay on his breast said, "There He is, Milton, coming unto His own and His own received Him not." 'There He is," says Luke, "going around doing good, opening the eyes of the blind, making the lame walk and healing all manner of diseases." Mark says, "There He is, being deserted in His hour of trial…being betrayed by Judas, denied by Peter, and abandoned by His friends." "There he is," cries Matthew, "with the weight of the cross on His shoulder…stumbling and falling up Via Dolorosa, bleeding, wounded scorned and misunderstood." The gospel writers were united in seeing how they took off His clothes and mocked Him…slapped Him…spat on Him…going to His father; seared… marred …mocked…bruised…wounded…and somehow we as Christians cannot stand being misunderstood.

No wonder Lucie E. Campbell cried out one day singing, "If

when you give the best of your service, telling the world that the Savior is come; Be not dismayed when men don't believe you; He understands, He'll sat well done. Misunderstood, Hung on the cross; He was God's only Son; Oh! Hear Him calling His Father in Heav'n, Not my will, but Thine be done. But if you try, (here she is making it personal) and fail in your trying, Hands, sore and scarred from the work you've begun; Take up your cross, run quickly to meet Him; He'll understand, He'll say well done."

Dr. MLK with Dr. Reid on one of many "marches".

CHAPTER XII

MARCHING WITH MARTIN

"A New Day Dawns"

Marian and I were invited to attend the twenty-first annual Martin Luther King, Jr., Memorial Breakfast in Hampton by a very dear friend, Alfred P. McQueen, Ph.D., a professor of biology at Hampton University. Delta Beta Lambda Chapter of Alpha Phi Alpha Fraternity, Inc. of Hampton, Virginia, sponsored this breakfast. Dr. McQueen, a member of our weekly Bible Study Group, invited me because he discovered that I was an Alpha when we had a class session in his lovely home. I had completed my memoirs but had not sent them to the publishers. I heard a powerful speaker, Frederick S. Humphries, Ph.D., past President of Florida A&M University in Tallahassee, Florida. He used as a subject, "Come Before Winter," and as his message vibrated throughout the auditorium everyone was both sincerely challenged and thrilled. I made my way to congratulate him and was happy to tell him that I had worked with Dr. King, who preached my sermon of installation at New Calvary Baptist Church in Norfolk in on October 30, 1966, just about a year and a half before he was assassinated on April 4, 1968. I had been appointed by Dr. King to serve as the Virginia Coordinator for the Poor Peoples Campaign. He was scheduled to meet with the interfaith and bi-racial coalition and me on the Saturday of the week in which he as assassinated. I was on the Board of Directors and serving in the capacity of part-time staff as Southeastern Regional Director of the Southern Christian Leadership Conference. I was appointed to that position in 1963, while serving as Pastor of First Baptist Church in Petersburg, and the Rocky Branch Baptist Church in Southerland, Dinwiddie County in the suburbs of Petersburg. I resigned as Pastor of the Rocky Branch Church and accepted this position with SCLC.

I met Dr. King in the fall of 1959, when he made a visit to Petersburg. He was a very personable man, somewhat pensive and mystical at times, but he loved a good joke. I haven't met anyone in life who enjoyed a good laugh as much as Martin. He could laugh at times at his own jokes when delivering a speech or a sermon but he had another side that reflected his said somewhat pensive and mystical quality. He was always alert and appeared fresh when he met the press because he was speaking as if he were hooked up to eternity and speaking to God's world, not just the press. When he first met me he asked me to work with him on the board of directors of the Southern Christian Leadership Conference. I agreed but it was during the springboard meeting in 1960, when the board accepted me as a National Board member. I encouraged Dr. Curtis Harris of Hopewell to join the board as he had been in a longtime fight with the labor unions in Hopewell. Curtis was with me the snowy night we left Lynchburg, Virginia, with Martin and Dr. Ralph D. Abernathy, his right hand man, and drove on into Petersburg. Both Martin and Ralph stayed at my home that night and Martin fell in love with Marian's cooking. He raved about it. He did the same thing when he had dinner in our home in Norfolk years later. I told my Marian that she had prepared a sumptuous and great meal and that I was going to write her a check. I continued (looking at Martin) by stating that anybody who enjoyed the meal as well as I did should feel some obligation to follow my generous actions. As I was feeling my pockets for my checkbook Martin said, "Marian, I wouldn't think about insulting you by writing you a check for this great meal. Any price that anyone puts on a meal like this would be an insult; you couldn't buy a meal like this in heaven!" I had no come back on that one. Martin's remarks were so smooth and timely that I believe to this day he had either heard it or practiced it before.

I was with Martin on most of the major marches in the South and in the North. I was in Danville Virginia, when the Birmingham movement picked up in 1963. The local group wanted Martin to come to Danville but so did everybody else everywhere. Martin sent me to Danville. I was then serving as the regional representative of SCLC. Danville was a duplicate of Birmingham. It looked like Bull Conner was playing quarterback against the protesters in Birmingham and by phone he was directing the movement to Chief McCain in Danville. I would be in Danville during the week and come home on the weekends. Every time I would leave town the police would be looking for me. We held meetings at the High Street Baptist Church that was somewhat the headquarters for our meetings. When I arrived in Danville I called the Holiday Inn and made a reservation for a place to sleep that night. Now you may call that action "crawling curiosity or creative courage". it is your choice. It was about 1:00 A.M. when I drove up, "black, big and burley", to check in. The clerk asked me my name and sheepishly told me I didn't have a reservation because my name wasn't listed. I looked over the counter at the manifest and said, "Yes, I do, there is my name right there!" She said there must be some kind of mistake, I cannot give you a room, all the rooms are taken. I immediately asked for the manager. She was happy to call the manager, not knowing what else to do. The manager came and talked with me like a consoling father. He explained that he was from Connecticut and some of his closest friends were colored but this was the policy here. I reasoned that here I was attempting this in the last seat of the Confederacy. He invited me to his home to spend the night. I said, thank you but no thank you. I am going to stay right here on this sofa and I began to disrobe. It was summer and I didn't need any cover. More than that, it is now about 2:00 A.M. and I was both tired and sleepy. As I lay down I discovered that I was a little uneasy also. So I nodded with one eye half opened until daybreak. As folk began to check out, I got up without saying a word, put on my clothes, and went to the restroom. I took care of business, washed up, and something in me reminded me that I was hungry and I went into the restaurant. As I took my seat all eyes were trained on me. A waitress came about ten minutes later and took the tablecloth off, she took the condiments off, and the little vase with flowers in it. Across from me there sat an old White man who was staring at me with daggers in his eyes. He looked at me and I looked back at him until he couldn't take it any more. He lost his appetite, got up and stormed out of the restaurant. His food was untouched. I got up and put his food on my table, said my grace, thanking the Lord for the gift of food, and proceeded eating. To the amazement of everybody, I heard the question raised, "who served him, who served him?" After I finished eating I stopped by the table where I had taken the food and picked up the napkin, wiped my mouth, drank my coffee, and went out to my car, thanking Jesus my revolutionary Lord for a night's sleep with his protection and a breakfast for which I didn't have to pay. I felt great! After the mass meeting and the strategy session one night at the High Street Baptist Church the police came looking for me. We locked the doors following the meeting. The police battered in the door of the church and I was ushered out the back door and put in the trunk of my car and was driven out of town.

This was a strange escape and one that I suppose I will always remember. We went a few miles out of downtown Danville to a home in Pittsylvania County. It was a safe place I was assured and that the police would never find me. It was a boot legger's nip joint and when the door was opened I saw two Danville policemen in uniform lying back nipping and telling jokes. Now this was on a Friday night and I was scheduled to preach on Sunday morning. "Would the police arrest me here, I asked myself if I give my correct name and profession?" I agreed with my driver that I would be Attorney Jones from Washington, DC. I was so presented and went to the dining area where I laid down on a sofa until daybreak. Did I stop to preach to them and have them arrested? No, No. I was just happy to be delivered into "loving hands of those sinners while God was preparing my way of escape."

After a pretty good nap I woke up to make the long dash into Petersburg and I stopped to call my Marian. She told me in panic, "Don't come here, the police have been circling the house all night looking for you. It is on the radio and in the papers." I kept on past Petersburg and went to my brother-in-law and sister's home in Chesterfield. When my sister came to the door I was an unwelcome fugitive. She started yelling, "Get away from here, the police are looking for you!" I got in my car and went to the Howard Johnson Motor Lodge on Route 10 just off route interstate 95. I called back and told my brother in law, LaSalle McCoy, where I was. He brought me a lovely dinner prepared by my sister, Ella Mae McCoy, after she cooled off. Now Ella Mae Reid McCoy was not alone in her feelings about the civil rights movement. As a matter of fact she was where a majority of the traditional church was and after all of these years, many still are. They believed that God was going to "fix it" bye and bye. If you remember that is where my loving father was when I raised the question about our having to walk to school while White children rode the bus. I had another sister who was just the opposite. When I came back from Libya, speaking on the occasion of the 15th anniversary of their Revolution, my sister Trudy, who was a nurse in New York, told all of her friends that her brother was invited to speak in Libya! Most of the folk she told were shocked and amazed. They began to look at her differently and she wondered why. I told her that I found out after getting to Libya that our government had listed Libya as an "outlaw state" and travel there by American citizens was prohibited.

After preaching that Sunday morning I went back to Danville that Monday. Curtis Harris accompanied me to Danville. On our way we stopped in South Hill, Virginia, and sought to desegregate a Horne's restaurant on US High Way 1 south of downtown South Hill. We finally did after weeks of trying and negotiating. I found out in the rural township of South Hill, Virginia, that White folk get nervous in their enforcement proceedings of discriminatory statutes and become defensive as hell. When we sat around the table negotiating with management about calling off our demonstrations and the boycott of his business, he provided lunch for Curtis, the employees who had walked off the job and me. We were about to eat when I raised the question, what about grace? That White man turned red and said to the other employees, "Where is grace, go get grace!" I was only asking that we would say grace or offer a word of blessing and thanks before we ate. I don't remember who prayed but it was a very short prayer and we went on with the business of setting the record straight and we were successful.

When we arrived in Danville later on that day we went to Main Street where demonstrations were taking place. Recognizing my car some one told the chief of police, "There he is now!" The chief came over to my car and asked in a mean voice; "Are you Reverend Milton Reid?" I said, "No, Sir." The chief looked around and they cried out all the more, "Yes it is, Chief, that is Reverend Reid." The chief asked again, "Are you Reverend Milton Reid?" I answered again, "No, Sir, I am not." They yelled out again, "That's him; dat's him!" The chief, now thoroughly confused, asked me the third time; "I said are you Revered Milton Reid?" I said, "No, Sir." "Well who are you then," the Chief growled? I said, "I am Doctor Milton A. Reid." He said, "You are a smart nigger, 'aintcha'?" I never said another word as he grabbed me by my arm and escorted me to the paddy wagon and off to jail I went. This was to be followed by three more jailings in Danville. When I wasn't in jail I stayed in the home of two very fine people who lived out on Piney Forest Road. Both were educators in the school system. They were Christopher P. "Jeet" Banks and his lovely wife, Doris. Mrs. Doris Banks was helpful in my doing some research on the movement in Danville. I met Mrs. Louise Pinchback again, a strong and committed leader in the Danville movement, and Dr. Joyce Glaise, who had completed her doctoral thesis on the Danville movement. I met some wonderful friends in Danville and all were supporters of the movement, especially Bishop Lawrence Campbell of the Bible Way Church, Worldwide, the late Reverend Dr. L.W. Chase, who headed the movement for a while and was Pastor of the High Street Baptist Church, the late Dr. Doyle Thomas, at Loyal Baptist, Reverend A. I. Dunlap, at the St. Paul AMEZ Church, the late Dr. H.G. McGhee, who was at Greater Triumph Baptist Church, Reverend Thurman Echoles, at Memorial Hill Baptist Church, and there were others.

After demonstrators were beaten up and stretched out in the "colored" Winslow Hospital, down the corridors and in offices after all rooms were filled, Dr. King finally got a break away from Birmingham and came to Danville. It was one of the most intense rallies ever held in the summer of 1963, when he spoke at a mass meeting at the High Street Baptist Church. Before the Danville moment I joined with Dr. King in Albany, Georgia, in 1962, where nothing much happened in our favor. I went to jail there too. This is the only time I was in jail when Martin was in jail. The men and the women (just like Birmingham would be in the next year) were stacked together in the same cell. There was one toilet for about twenty-five or thirty per cell and other cells were equally packed with one toilet available. There was no privacy, no respect, and no dignity. It was almost as bad as it was for our forefathers who came to this country on slave ships. The only difference was that we were not chained down and we weren't days at sea. Dr. William G. Anderson, an osteopath, had what seemed to be a small practice in Albany. I didn't know it then but I wish I had talked to him about my back pain that turned out to be diagnosed as spinal stenosis. But like most civil-rights activists we did not cry out regarding personal pains unless they were extreme. My back pains were not extreme. Dr. Anderson was heavily involved in the civil-rights movement. His practice suffered. He was to move his practice North, I believe to Detroit.

During the March on Washington, as a National Board Member I was there helping with the planning and the strategizing. Curtis and I were together the night before and we stayed in a small Black hotel called the Belmont, operated by an entrepreneur from New Orleans. We had to go to the Lincoln Memorial following the strategy session and we worked until the break of day. When the people were gathering the lack of sleep was catching up with both of us. We fought to stay awake. Around 11:30 A.M., we just couldn't take it any longer. Curtis called upon a former member of his church, the Little Gilfield Baptist Church in Ivor, Virginia. Mrs. Edith Lipscomb was young, beautiful, vibrant and a helpful sister. She put a small TV in our room so we could watch the march. We had intended to sleep for an hour and return to our favorite spots on the steps of the Memorial. When I woke up Dr. King was giving his "I Have A Dream" speech. We soon concluded that by the time we got back to the Lincoln Memorial, with some two hundred and fifty thousand people to wade through, Dr. King would have finished his speech and our efforts would have been in vain.

I was with Dr. King during the Selma to Montgomery March for the passage of the Voting Rights Bill of 1965. I wasn't so privileged as the millions of Americans who watched the unfolding of this march on television from the comfort of their dens, bedrooms, or living rooms. I was in it all the way from Selma to Montgomery. I was not in that initial lineup of over 700 demonstrators trying to march to Montgomery. Nor was I in that second lineup led by the Reverend Hosea Williams and Mr. John Lewis, a benefactor, and now a Congressman from the State of Georgia. No, I was not there on "Bloody Sunday."(I had to preach at home that Sunday, ahem) I was there two days later when Dr. King led another March of an estimated fifteen hundred across the Edmond Pettus Bridge. I had crossed that bridge in 1951, as a paratrooper with the 82nd Airborne Division. While passing through Selma I preached at the Green Street Baptist Church. When Martin led the demonstrators across the bridge I was up front on the left side of the march when about 200 state troopers and law enforcement officers stopped us. When we were stopped the head of the state police told Dr. King that he would have to turn around and go back. Dr. King insisted that we had a right to address our grievances before the government. That argument didn't get us anywhere. Then Dr. King called on a priest from the Greek Orthodox Church to lead us in prayer. In the meantime a deputized law officer, in civilian clothes, a helmet, with an electric prodder, a bully stick and a loaded pistol, was standing there with his eyes on me in "angry disgust." Remembering Bloody Sunday and the death of Jimmie Lee Jackson, I felt very strongly that my time was coming to an end. I received no comfort from the prayer of the priest because he was praying in Greek. I didn't know what he was telling God and he was White too. After his prayer Dr. King called on a rabbi to offer prayer. I still didn't get any comfort because I wasn't conversant with the Hebrew tongue. Then Dr. King called on Reverend Dr. Fred Shuttlesworth to pray, a Black Baptist minister that had been jailed and beaten and his church had been bombed in Birmingham, Alabama. I immediately began to feel a little better because at least I knew God heard a "real life experience prayer in English." While Fred was praying Andy Young came up to Martin and whispered something of great significance. President Johnson had called and suggested to Martin to call off the march for that day because he was federalizing the State Police and the National Guard and was ordering them to protect us on our march to Montgomery. Now I don't know which prayer God heard (it could have been all of them) but the answer came while Fred Shuttlesworth was praying. Even now, every once in a while I just holler out "GLORY" and folk immediately call my sanity into question. They don't know how you feel when you come out of the wilderness of a threatening infliction of violence from an organized group of law enforcement officers, only to be delivered by faith through fear and the power of prayer.

There was hardly a day of genuine relaxation in Martin's life between his rise to fame in Montgomery, Alabama, during the bus boycott, to his untimely death in Memphis, Tennessee. People were calling him from almost every section of the nation and many parts of the world. He was in demand. Martin couldn't make them all. On our way to Selma I was supposed to speak at our headquarters church in Selma and Martin was on the West coast. He was also scheduled to speak in Montgomery but he couldn't make it. Martin called and requested that I would go to Montgomery and the Reverend James Reeb spoke in my stead in Selma. When I got to Montgomery I was taken to a hotel downtown where they had an elevator operator to take me to my floor. When I got there and saw the room my hopes fell and my parading spirits took leave. There in the middle of the floor was what I thought to be the first bed that was ever invented or made, with a light bulb, almost totally covered with fly specks, hanging down on a long electric wire. I sat on the side of the feather-ticked mattress and the head of the bed and the foot of the bed stood up and took a bow as a way, I suppose, of greeting me. I sat there and cried out to the Lord saying, "Lord, is this what we have been demonstrating for?" I don't remember what I said that night or how the meeting turned out. I do know that "flunk" was upon me. Noticing how down I was a young movement sister drove me back to the hotel following the mass meeting. She came upstairs to my room of desolation and wanted in some way to cheer me up. I thanked her and declined her offer. As nice and as willing as she was, her appearance and demeanor matched the room and I felt I was in double jeopardy in Alabama and there was no way she could have been of further assistance.

We resumed our March to Montgomery and upon getting there Dr. King, who had been up nearly all night, gave a speech on the Capitol steps and I was right there on the makeshift platform supporting him with loud "Amen's" and "speak, Sirs!" Dr. King climbed a stiff hill that day because he was nearly exhausted. We handed Governor George Wallace a petition, demanding voting rights for African-Americans. Following that presentation we all congregated at the Dexter Street Baptist Church where my first mentor, the late Vernon Johns, had served as pastor, and was followed by the call of my second mentor, Dr. Martin Luther King, Jr. He by now had electrified both the nation and the world. In the basement of the Dexter Street Church refreshments were being served to the demonstrators who had made the march from Selma to Montgomery. It was there where I first met Viola Liuzzo. I was eating an apple and she asked for a bite. I told her, "that is the problem with our movement, when White folk join it they want to eat up all of our food," as I was handing her my apple. She knew I was joking so she took her bite and gave it back to me.

I left Montgomery that night, along with the Reverend Will Judge, who was then pastor at the historic 3rd Street Bethel AME church in downtown Richmond, on a charter flight that was going to Philadelphia. When we got off the plane in Philadelphia, Viola Liuzzo's picture was on the front page as having been shot and killed while leaving Montgomery heading back to Selma with more demonstrators. I remember vividly leaving Montgomery that night after I spoke for Martin and was being driven by a movement brother. He noticed that a car was following us loaded with White men that he deemed did not mean us any good. His was an older model car and I was sitting on the edge of the seat (at least in my mind). Highway 80 between Selma and Montgomery is a hilly road to travel. As we were going down one hill at about seventy-five miles an hour an eighteen-wheeler tractor-trailer was speeding down the hill coming toward us. The hood on the car in which we were riding popped loose and came flying up, covering the windshield. Now I knew I was a goner because the road had vanished before our eyes and my driver had cut off the headlights, trying to escape. I was praying out loud in English! The driver brought the car to a stop on the right hand side of the road. I said, "Man, how on earth did you do that?" He said, "I just remembered what I saw when I could see, and when I couldn't see, I jest "hold on." Now you might have guessed, as a Baptist Preacher, I have used that illustration many times. "Hold on in the dark when you can't see the light you saw, when you could see the light."

Dr. Martin Luther King Jr., had been to Virginia many times at my invitation on behalf of the Virginia State Unit of SCLC that I organized in 1960, while I was the pastor at the First Baptist Church on Harrison Street in Petersburg, Virginia. It is a fact that Dr. Wyatt Tee Walker, active in the Petersburg Virginia, movement and Executive Secretary of SCLC from 1960 to 1964, helped in his decisions to come. I invited and coordinated the first meeting of the Southern Christian Leadership Conference in Virginia, the convention before the "March on Washington." It was held in Richmond, Virginia, with both Roy Wilkins, and Adam Clayton Powell among our national leaders participating. It was following this convention that Dr. King dispatched me to New York to talk with Roy Wilkins, A. Philip Randolph and Whitney Young, of the National Urban League, in and effort to have this march on Washington. I am sure it wasn't my presence or influence or even the call from Dr. King that assured the march's success. The time was right. Dr. A. Philip Randolph had wanted this march as far back as 1942, when Mrs. Roosevelt intervened and caused her husband to make steps toward desegregating the armed forces. This delayed Brother Randolph's push for a March on Washington. It seems like all of our lives something or someone gets in the way of our full freedom by trying to help, while waiting on the goodwill that just doesn't exist, but tends to take the place of God's Will. I had just led a Statewide Pilgrimage of Prayer to Prince Edward County, Virginia, that had closed its schools rather than to desegregate them in the Supreme Court's decision of May 17th, 1954. Schools were also closed in Norfolk, Warren County and in Charlottesville, Virginia. I also invited and entertained the convention in August of 1979, when the Norfolk Chapter of SCLC hosted it during the administration of President Jimmy Carter. It was during this convention that it was announced that Ambassador Andrew Young was forced to resign. He was terminated for doing what America and the U.N. were ultimately forced to do and that was to talk with the Palestinians. They didn't understand even then that Ambassador Young was serving the God of the Ages and the Christ of Glory.

Following that first Virginia Convention with the National Office Dr. King, others and I went to the Department of Justice to meet with then Robert Kennedy, the Attorney General and brother of the President. I had run for the City Council in Petersburg and also the State Senate from the Eight Senatorial District in Southside, Virginia. With the passage of the Voting Rights Bill that was signed into law on August 6, 1965, we had heard President Lyndon Baines Johnson say over the airways, "We shall overcome." Here it is nearly forty-five years later and there are those in Congress and in state houses across America who still haven't accepted the message. I served on the staff of the White House Conference to Fulfill These Rights, in 1964, where we had discussions on not only the "Law," but also the "Spirit of the Law." This too seemed almost fruitless as I look back, compared with the sufferings and the deaths it took to get the law.

When Dr. King came to Norfolk at my invitation to preach the installation sermon for me in October of 1966, he used for his sermon that famous sermon of his, "A Knock at Midnight," I was so caught up in the spirit of the day that I failed to delve into the deep, theological and philosophical meaning of this sociological challenge. I still didn't get it when he gave his last major sermon in Memphis, "I don't know what will happen now. We've got some difficult days ahead. I've been to the mountaintop. And I don't mind. Like anybody, I would like to live a long life; longevity has its place. But I'm not concerned about that now. I just want to do God's Will and He's allowed me to go up to the Mountain. And I've looked over, and I've seen the Promised Land. I may not get there with you. But I want you to know tonight, I'm not worried about anything. I do not fear any man; 'Mine eyes have seen the glory..." As I reflect on his sermon in Norfolk and his last sermon and review my experience in the civil-rights movement and the church trying to do Liberation Theology, I now see what Dr. King saw, i.e., How Black the Midnight is in our nation and the world. It is still midnight in the traditional church that worships the God of the West rather than the God of the Ages, and the Christ of Glory.

The Biblical March with Jesus

Many of us tend to forget that Dr. Martin Luther King, Jr., was an ordained, called, educated and trained Baptist Minister of the Euangelion (Greek) or the Gospel, the good news. Let's not get so far involved in his civil rights activities that we forget that. Everything he did and everything he wrote, and in every speech he gave, we must keep that perspective in mind. So to march with Martin even today, we must first of all "get in step with Jesus", our glorified Lord. I have said it differently in a sermon. "To March With Martin" you must first march with Jesus. Jesus told those who would march with Him that, "You are the light of the world. A city located on a hill cannot be hidden. People do not light a lamp and put it under a basket, but on a lampstand, and it gives light to all in the house. In the same way, let your light shine before people, so that they can see your good deeds and give honor to your Father in heaven" (Matthew 5:14-16 NET). This is why Dr. King said the church is the light of the world, but it had become the "tail light rather than the headlight." He also stated that SCLC was the social arm of the church.

Many so-called Christians are serving the God of the West with a watered down concept of Jesus, the Christ; out in the fields, with white sheep and holding white babies while entertaining them with his matchless words of comfort and beauty. This is far from the revolutionary Lord of Glory who went to Calvary to deliver man from the world of Aion, "the endless world of men to Kosmos, the world of perfect order and everlasting joy, where the fruition of our faith leads. The Bible teaches, "From one man he made every nation of the human race to inhabit the entire earth, determining their set times and the fixed limits of the places where they would live, so that they would search for him and find him, though he is not far from each one of us. For in him we live and move about, and exist, as even some of your own poets have said, for we too are his offspring" (Act 17:26-28 NET). Dr. King's journey on this "Island Isthmus" between life and death had its genesis in the God of the Beginning, who is the God of the Ages, not this man-made God of the West. He states the reason he violated man's law of segregation and discrimination is because he was under a mandate from a higher moral law of the Universal God. And he was willing to pay the penalty for violating man's law to satisfy the appeal, the calling, and the directions of a higher Law. That is what was behind our sit-ins, kneel- ins, wade-ins and walk-ins of the civil rights movement. King followed in the traditions of Jesus, Gandhi, John Bunyan, and the apostles, who refused to stop teaching and performing miracles in the name of Jesus in defiance of the law and even Aristotle in drinking the hemlock.

The March Against Violence

The second focal point in the March with Martin was a march against violence. Dr. King once said, "The greatest purveyor of violence on planet earth is my own government." What should have been the best stance for America became a stumbling block for our national leaders, a few uprooted preachers of the gospel, and several in the civil-rights community. It seemed that his philosophy of non-violence was tolerated for the demonstrators when they were marching against the policies and the ordinances of discrimination but when it came to the policies of our nation at home and abroad, the thought in some circles was that Dr. King had overstepped his bounds. He was not supposed to be delving in "Foreign Policy." They didn't know that Dr. King was an appointed and a called ambassador, representing the "Homeland of the Soul." I have heard several speakers who cited Dr. King's first outrage with the war in Vietnam as being from different places. On his way to speak at the Riverside Church in New York, Dr. King came to Petersburg, Virginia, in August of 1965, for the Virginia State Unit of SCLC, and in his speech he said, "The war in Viet Nam must be stopped." He made this statement in Rogers Stadium at Virginia State College. This statement on which he agonized before making, caused the loss of thousands of dollars in contributions that dried to SCLC and it ultimately caused me as a part time staff person to lose my staff job. Although there was no pay I remained on the National Board and did whatever I could to keep the movement going. Dr. King declared that he was disappointed in America. The war efforts were drying up resources that could have been better used in a domestic policy because it took money and attention away from the anti-poverty program that incidentally had been launched by President Johnson.

Dr. King would say, "If we continued under the old ideology of an eye for an eye and a tooth for a tooth, it would leave us in both blind and toothless in the world." While that was law under Moses it was not in the teachings of Jesus. The late congressman, Adam Clayton Powell, once glibly remarked on Dr. King's teaching on non-violence and said: The Bible does say: Whoever strikes you on the right cheek, turn the other to him as well." But after you turn the other cheek, the Bible is silent and you should "go for your self." When he said that he was chiding Dr. King. When Dr. King spoke of violence it wasn't limited to warfare and fistfights. He thought when you lived in America, the richest nation on earth in a sea of opulence, and see here and there islands of poverty, that was violence. When you live in an affluent nation, abounding in prosperity, and there are babies crying every day and hungry every night while dying of malnutrition, that is violence at its lowest. When you live in a nation where the rich keep getting richer and the poor are still getting poorer, that is an act of legislative violence. When Jesus said, "the poor you will have with you always", that was not a mandate or a directive from heaven; that was human reality based upon the hardness of our hearts, our unwillingness to share and our greed for gain. I was invited to give a lecture on Dr. Martin Luther King, Jr., on a King's Day celebration at Langley Air Force Base, Virginia. I debated long and hard about really saying how Dr. King felt about military violence. I had not made a decision to change my speech and I came upon it in the speech before I realized it. I didn't see a rebellion in the making but I think the Post Chaplain did. When I said that Dr. King was against even the violence of war, a White face in the audience turned red. Of all the folk who came by and shook my hand, that chaplain was not in the number. If I had been reported to the NSA or some other government agency, I am sure they responded, "We know him, he is already on our list to be watched."

Knowing the world as he did I don't think Dr. King would have his congregation raise money and give it to the Red Cross to help with Katrina evacuees. He would have organized a movement as he did in 1967, a movement for churches to respond and many of them did. I organized a food and clothing drive for the children in the Delta of Mississippi and drove there following the 18 wheeler truck that we had leased and delivered the clothing, the food, the medical aid, the shoes, etc., with my wife Marian, and the Chairperson of the Missionary and Benevolent Commission of New Calvary Baptist Church. This was a battle in the war against the violence of hunger in which our church was committed. We need to do more than to grunt and shake our heads about the violence in our communities. I have a relative who spent 13 years in prison on a charge of killing his wife. He is finally out of prison but as I understand it, he refuses to consider taking a job doing "labor." His reason is that he gave 13 years of his life to the state and he is not giving them any more. This information came to me through two concerned relatives I suppose with the hopes that I would do something. As a relative and chairman of the national board of the Dr. Martin Luther King, Jr., Family Life Institute, I have already talked with his mother and I am trying to get to see him to have some sessions with him. It is a matter of personal self-inflicted psychological violence when one who is able and capable of working, refuses to do so. Biblically speaking, work is the first order of God, following man's fall. Dr. Martin Luther King, Jr., even dignified a street sweeper's job. "Even if you are a street sweeper, sweep streets like Michelangelo painted pictures. Sweep streets like, Beethoven composed music...Sweep streets until some body will say, There goes, a great street sweeper."

Marching in Peace and in Love

This is the ultimate in the message of Martin, the development of the beloved community." He writes about this in his book, "Where Do We Go From Here?" I almost wish sometimes that I had been in Memphis with him on that memorable night when he delivered his final message to the world. Martin is still on the march in America despite the fact that he died on April 4th, 1968. There is a scriptural passage that says, "Blessed are the dead, those who die in the Lord from this moment on! `Yes,` says the Spirit, so they can rest from their hard work, because their deeds will follow them" (Revelations 14:13, NET). Martin's work continues in many forms and through many venues. There are Martin Luther King libraries, schools, churches, streets, interstate and local highways in just about every major city in America. I spoke on at least two occasions at the Martin Luther King Center in Havana, Cuba. I regret that physically, my marching days are about over. But I do have a heavy duty electric wheelchair that will carry me if I am called on to go, although I would hate to face for the first time the admonition of my dear wife and children who would remind me that I did what I could, when I could. But somebody has to wave the peace flag, and we need to raise it now all over this nation.

Dr. King says "peace" is not merely the absence of tension but is the presence of justice. That is the level of peace we should be seeking. Jesus said in his Sermon on the Mount, "Blessed are the peacemakers, for they will be called the children of God" (Matthew 5:9 NET). Just eleven years after the death of Dr. Martin Luther King, Ebony Magazine published a special issue dealing with Black on Black Crimes. I found it difficult to put the article down after reading the first sentence that said "More blacks were killed by other Blacks in the year 1977 than died in the entire nine years of the Viet Nam War. Most of the 5,734 Blacks killed on the battlefields of Black America in 1977, could have survived Vietnam, since the Blacks who died there, being some 5,711, for an average of only 634 per year." Before I could finish reading the article I received the message that another brother had killed a 30-year-old Black publisher/editor of a weekly newspaper in Danville, Virginia. I found myself in the pulpit of Camp Grove Baptist Church in Danville, attending Louise's funeral and heard Bishop Lawrence Campbell say, "As Black people, we must find other ways to vent our frustrations. We must put down the guns and put down our knives." Then the pastor of Camp Grove Baptist Church, the Reverend Dr. Toomer, delivered a beautiful eulogy that was more meaningful, relevant and appropriate to me than any I had heard in a long time. One of the critical things he said has bothered me throughout the years of my ministry. He said, "Most of you are going to leave here today without any intentions of changing or improving upon your behavior…right in the face of this tragic death…a needless death."

How can the church engage in peace making in the world if it has only a semblance of peace within her walls? Jesus said, "I am leaving you with a gift – peace of mind and heart. And the peace I give isn't like the peace the world gives" (John 14:27 LASB). Throughout his life Dr. King operated on the peace from God that surpasses all understanding. The peace of Jesus Christ is contagious. I caught it in the struggle after I saw how it was working in his life. Thank God for "maturing grace." It is redemptive and His love grows out of His grace. Dr. King would tell us today in order to really march with him, you have to march in grace, and in love. The Greeks would say you have to march in "Charis and Agape." That means, standing in "Divine favor and in eternal, unfailing love."

As I come to the close of this chapter I want you to know that Martin taught me how to walk with God, with the love and the grace of God. Love attracts love. In our effort to make `love` a word of action The Martin Luther King, Jr., Family Life Institute has issued a call for a Global Family Day. This proposal has attracted the attention of several governors as well as numerous big city mayors (some of them are listed on our Web site: drmlkjrfamilylife.org). On December 15 and 16 of 2005, resolutions were signed in Congress calling on the President to sign in on the bill calling for a Global Family Day. With all of the discord in the world, with nations rising up in warfare against nations, the earthquakes, the hurricanes, the tsunamis, the flu viruses, and scientists struggling to find the right medications or serums to combat these diseases, with the violent warfare in the streets and our bulging prison walls, families need to come together to assimilate the family of God on earth as it is in heaven. We all have this one thing in common, i.e., "we all came from God through a family of the earth and we will all be returning to God for His eternal dwelling with us." We were invited to the United Nations for their annual Family Day symposium. While there we were asked to join the United Nations as a non-governmental organization.

When Dr. Martin Luther King, Jr., came to Norfolk on October 30th, 1966, to preach my sermon of installation, for some strange reason I sang a solo before his sermon that had just dropped in my spirit. When my daughter, Maravia, came to the Immigration Court on the day that my grandson and her step-son was finally given American citizenship she gave me a clipping out of the daily newspaper of an article that was written about Dr. King's visit. That song again dropped in my spirit as a review. I was in Federal court and I didn't dare hum. It occurred to me why I was bothered by that song. Attorney William Smith, a good friend of mine and a former classmate at Virginia Union University in Richmond, and the painstaking editor of this book, reminded me that this song was written by Thomas A. Dorsey, who also wrote, "Precious Lord, Take My Hand," which was also a favorite hymn of Dr. Martin Luther King, Jr. (I am reminded here that, on the night before he died he requested that song to be sung). As I look back on my "journey on the isthmus island between life and death," I am still wondering if I were singing that song for me or for Dr. King? The beautiful song that that haunted my mind is, "When I've Done The Best I Can:

> When I've done the best I can, if my friends don't understand
> Then the Lord will carry me home
> After I have done my best, I will find a peaceful rest,

When my Savior carries me home
Many griefs and sorrows I have witnessed on my part.
On that bright tomorrow, He will mend and heal my broken heart
When the best I've done for Thee, Then the best comes back to me
When my Savior carries me home.

I believe Dr. King did his best and I know I have done my best. When I have completed my journey here I want to leave here with joy bells ringing. That song by the late Thomas Dorsey is too somber for me. I couldn't even handle it that day in court just thinking about it.

At my homegoing I want a selection from Handel's "Messiah" sung. I want somebody to sing, "Great Is Thy Faithfulness", I want everybody to sing for me,

"Some glad morning when this life is over, I'll fly away.
To a home on God's celestial shore, I'll fly away.
When the shadows of this life have grown, I'll fly away
Like a bird from prison bars has flown, I'll fly away
Just a few more weary days and then, I'll fly away
To a land where joys shall never end, I'll fly away."

Until then, for the God of the Ages' sake, and for the Christ of Glory's sake, let us all march with Martin till traveling days are done. Then we all can really sing with Martin, "Free at last, Free at last, 'Thank the God of the Ages for the Christ of Glory,' we are Free at last."

Key Persons in the 2006 Martin Luther King, Jr. Global Family Life Breakfast in Portsmouth, VA.

CHAPTER XIII

BEYOND THE ACHIEVEMENT GAP IN BLACK HISTORY

Forgetting the things that are behind and reaching out for the things that are ahead, with this goal in mind, I strive toward the prize of the upward call of God in Christ Jesus.

Philippians 3:14

THE HAND OF GOD

"Be under no illusion, you shall gather to yourself the images you love. As you go, the shapes, the lights, the shadows of the things you have preferred will come to you, yes, inveterately, inevitably, as bees to their hive. And there in your mind and spirit they will leave with you their distilled essence, sweet as honey or bitter as gall, and you will grow unto their likeness because their nature will be in you.

As men see the color in the wave so shall men see in you the thing you have loved the most. Out of your eyes will look the spirit you have chosen. In your smile and in your frown the years will speak. You will not walk nor stand nor sit, nor will your hand move, but you will confess the one you serve, and upon your forehead will be written his name as by a revealing pen. Cleverness may select skillful words to cast a veil about you, and circumspection may never sleep; yet you will not be hid, No.

As year adds to year, that face of yours, which once like an unwritten page, lay smooth in your baby crib, will take to itself lines, and still more lines, as the parchment of an old historian who jealously sets down all the story. And there, more deep than acids etch the steel, will grow the inscribed narrative of your mental habits, the emotions of your heart, your sense of conscience, your response to duty, what you think of your God and of your fellow men and of yourself. It will all be there. For men become like that which they love, and the name thereof is written on their brow."

This poem by Oswald W.S. McCall, "THE HAND OF GOD," should follow you throughout this presentation and, if you listen closely, it could follow you for the rest of your life. For men and women, regardless of race, creed or color, will become like that which they love. What do you love? How high, how deep, and how wide is your love? What are your goals as you take flight in Black history? There is no need to merely reflect upon the past, or to close the achievement gap between Blacks and Whites. I have been to several Black History events, and have even worked with my wife and her sorors on some of them where the theme was, "Closing the Achievement Gap between Blacks and whites." This may be a fair secondary goal but it should not be our primary goal. Let us just think for a moment. Suppose we did close the achievement gap racially. Just suppose all Black students actually dug in, passed all tests and the SAT scores went off the chart and we were even with everybody else in America, where would we be? Would that be equity and justice? Do you think George Washington Carver, who was born in slavery, had his mind on closing the gap when he was researching the peanut and became one of the greatest scientists who ever lived? What about Mary McLeod Bethune, Frederick Douglass, Nathaniel Paul, Martin Luther King, Jr., Thurgood Marshall, A Philip Randolph, James Farmer, Rosa Parks, Coretta Scott King, and Carter G. Woodson, of all people, spent their lives trying to close the achievement gap between Blacks and Whites? Suppose they had stopped at being equal to whites; would we be celebrating Black history month every February? Take another look. Let's look at the highest elected office in America. Would you want us to close the gap to become equal to the Honorable George W. Bush? I am aware that there may be some Republicans in our midst, but what do you do when you close the gap? Do you start singing, "So glad I am here, so glad I'm here, so glad I'm here in Jesus name?" I don't think so.

When Paul was commissioned to minister to the Gentiles I didn't hear him say, "Now I want you Gentiles to close the achievement gap between Gentiles and Jews." Here this lawyer of lawyers, who studied at the feet of Gamaliel, this Hebrew of Hebrews, this Pharisee of Pharisees, this linguistic major said something else. He said something that I think we need to hear today. "Not that I have already attained this-that is, I have not already been perfected – but I strive to lay hold of that for which Christ Jesus also laid hold of me. Brothers and sisters, I do not consider myself to have attained this. Instead I am single minded. Forgetting the things that are behind and reaching out for the things that are ahead, with this goal in mind, I strive toward the prize of the upward call of God in Christ Jesus."

Now before you go south on me… before you go sour – south, this passage has nothing to do with Morgan Freeman. I am not telling you to forget about Black History month. You don't have to go there at all. Let me tell you something. You cannot live in the past neither can you live in the future. You can only live in the present, for in the present you will have the past and the future. Let me see if I can make this plain. I am a Virginia native. I was born in Norfolk County, which is now the City of Chesapeake. Chesapeake was not only racist but it was also klanish. In spite of the fact it has had a Black Ph.D mayor for several years, there are pockets of racism and klanism still present. I just moved back to Chesapeake two years and a month ago. Following high school in 1948, I left Chesapeake and went into the military. I went on to college and the seminary. I went on to Boston University and earned a Doctor of Ministry Degree in Liberation Theology with honors. I was on the national board of directors of the Southern Christian Leadership Conference for 42 years. I was jailed 11 times, four times down the road in Danville, and once in Lynchburg. I traveled around the world with my wife of 55 plus years and I have preached on five of the seven continents of the world. I have met with presidents of several countries and leaders of several nations. After 59 years of absence I came back to Chesapeake and went to the diagnostic center of Chesapeake General Hospital for some lab work. My wife looked as we checked in and said we will have a 40-minute wait. I said, well okay, we'd just sit it out. Several White persons who came in after we were waiting got served and went on about their business. It was a two-hour wait but finally my name was called. When I looked at the registration paper I saw two items that puzzled me. The first thing was religion…NPO…and race…#2. and it required my signature. I had to inquire. I asked the lady what they meant and she shrugged her shoulders and said, "I don't know." She called across the hall and asked, "what does religion NPO mean? The other employee, who was Black said, I think that means what religion are you. She turned around and said, "Dr. Reid, did they ask you what religion you were?" I said, "no." She asked, "What do you want me to put down?" Now when she said Dr. Reid, (which wasn't on the sheet) I got the feeling that she either knew me or at least knew of me. I said, well I am a retired American Baptist Pastor; she said, "Baptist, okay, I'll put that down." I ask the lady who had drawn my blood, and what does race #2 mean? With a broad smile on her face she came over and patted my hand and said, "that means colored. Number 1 is white, and number 2 is colored!" Go on and fight on the battlefields of the world, you are still number #2. Earn your doctorate degrees, as long as you are Black you are still number #2. Build your home in the new subdivision, and pay your taxes on a six figured income, if you are Black, you are still number two. Become the Secretary of State and rely on information that they give you to report to the world, and do a great job doing it, but if you are Black, you are still number #2. Discover blood plasma, and get in an accident, go to the hospital needing blood but cannot get because you are Black. This discoverer, a Black doctor, ironically couldn't get it because he was number 2. Dr. Joseph Lowery said it again at Coretta's funeral, "Yes, everything has changed, and nothing has changed." So we must go beyond closing the gap in Black history, we must reach out and press on for the mark of the high calling in Christ. Why press for this mark?

1. COME FIRST AND SEE THAT WE ARE PILGRIMS PASSING THROUGH THIS BARREN LAND, THIS WORLD IS NOT OUR HOME, WE HAVE BEEN CALLED BY GOD TO PRESS ON.

For about the last twenty years of my life I have been writing commentaries on the church school lessons that are published each week in the New Journal & Guide, the third oldest Black weekly in the nation. Several weeks ago the lesson to Timothy from Paul was entitled, "Follow a Good Mentor." A good mentor is a wise and trusted counselor. When I am convinced that I have hit a home run on the lessons I usually e-mail them to friends or whomever I am led to send one. I sent the one on "Follow a Good Mentor" to my niece in Brooklyn and forgot that I had sent it. My niece called me several days later to thank me and she broke down on the phone crying like a baby. I said, Angel, what is wrong? She said, sobbing, "I needed that lesson, I needed that lesson. Here I am having past my fiftieth birthday and I don't have a wise and trusted counselor, I don't have a mentor!" Here she is in Brooklyn, New York, separated from a husband of inconveniences, having one son who was recently released from prison, her mother, my closest sister, and her father now deceased, (I eulogized both of them at the Cornerstone Baptist Church in Brooklyn), she is working, trying to hold things together and she doesn't have a trusted and wise counselor. I told her, "Listen, you need more than a mentor, you need a prayer partner who knows the Lord, who can get a prayer through beyond the achievement gap, and I will be your prayer partner." You see, I know that "I love the Lord and he has heard my cry, and pitied my every groan." And as long as I live, when troubles arise, I'll hasten to his throne. Too many of us have become disappointed and disillusioned with the witness of the traditional church. And there may be some rationale for that which I know is legitimate. The traditional and mainline churches have been co-opted in serving the God of the West, a man-made God, rather than the Christ of Glory, our redeeming Lord. The God of the West permits slavery, economic exploitation, under the disguise of capitalism, discrimination, and injustice. It provides warfare, political corruption, personal and institutional racism extremism, and Humanism with a capital H. Closing the achievement gap between Blacks and Whites has been seen as a notable goal of the highest good. Our sights in Black History must go beyond closing the achievement gap; we must close the gap between man and God. We were created in the imagoes Dieu, the image and the likeness of God, and as creatures of His creation we must set our sights on the Pontifex Maximum, the Bridge builder, that brings us to an at-one-ment with God. John says, "See what sort of love the Father has given to us that we should be called God's children-and indeed we are!" For this reason the world does not know us. The world sees the color of our skin and we become a number and that number is 2 and that is because it does not know him. "Dear friends, we are God's children now, and what we will be has not yet been revealed. We know that whenever it is revealed we will be like Him, because we will see Him just as He is, and everyone who has the hope focused on Him purifies himself, just as Jesus is pure" (1 John 3:1-3 NET). Being number 2 down here doesn't bother me at all when I go to the word of God. Jesus said, "And whoever has left houses or brothers or sisters or father or mother or children or fields for my sake will receive a hundred times as much and will inherit eternal lie. But many who are first will be last, and the last will be first" (Matthew 19:29,30 NET). Our past is our present. Everything has changed, yet everything remains the same. Paul said, "Therefore we do not despair, but even if our physical body, (our outer man) is wearing away, our inner person is being renewed day by day...for we know that if our earthly house and tent we live in, is dismantled, we have a building from God, a house not built by human hands that is eternal in the heavens."

2. COME FINALLY AND SEE THAT WE MUST GO BEYOND CLOSING THE ACHIEVMENT GAP BETWEEN BLACKS AND WHITES TO PERFECT OUR WITNESS.

There is always the temptation of secondary achievements to reach a humanistic goal that makes us feel good in a temporary fix. Our struggle is far from being over. When Coretta Scott King was born in Marion, Alabama, her mother and father were fighting the Klan, segregation, and racial discrimination. At her funeral the other day, the skinheads and the Klan were outside on the edge of the highway for all to see as we approached the church, holding up signs protesting her life with her picture on them that read, BURN IN HELL...GLAD SHE'S GONE...KOONS GO BACK TO AFRICA. I was sitting beside my wife who could feel my blood pressure rising and as she saw "me" turning red she whispered, "Be godly now, be godly." You see, to be godly, you have to rise above your circumstances by the grace, or as the Greeks would say, beyond the Charis of God by His redemptive love, and not allow the devil to suck you back down into bitterness. I don't have any antidotes against the evils of this world; they will be here always. Neither am I insulated against arrogance and indifference.

Paul says in the seventh Chapter of 1 Corinthians, "When I would do good, about all I can produce is bad." Jesus tried to calm me when He said, "In this world you will have trials and tribulations; in this world, you are going to have despairing moments of gloom and doom, in this world, you will have what will feel like more of your share of trials and tribulations, but be of good cheer, for I have overcome the world." But I have come to tell you, "There is a balm in Gilead, to make the wounded whole, There is a balm in Gilead, to heal the sin sick soul. If you cannot sing like angels, if you cannot preach like Paul, you can tell the love of Jesus, you can say he died for all." Now you cannot tell the Love of Jesus if you don't live the Love of Jesus. You tell His love from a new plane, from another perspective. You don't view the world through the humanistic eyes of the world. If you have been born of His Spirit and washed in His Blood you now see the world through godly eyes. You don't stop at deluding goals like the road maps to peace and the workfare of warfare.

We have to follow examples like President William A Keen of the Virginia State Unit of SCLC, who went out on a limb in supporting the cause of the Dixon Brothers in Dixie, who were jailed based on a lie. I understand that the judge in this case has recused himself. Brother Keen could not get the support he needed from some clergy because these brothers were Muslims. What did Jesus mean when he said to His disciples, "…and when you pray, say Our Father." I'll tell you what he meant. He meant just what He said. God, the Creator of life and the Sustainer of life is Father to red, white, black, brown, yellow, and all colors in between. He is Our Father and all men and women of the earth, regardless of race, creed or color, are brothers and sisters, whether Jew, Muslim, Christian, Black or White, He is Father of us all. Paul said out on Mars Hill, "From one man, he made every nation of the human race to inhabit the entire earth, determining their set times and the fixed limits of the places where they would live, so that they would search for God and perhaps grope around for him and find him, though he is not far from each one of us. For in him we live and move about and exist, as even some of your own poets have said, 'For we too are his offspring'

"(Acts 17:26-28 NET). Let us not go back in Black history and pull out that provincial ignorance that says only Baptists are right, or only this denomination or that denomination is right. We are all sinners. "All have sinned and fallen short of the glory of God. And God sent not His Son into the world to condemn the world but that the world through Him might be saved."

We need to check out ourselves in Black history. Were we born Black or were we born Free? David said, "Look, I was prone to do wrong from birth; I was a sinner the moment my mother conceived me"(Psalms 51:5, 6, NET). "Then Jesus said to those Jewish people who had believed him, if you continue to follow my teaching, you are really my disciples, and you will know the truth, and the truth will set you free" (John 8:31, 32, NET). We need to be reevaluating our faith to see if we are serving the God of the West, who is at war with the Christ of Glory. In other words my book will help you to identify your location, "as whether the God you worship and the Christ you practice are the same or not!" We should not leave here today as we came. Don't leave here upset with me either. We must go beyond closing the achievement gap between Blacks and Whites. I am afraid when we close this gap you will be raising the question if this all for which I have been striving. Now I have never been that good in math. Here I am just about to cross the swelling tide and several years ago I turned my checkbook over to my wife. I don't like numbers and I have rejected the racial designation of being number 2. Call me what you will but I am not a number of any description. I have committed my life to joining that number that John saw and it was a number that no man could number.

You may have to speak to your sons and daughters in the poem that Langston Hughes penned:

> "Well son, I'll tell you, Life for me ain't been no crystal stair,
> It's had tacks in it and splinters and boards torn up,
> And places with no carpet on the floor...BARE
> But all the times I'se been a-climbing on and reaching landins,
> And turning corners, and sometimes goin in the dark where there ain't
> Been no light, So boy, don't you turn back...Don't you set

down cause you find it kinda hard…Don't you fall now- For I'se still goin honey, And life for me ain't been no crystal stair." Look at our history, look at Black slaves being sold by Black men to White Christians. Look at them throwing themselves over board saying, "Before I'd be a slave I'll be buried in my grave and then go home to my Lord and be free." Look at the revolutionaries who stood up against the godless institution of slavery. Look at your foreparents being stamped, beaten into submission, and sold like cattle. There are others who fought and died for a freedom in this nation that they were denied at home. Look at the martyrs who were assassinated and murdered. Then there are the civil-rights leaders, such as Vernon Johns, Martin Luther King, Jr., Ralph Aberthany, Fannie Lou Hammer, Roy Wilkins, Thurgood Marshall, Rosa Parks, and Coretta Scott King. Then there are the Martinsville Seven, M.C. Allen, and others. There are Peter and Paul saying, "Get up, get up, get up…Therefore we are surrounded by such a great cloud of witnesses, let us throw off everything that hinders and the sin that so easily entangles, and let us run with perseverance the race marked out for us…. fix our eyes on Jesus, the author and the finisher of our faith…" I am nearing the shore. Somehow I hear Dr. Martin Luther King, Jr., in the grandeur of eloquence saying to us:

"Fleecy locks and Black complexion, cannot forfeit nature's claim
Skin may differ but affection dwell in Black and White the same.
Were I so tall that I could reach the pole or grasp the ocean at a span…
I must be measured by my soul, for the mind is the standard of the man."

We must go beyond closing the gap that is mundane or earthly. We were not created or redeemed to reach only terrestrial goals. We must go on to celestial heights. This world is not our home; we are pilgrims here on a journey of faith. And then and only then can we sing that futuristic unlined hymn of our foreparents, "How I got over, How I got over, My soul looks back and wonders, how I got over. As soon as my feet strike Zion, I'm going to lay down my heavy burden. Put on my robe in glory, going to shout and tell the story. Coming over hills and mountains, up to the crystal fountain, then I'm going to shout, hallelujah, I'm going to shout, hallelujah, I'm gonna shout hallelujah and never good-bye.

The 2006 Group Shot. The MLK GFD Breakfast in Portsmouth, VA.

More Stops along the Way

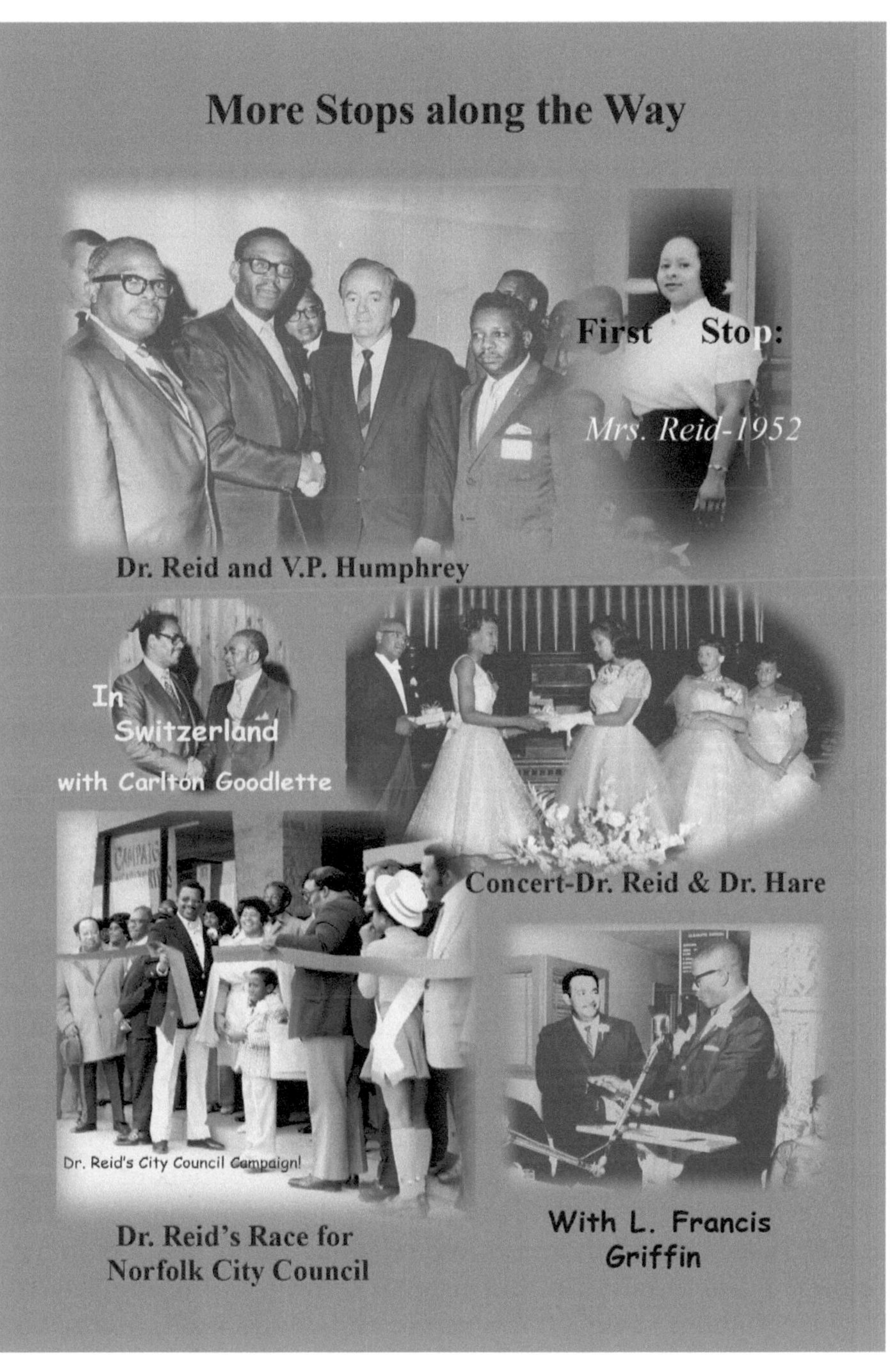

Dr. Reid and V.P. Humphrey

First Stop:

Mrs. Reid-1952

In Switzerland with Carlton Goodlette

Concert-Dr. Reid & Dr. Hare

Dr. Reid's Race for Norfolk City Council

With L. Francis Griffin

CHAPTER XIV

OUT OF THE BOX MINISTRIES

"Philip went and found Nathaniel and told him, We've found the One Moses wrote of in the Law, the One preached by the prophets. It's Jesus, Joseph's son, the one from Nazareth!" Nathaniel said, "Nazareth? You've got to be kidding." But Philip said, "Come, see for yourself."

John 1:46 THE MESSAGE, REMIX
Eugene H. Peterson

After John was arrested, Jesus went to Galilee preaching the Message of God.
"Time's up! God's kingdom is here. Change your life and believe the Message.

Mark 1:14 THE MESSAGE, REMIX

INTRODUCTION: Mark's biography of Jesus begins with the proclamation of the euangelion, the good news or good tidings of the Kingdom of God and of salvation to all mankind everywhere. That in its self suggests to me that the gospel is neither restricted nor limited to kindred or kinds, customs, or class, but as God's Word to the world. It establishes salvation to all of humankind. Had this word come to us from Rome, the capital city on seven majestic hills of power, the seat of authority for the civilized world of its day, maybe it would have been accepted or understood more. Had the euangelion, the great tidings of great joy come to us from the Holy City, the city of David, Jerusalem, where the prophets of the Lord had been slaughtered and slain, possibly the Sanhedrin, the Scribes and Pharisees, the High Priests and religious authorities would have respected and honored it. But from Nazareth, as Eugene Peterson interprets Philip saying, "You've got to be kidding. Can anything good; can anything noteworthy, anything worthwhile come out of a town like Nazareth? Nazareth is not a king's town. It is not the seat of authority. It has no army, no military, and no major industries other than fishing. Fishing? Did you say fishing? Yes, I said fishing, but you come and see. Jesus, the one of whom Moses wrote about in the law; Jesus, whom Isaiah, that eagled-eyed prophet saw coming more than 700 years before His earthly birth, was born in a stable while His parenthood was still being questioned, but He actually did not have His genesis in Bethlehem or Nazareth. I know many of us go straight to Bethlehem, but John said He was in the beginning with God. In other words, "In the beginning was the Word and the Word was with God, and the Word was fully God..."All things were created by Him and apart from Him not one thing was created that had been created. In Him was Life and the Life was the Light of humankind. And the Light shines on in the darkness, but the darkness has not mastered it." Not only was God that light but also He sent that light and has called on us, the children of Light, to light up this world of darkness.

He grew up in a fishing town, calling unlearned disciples to become fishers of men. He began a ministry outside of the box, not calling bishops, deacons, pastors, churchmen, or religious leaders, but He called fishermen to a fishing ministry. One night they had fished all night and had caught nothing. He came to them one morning, as day was breaking, saying, "how goes the fishing?" They said, Master, it is not going well. We have fished all night and caught nothing. Jesus got into Simon's boat and asked Him to put out into the deep water and lower your nets for a catch. Simon said, Master; we worked hard all night and caught nothing! But at your Word, I will lower the nets. Jesus is the Master Fisherman. He's Master over the waters and the fish and He knows where they are. All we have to do is to fish at His directions, and don't fish in dead waters. I had the experience once of going deep-sea fishing in the Caribbean, from the island of St. Thomas. The captain told us to rest and relax because it would be about an hour and a half before we got to where the fish were. I went down stairs to the berthing area and I picked up a little paperback book with the title, DEVIL'S TRIANGLE. I read for about two hours before I went back upstairs and raised a question with the captain concerning the location of the devil's triangle? I had read about the fifty missing ships and twenty planes that had gone down in the Devil's Triangle, and about several other mishaps of mystery like the mysterious water spouts. The captain looked at me and smiled, noting the book that had caught the "trembles" in my right hand as I was waiting for his reply. He said to me, "We have been in the devil's triangle for the last hour and a half." I looked around and there was absolutely no sight of land. The Captain said, "If you want to find the fish you have to go where the fish are, and we are just about there!"

Jesus said to Simon, "Launch out and let down." The entire world is in the Devil's Triangle and fish are everywhere. There are divine geometric lines at each point. I see the Trinity in the triangle, the Father, the Son, and the Holy Spirit. Don't get upset with the apparent success of the mega churches. Every church can be a mega church called out of darkness and walking in the Light of His Love with the presence of Jesus in the midst. Can anything good come out of Nazareth? Can anything good come out of the Devil's Triangle? Can anything good, worthy or worthwhile, come out of the Church today? Philip said, "COME AND SEE, BUT WE HAVE TO COME OUT OF THE BOX!"

I. COME FIRST AND SEE, WE MUST COME OUT OF THE BOX OF RELIGIOUS TRADITIONS AND PRACTICES WITH JESUS BECAUSE THE DAY OF THE LORD HAS COME.

This is it. This is the day that the Lord has made, let us rejoice and be glad in it. I remember speaking a prophetic word in a sermon one Sunday morning, not knowing how profound and accurate I was. I stopped in the middle of a sermon at the New Calvary Baptist Church of Norfolk and said, "If you all knew what I was really saying to you, you would put me out of here!" They finally got the word and with the help of the offspring of the City fathers, they finally put me out. I have never regretted that prophecy because I knew then that God had called me before the church called me. Here I am now, as Dr. Gardner Taylor would say, "With my hair turning white by the snowfalls of many winters, and my eyes are growing dim with the twilight of old age," with many of my organs slowing down and my steps getting slow and tender as I peek by faith beyond the veil, like Nolan Williams who sang out one day, "I've seen the lightning flashing, and I've heard the thunder's roar. I've felt sin breakers dashing, trying to conquer my soul. But I heard the voice of Jesus, saying to me to fight on, for He promised never to leave me, never to leave me alone." They didn't promise me, but He did! He who supplies my every need according to His riches in Glory...He did! He did, who is my way maker, my burden bearer, my Light in darkness, He who is the Eternal I Am in both the Old Testament and in the New Testament, He promised never to leave me, never to leave me alone.

Being put out for practicing what I preached has never bothered me. God has spared me from going around hoping for an opportunity to preach and to receive an "after offering" as a put out, a has been, and a use to be., "No such thing." I am approaching my seventy-eighth birthday and I am still going to weight watchers and the gym. I am; because He is, and He promised! He promised! He promised never to leave me, never to leave me alone. Don't feel bad because you get put out; remember Jesus was put out following His first recorded sermon in Nazareth. He was put in the blasphemous box with certain condemnations, and left alone in a solitary place to plead with His Father. He confessed that, "I am not alone, for my Father is with me." Jesus never did get in the box of religious traditions and made it clear in His Sermon on the Mount. He was on a mission, sent by God His Father, as a Bridge Builder between God and Man. In other words, He is the Pontifex Maximun, who atones for our sins, and brings us into a fellowship relationship, what the Greeks called the Koinonia, in a divine geometric triangle with God, the Father, God, the Son, and God, the Holy Spirit. Jesus was caught up and inextricably bound up in God, and that is where we must be! He would never lock Himself in the temple of His day or the culture of His day, or any day. He called our bodies the temples of the Holy Spirit. That's why he called us to holiness. "Be perfect, as your Father in Heaven is perfect. How can your really serve God, locked in a box, whether it is the box of traditionalism, or the box of outmoded practice in religion? Jesus said, you have heard it said, "An eye for an eye, and a tooth for a tooth, but I say! Don't hit back at all. If someone strikes you, stand there and take it. If someone drags you into court and sues for the shirt off your back, gift wrap your best coat and make a present of it."

In other words grow up, grow out, break out of the box of

limited religious traditions. We are called on to be witnesses of Him. There is an interesting Greek word here, Martus, or Martur, from whence we get our English word, martyr. It means taking a stand or bearing witness even if it costs you your life! Creature comforts just cannot be your priority, but seeking first the Kingdom is, and then the things shall be added unto you. In an "Out of The Box Ministry you will have to trust in God. W. C. Martin, the hymnologist sang out one day, " I trust in God, wherever I may be, Upon the land or on the rolling sea; For come what may, from day to day, my heavenly Father watches over me. He makes the rose an object of His care, He guides the eagle through the pathless air; and surely He remembers me, my heavenly Father watches over me. I trust in God, I know He cares for me, On mountain bleak, or on the stormy sea; Though billows roll, He keeps my soul, My heavenly Father watches over me." Jesus was involved in an "Out of the Box Ministry" and he founded His church as a call to out of box ministries. And He said to old "shaky" Peter, denying Peter, out spoken Peter, that despite all of the negatives, you are Petros, the rock on which I will build my church, and the gates of Hades will not overpower it." Let us understand that the church building is not the church or the rock of faith that Jesus was talking about, no matter how many millions you spent and borrowed to build it. "Petra", in Greek, denotes a mass of rock, which could signify a church building. "Petros", in Greek, is a detached stone or boulder, a stone that might be thrown or easily moved, and signifies a person just like Peter, who could, with the help of God, affirm Jesus on the Mount of Transfiguration as the Christ, the Son of the Living God, and then deny Him in Pilate's judgment hall, taking his seat among the prosecutors, warming himself by their fires. "That" is the foundation on which the Ekklesia, the Church, the called out, the sanctified, and the soon to be glorified, is built by faith. We picked up a "biblically based" and a "theologically sound song" that said, "We're going to do what the Spirit says do, we're going to do what the Spirit says do, we're going to do O' lord, we're going to do, O' Lord, we're going to do, what the Spirit says do. In Out of the Box ministries we must do what the Spirit of God says do.

2. COME FINALLY AND SEE THAT IN OUT BOX MINISTRIES, WE HAVE TO BE GUIDED AND DISCIPLINED BY THE HOLY SPIRIT, TO MAKE A HOLY DIFFERENCE BEFORE A HOLY GOD.

In speaking of Jesus, Eugene H. Peterson says in the Message Bible translation, "God's Spirit is on me, He's chosen me to preach the Message of good news to the poor, sent me to announce pardon to prisoners and recovery of sight to the blind, to set the burdened and battered free, to announce, this is God's year to act!" The Holy Spirit is not locked in or boxed in to the limits and confines of denominational understanding, or misunderstanding. In "Out of the Box ministries we cannot allow "what we use to do" to sidetrack us from what we ought to be doing. In 1972, I was on an American Baptist Mission tour with several other American Baptist Ministers. On that tour I met Dr. Lucius Walker, who was then the Executive Director of the Interreligious Foundation for Community Organization, headquartered in New York. Lu invited me to serve with him on the board of directors and I did for 26 years. I found myself doing community organizing around the country, empowering the poor, and sharing with them a sense of worth and dignity based on the New Testament teachings of Jesus. I was elected Vice Chairman of IFCO Pastor's for Peace, with the determination of breaking the blockade that our government had placed on Cuba by trying to starve Cuba into submission to American authority. We did that successfully for about twenty years, up to the time of this writing. We were witnessing under the social imperatives of the gospel as Matthew 25 points out. We have taken, across the years, several hundred tons of supplies to the churches of Cuba, including busses, trucks, medical supplies and equipment, food, building materials, Bibles in Spanish and in English, clothing, computers, and computer medical technology equipment. We answered the Macedonian call of our sisters and brothers. The question that one usually raises regarding this so-called "Out the Box" or "Liberating Ministry" was, and is, why break the Law? We need to ask, whose law? Does not the authority of God supersede the authority of man? Outbox ministries must always be driven by the Holy Spirit, to do works of faith that established the Kingdom that is within us. It just might put us on the mountain with Abraham and Isaac, and find us suspending the ethical, (the socially expected norm) for the teleological, (the doctrine that final cause exists, the study of the evidence of design or our purpose in nature). Abraham went up on the mountain with Isaac, to do what the social norm of his day expected of him and that was to sacrifice His only son, his longed for son, his prayed for son that was miraculously given to him in old age. In his day, everyone proved their faithfulness to their God by sacrificing their son. As he walked with Isaac up the mountain Isaac raised the question, Father, we have the flint and the wood but where is the sheep for the sacrifice? Abraham said, "Son, God will see to it that there's a sheep for the burnt offering." My sanctified imagination tells me that God had no problems with sacrificing a son, but this son was the wrong son to be sacrificed. "But when the time arrived that was set by Him, GOD SENT His Son, born among us of a woman, born under the conditions of the law so that He might redeem those of us who have been kidnapped by the law"(Galatians 4:4-7 The Message by Eugene Peterson). And they went up together. In Out of the Box Ministries we need to go up together, not knowing what may befall us, but we go up trusting God because God said, Go! We have to trust God as never before. When U.S. customs officials seized a little yellow school bus with our Bibles, computers, medications, medical supplies, and other cargo that was being delivered to the churches of Cuba for distribution, we went first to God in prayer. Ultimately, we got it all back and our brothers and sisters are utilizing it in Cuba in their struggle for liberation from a so-called Christian nation. We felt compelled to be disciplined in discipleship under the mandates of the Holy Spirit, and we overcame all obstacles.

We all are indebted to the people in the State of Alabama, down in the heart of Dixie, where we discovered that Dixie didn't have a heart. The late Dr. Vernon Johns, one of my mentors and a dear friend when we both lived in Petersburg, Virginia, laid the "golden egg" of the civil rights movement in Alabama that was hatched by the late Rosa Parks. The late Rosa Parks was compelled to sit on it and Dr. Martin Luther King, who succeeded Dr. John's as pastor of the Dexter Street Baptist Church, helped in its hatching. This came to light when eight clergymen, boxed in darkness, wrote an open letter to Dr. Martin Luther King, Jr., who nurtured it to life. These so-called God-sent proclaimers of the gospel were expressing their disapproval of his leading the civil rights movement in the streets with demonstrations, boycotts, demanding justice and a change in the way of life for the citizens of Alabama. They had no concept of the fact that they were proclaiming and practicing an "In the Box ministry" that was seeking to maintain the status quo, thereby postponing our liberation until we got to the "colored section" in heaven. As Christians, we are called by Jesus to be witnesses of Him, not only in proclamation, but also in practice. We are not to ever satisfy ourselves with the delivery of the Word; we must move like Jesus to the "Doing of the Word." Dr. Martin Luther King's Letter from A Birmingham Jail, in April of 1963, explains to the clergy, the nation and the world what "Out of the Box Ministry" was about, "Saving the soul not only of America, but of the world, (Aion, this fallen world of men). I have spoken on several occasions around his birthday celebration, and I have never heard any mention of Dr. Kings' letter to the clergy of Alabama. Almost everybody in the country and around the world has become acquainted with his "I HAVE A DREAM SPEECH," delivered in August of 1963, but I have only heard passive mention about his Letter from a Birmingham Jail. This letter, which inspired his "I Have a Dream Speech," should be everybody's dream. It is more in depth and speaks to the witness of Jesus in works of love and faith even more so, out of the box. Had we really understood his letter to the clergy of Alabama and acted on that, His August speech in the nation's capital could have been changed to, "I HAD A DREAM." My analysis of his letter to the clergy was in sync with that model prayer that Jesus taught His disciple, when he said, "THY KINGDOM COME, THY WILL BE DONE ON EARTH AS IT IS IN HEAVEN." Out of the Box ministries not only compels one to hear the word, but to "DO" the word. It appears that many churches are caught up with the idea of getting happy, dying here and going to heaven immediately without any real commitment to do the work of the Kingdom in the here and now if it is not socially acceptable or politically plausible. Some are still "waiting on the Lord who has already come in the flesh, in the Person of Jesus, the Christ. What are we supposed to be doing between the gates of hell and the pearly gates in glory?

Many of our youth are following their peers, and in some cases their parents, into utter theological oblivion because they are not rooted in the discipline of a God of Deliverance. There is not too much difference between the Jewish synagogue of yesterday and the so-called Christian Church today. Many active church adults fail to see the cultural captivity of the church that is more concerned about going to church then being the church. We are more prone to having an emotional good time in worship on Sunday morning, with no challenge for the real witness of Jesus between Sundays. We don't come to the house of prayer to have a "good time." We must break away from the religious traditions of the past and commit ourselves to the way of the Christ, and effect changes in the world order that is creative, liberating and redemptive. We have developed a junior church or a children's church, as an add-on to our worship, and in some cases it has become an extension of the box in which we have become accustomed. We do not have sufficient leaders in the Junior Church to teach our children in "Out Boxed Ministries." If you take away the missionary society in the local church, the annual Men and Women's Day services, Father's Day, Mother's Day, the pastor's aid club, and a plethora of anniversaries and entertainment signing, and many times preaching and dancing, what is left for the church to do? We have been guilty of doing the same thing over and over, year after year; century after century, expecting something to happen that is new and different, with a lukewarm commitment to Christ and a steadfast commitment to our secularized culture. We tend to justify our action and our inaction by noting, "Jesus Christ is the same yesterday, today and forever!" That is true but our witness of Him should reflect our growth in His will and His way as we seek to become like Him and not like one another! We cannot become like Jesus in the "Box of religious traditions." Jesus was not in that box. He came from God, and was God, all the days of His life. Every time Jesus went to the synagogue, something new happened. Simeon, the High Priest, cried out, "God, you can now release your servant, release me as you promised. With my own eyes, I've seen your salvation; it's now out in the open for everyone to see. A God-revealing light to the non-Jewish nations, and of glory for your people Israel."

When He was left in the temple after the feast of the Passover, at the age of twelve, He was confounding the priests, scribes and the

Pharisees with His knowledge of God and the New Way of life that He had come to proclaim. He started in the temple but the religious leaders, amused by him, said, "NO WAY, HOSEA. John tells us that He was in the Temple driving out the trustees, the finance committee, the tellers, along with the sheep and oxen, scattering the coins of money changers, and overturning their tables, declaring, you cannot make my Father's house a market place, or a den of thieves and robbers! Dr. Wyatt Tee Walker, a close friend of mine, entitled one of his many books, "Common Thieves," which suggests to me that there is more stealing, robbing and thieving in God's church then there has ever been in the corporate world. Don't point your finger at Ken Lay or the Enron Corporation that failed; look at the stewardship failings in the body of Christ! No wonder Jesus said, "Enter through the narrow gate because the gate is wide and the way is spacious that leads to destruction, and there are many who enter through it. But the gate is narrow and the way is difficult that leads to life, and there are few who find it."

CONCLUSION: Nazareth? Nazareth? Nazareth? Can anything good come out of Nazareth? You've got to be kidding! Philip says, "Come and See!" Nazareth is everywhere. Sometimes sections of Nazareth are more pronounced in towns like the goshens of Egypt, or shanty towns in South America and South Africa, the tent cities in the overflow of Darfur in East Africa, or the ghettoes in America. Nazareth is everywhere, even in our stagnate state of mind. Can anything good come out of Nazareth? Jesus was born in Bethlehem, the House of Bread, but He grew up in Nazareth, a poor man's town. "He's the one that Moses wrote about in the law. He's the one that Isaiah saw coming from Edom wearing Edomite dyed garments, dressed in bright red, coming from Bozrah? Who is this one wearing royal attire that marches confidently because of his great strength? It is I who announces vindication, and who is able to deliver! Isaiah, I know you know, but allow me to tell you what I know. Come and see that He, who comes out of Nazareth, is still walking. He is still walking and knocking on the doors of your heart saying, "Listen, I am standing at the door and knocking! (Come, out of that box) If anyone hears my voice and opens the door I will come into his home and share a meal with him and he with Me" (Revelation 2:10 NET). In the last revival we conducted while I was the pastor of the New Calvary Baptist Church in Norfolk, an "out of the box, no nonsense preacher" from Brooklyn, New York, came to town at my invitation and said something that I have never forgotten. I think he was preaching from the 1st Psalm when the said, "Be careful of who you listen to, especially when it is between you me and the gate post." When you listen to everybody, and everybody is pointing you toward another way out, you are in the second phase of eternal lostness. When you listen to everybody it won't be long before you will find yourself stop listening to the Word of God! When you listen to everybody, you'll soon discover that you are not listening to your grandmother. Everybody has or has heard of such a grandmother. If she hadn't been here, then none of you would be here. If you forget about your grandmother, it may not be too long before you will forget to listen to your mother or your father. You might be in a state of glistening, but you won't be listening. You might find yourself back in the days of the judges in Israel. The Scriptures teach, "In those days there were no kings in Israel. Each man did what he considered to be right" (Judges 21:25 NET). Come out of the box of selfish concerns. In talking to some of the believing disciples of the Jews, Jesus said, "If you continue to follow my teachings, you are really my disciples, you will know the truth, and the truth will set you free" (John 8:31 NET). When you become free in Jesus you will come out of the box. When Jesus sets you free, you are bound, united, tied up with Him. No man-made institution can hold you. The state can't stop you, the jails cannot hold you. Water can't drown you and fire cannot burn you. When Jesus sets you free, you are free indeed. If you are so free, why don't you come out of the box so God can use you and your testimony? Jesus said, "If any one wants to become my follower he must deny himself, take up His cross and follow me. Follow me who art still John's Lamb of God that takes away the sins of the world. Follow me, for I am a balm in Gilead that heals a sin sick soul. Follow me, for whoever wants to save his life will lose it, but whoever loses his life for my sake and the gospel, will find it unto life everlasting. Follow me, and I will make you fishers of men. Follow me, and I will supply all of your needs according to my riches in glory. If you would just delight yourself in my words, I will give you the desires of your heart. Follow me, and trust me with your tithes and offering. And see if I won't open the windows of heaven and pour you out blessings that you won't have room enough to receive them. Just try me and I will make your enemies your footstool. Try Me; I'll be your bridge over troubled waters. Try Me, and I will make a way for you. I'll be because I am. I am all that you will ever need. I'll be your burden bearer and your sorrow sharer. Try Me... Try Me... Try me! If you are going to try me you will have to come out of the box.

CHAPTER XV

THE BONES OF JESUS, OUR GLORIFIED LORD

"Where is Jesus today and what happened to the Church He founded?"

Did they really find the bones or remains of Jesus in a tomb? "They may have," says a contextual student of the Bible from the viewpoint of Liberation Theology; the Scriptures support such a possibility. Think about this just for a moment; "What would Jesus be doing in heaven seated at the right hand of God, in bones, flesh and blood, when Jesus Himself said, "He is `Spirit?" After the resurrection of Jesus, how do you think He came in the room with His disciples through locked doors and closed windows? Was that a physical body or was it a Spirit Body? Doesn't the Bible teach, "Flesh and Blood cannot inherit the Kingdom of God?" Have we not understood that the language of the Bible is written in metaphors, parables, miracles, figures and the unspeakable groaning language of the Spirit? Are we still looking through a glass darkly, taking literally all that we believe and skipping over what we don't? Perhaps, if we keep on studying from a contextual reference in the Spirit, one day we will see it face to face!

Personally, I don't believe for a moment the exposure of Jesus and his alleged wife and child, as the da Vinci code represents Him and them. Consider Jesus, the Creator, as the Apostle John in the following Scripture represents him: "He was in the world, and the world was created by Him, but the world did not recognize him. He came to what was His own, but His own people did not receive him. But to all who have received him – those who believe in His name – he has given the right to become God's children – children not born by human parents or by human desire or a husband's decision, but by God" (John 1:10-13 NET). Could not this Jesus have a spiritual resurrection and ascend to His Father and be seated at His right Hand as a Divine/Spiritual Being?

How difficult is it for us to grow beyond the anthropomorphic notion of God as man? God is a Spiritual and a Scientific Divine Being. Listen to the Apostle Paul:

"Think straight. Awaken to the holiness of life. No more playing fast and loose with resurrection facts. Ignorance of God is a luxury you cannot afford in times like these. Aren't you embarrassed that you've let this kind of thing go on as long as you have? Some skeptic is sure to ask, `Show me how resurrection works. Give me a diagram, draw me a picture. What does this resurrection body look like? ` If you look at the question closely, you realize how absurd it is. There are no diagrams for this kind of thing. We do have a parallel experience in gardening. You plant a "dead" seed; soon there is a flourishing plant. There is no visual likeness between seed and plant. You could never guess what a tomato would look like by looking at a tomato seed. What we plant in the soil and what grows out of it doesn't look anything alike. The dead body that we bury in the ground, and the resurrection body that comes from it will be dramatically different.

You will notice that the variety of bodies is stunning. Just as there are different kinds of seeds, there are different kinds of bodies – humans, animals, and birds, fish – each unprecedented in its form. You get a hint at the diversity of resurrection glory by looking at the diversity of bodies not only on earth but also in the skies – sun, moon, stars – all the varieties of beauty and brightness. And we're only looking at pre-resurrection "seeds". "Who can imagine what the resurrection "plants" will be like! This image of planting a dead seed and raising a live plant is mere sketch at best, but perhaps it will help in approaching the mystery of the resurrection body – but only if you keep in mind that when we're raised, we're raised for good, *alive forever! The corpse that's planted is no beauty, but when it's raised, it's glorious. Put in the ground weak, it comes up powerful. The seed sown is natural, the seed grown is supernatural – same seed same body, but what a difference from when it goes down in physical mortality to when it is raised up in spiritual immortality!"*

...*"I need to emphasize, friends, that our natural, earthy lives don't in themselves lead us by their very nature into the kingdom of God. Their very `nature' is to die, so how could they `naturally'" end up in the Life kingdom?*

But let me tell you something wonderful, a mystery I'll probably never fully understand. We're not all going to die – but we are all going to be changed. You hear a blast to end all blasts from a trumpet, and in the time that you look up and blink your eyes – it's over. On signal from that trumpet from heaven, the dead will be up and out of their graves, beyond the reach of death, never to die again. At the same moment and in the same way, we'll all be changed. In the resurrection scheme of things, this has to happen, everything perishable taken off the shelves and replaced by the imperishable, this mortal replaced by the immortal. Then the saying will come true:

Death swallowed by triumphant Life! Who got the last word, oh Death? Oh, Death, who's afraid of you now? With all this going for us, my dear friends, stand your ground. And don't hold back. Throw yourselves into the work of the Master, confident that nothing you do for Him is a waste of time or effort."

You may read this passage from any translation and it is equally as powerful. I omitted a few lines of the Scripture to shorten it for purposes of this book. It brought glory to my being in this translation taken from THE MESSAGE, REMIX, by Eugene Peterson, (1 Corinthians 15:34-58, with the two noted brief omissions.) I call this Paul's Eulogy for the Disciples of Christ, wherever they find themselves.

Many believers have become confused on biblical interpretations and have adopted a fundamentalist and literal interpretation of the Bible that God never intended. The Bible says what it says, many times, "in figures of speech, simile, metaphor, anthropomorphism, words of association, personification, euphemism, hyperbole, and irony." Check this out on the Internet. You can take a literal view from understandable passages, like the eulogy above, but when the literal interpretation bothers you, dig deeper. There is even biblical meaning in the darkness that will turn on its light through study, prayer and meditation. What I am saying about the "Bones of Jesus" will perhaps trouble some, but if anyone thinks that Jesus is in heaven today in "flesh and blood," after 2000 years, I would suggest further study and prayer. Getting the right understanding of the Scriptures is a process of liberation that demands deliverance from the shambles of sin and the arrogance of ignorance. It may sound harsh but I am not one for ' beating around the bush!'

To change our view today on death and dying would almost wreck the economy of this nation. Take a look at what we pay for "death, dying and burials!" We have been sold on the idea of seeing our mothers again, our fathers, wives, husbands, sisters and brothers, just as we knew them here on earth. I don't believe that we can find any support for that interpretation in the Scriptures. Be careful about the literal translations of what we want to believe. When Paul says, "When this mortal puts on immortality, and this corruption puts on incorruption and we shall be changed," I take that as a literal fact of "Biblical faith." Humankind has for centuries thought of a bodily resurrection, from the way we bury our dead. In ancient Egypt we dressed up the pharaohs, the kings and queens, mummies in standing positions, sometimes with swords and shields, uniforms, expensive shrouds, jewelry, favorite foods, wines, and drink, "just in case." The pyramids themselves are but monuments of grandeur commemorating death and afterlife. Even today we cater to "what was, rather than what is, in the realm of death and dying." When President Dwight Eisenhower made his request for a simple pine box with one flower, he knew that his remains were going back to the dust. Mature Christians do not look forward to seeing their love ones in physically resurrected bodies in the form of the biological forms that they once exhibited. Am I a Sadducee? By no means. I believe the "Good News of the Gospel." I believe that man's bones, his flesh, and blood, will return to the dust from whence it came. I want to see my mother, father, sisters, brothers, and kindred again, but not in physical bodies. We will have glorified, resurrected bodies.

To reverse this view now would involve a fight with centuries of unbelief – centuries before and after Christ. Note the way we dress up for our final departure and for our life to come, sometimes under the world, over the world, or beyond the world. When the biological cells die out in our bodies and the organs such as the heart and brain lose their power to function, it is all over for us in bodily form forever. The Scripture teaches (see Ecclesiastes 12:7, that ends with these words from the New English Translation, "... and the dust returns to the earth, as it was, and the Spirit returns to God who gave it." Recall Genesis 2:7, "The Lord God formed the man from the soil of the ground and breathed into his nostrils the breath of life, and man became a living soul." All of our lives we have been "body and soul, flesh and spirit, human and divine." When the human in us, the flesh in us, and body in us, are all gone, 'they're gone! Jesus, who was Spirit, and in the beginning with God (and incidentally was God), and who came to us born of Mary, by the empowerment of God, became flesh for us, so we could go back to God in the Spirit and dwell with Him forever. John tells us in Revelation 21:1 5 (NET Translation), Then I saw a new heaven and a new earth, for the first heaven and the first earth had CEASED TO EXIST, and the sea existed no more. And I saw the holy city – the new Jerusalem – descending out of heaven from God, made ready like a bride adorned for her husband. And I heard a loud voice from the throne saying, look! The residence of God is among us, among men and women. He will live among them and they will be His people, and God Himself will be with them and as God."(This is in Spiritual transformation). "He will, (perhaps a metaphor) wipe away every tear from their eyes and death will not exist any more crying, or pain, THE FORMER THINGS HAVE CEASED TO EXIST."

Please take time to read the prayer of Jesus in John 17:6-19. John said he wrote this gospel that we may "believe." If you believe this gospel, this good news, this euangelion, does it really make any difference to you if the bones of Jesus were found in a cave dating from more than 2000 years ago, or does it put you in a conflict of faith? The ascension of Jesus was in a Transformed Spiritual Body, just as He was in the beginning with God! He is now one with the Father in fullness, and with us in a spiritual body. Now hear this one last spiritual caveat; When Jesus walked on the water was He walking in a physical body or a spiritual body? (It could have been either). I think we all know that Peter wasn't ready when he wanted to walk on water to meet Jesus, yet stepped out in a physical body. The Bible doesn't give us any notice as to when it is switching from the literal language to a figurative language. Paul said in 2

Timothy 2:15, "Study and be eager and do your utmost to present yourself to God approved (tested by trial), a workman who has no cause to be ashamed, correctly analyzing and accurately dividing – rightly handling and skillfully teaching the Word of Truth" (The Amplified New Testament, Zondervan Publishers House, Grand Rapids, Michigan).

I trust that this biblical and theological analysis has at least provoked your thinking about the *Bones of Jesus* and our own bones. No matter where they are, my contention is that they are NOT IN HEAVEN! There is no place for a bone field in the realm of the Spirit. My last statement in this book is to admonish you to go to Ezekiel, Chapter 37, and please read verses 1-28. We will find that the bones could live, that there was a possibility if they heard the WORD OF THE LORD, AND GOD'S SPIRIT WOULD COME UPON THEM. Some bones even from that period are living today through transformation by the Spirit. The late Fanny Crosby, who lost her sight at the age of six months by an apparent medical error, was the author of more than 6,000 hymns. She had the vision to look beyond her blindness to see the beauty of God's redemptive love in life and after death. A Mr. John Sweeney gave her the melody and she prayed for the words to follow. "When my life work is ended, and I cross the swelling tide, When the bright and glorious morning I shall see; I shall know my Redeemer when I reach the other side, and His smile will be the first to welcome me. Oh, the soul – thrilling rapture when I view His blessed Face, And the luster of His kindly beaming eye; How my full heart will praise Him for the mercy, love and grace, That prepares for me a mansion in the sky. I shall know Him, I shall know Him, when redeemed by His side I shall stand; I shall know Him, I shall know Him, by the print of the nails in His hand."

What happened to the church that Christ, inspired by God, developed? Jesus is the same, yesterday today and forever more, but what happened to the church? Are we actually dealing with the total person in our pews, i.e, those who have lost their way but who give out of their substance?

OUR GLORIFIED LORD

Like our journey on the isthmus, we must never conclude this thought on the Bones of Jesus, in a buried grave in Jerusalem. From the earliest times of recorded history man has exemplified steadfast belief in a life that was eternally on going in one form or the other. I believe, along with thousands of others, that the "Cross" did not end the life of Jesus, just as the manger and Mary did not begin it. As Jesus said in the gospel of John and other gospels, "God sent Him, who was in the beginning with God." Both biblically and theologically, our very existence bears witness of our being rooted and grounded in God, who is Eternal and Always. The Bible itself could be rightfully called, "The Life and Love Book." When we live our lives outside of the Will and Purpose of God, we are engaging the darkness of death. Life begins with God and Love (which is God) who sees us through. We all have had preexistence with God, because, before He formed us, we were in the mind, the heart, and soul of God, as the Source of our being. When God said, "Let Us make Man," He was obviously talking to his created order. Whatever gasses minerals, i.e, substances of water, word and spirit, had to be in place before the creation of man, for it is by these, that life is made possible. God made us in His image and likeness, so that we could live a life of obedience that would bring Him glory and honor. He endows us with the "power of contrary choice," through a will that gives us the option of ascending as high as angels in Heaven, or falling low as devils in hell. Man fell from this lofty state, as John Milton has said in *Paradise Lost*, "nine times the space that measures day and night." But when the time arrived that was set by God the Father, God sent His Son born among us of a woman, born under the conditions of the law so that He might redeem those of us who have been kidnapped by the law. Thus we have been set free to experience our rightful heritage. You can tell for sure that you are now fully adopted as His own children because God sent the Spirit of His Son, into our lives crying out, Papa! Father" (Galatians 4:4-6 THE MESSAGE by Eugene H. Peterson.)

No, Jesus is not in Jerusalem in an age-old grave. His physical body, including his bones, has long gone back to the dust. And just what is dust? Dust, according to Webster's Encyclopedic Unabridged

Dictionary of the English Language says, dust is earth or other matter in fine dry particles; any finely powdered substance as sawdust. That to which anything, as the human body is ultimately reduced by disintegration or decay." Dust is both eternal and always. We can never get rid of it. Our bodies go back to the dust, and in that form, we will always exist. "For instance, we know that when these bodies of our are taken down like tents and folded away, they will be replaced by resurrection bodies in heaven – God made, not handmade – and we'll never have to relocate our tents again. Sometimes we can hardly wait to move – and so we cry out in frustration. Compared to what's coming, living conditions around here seem like a stopover in an unfurnished shack, and we're tired of it! We've been given a glimpse of the real thing, our true home, and our resurrection bodies! The Spirit of God whets our appetite by giving us a taste of what's ahead. He puts a little of heaven in our hearts so that we'll never settle for less' (2 Corinthians 5:1-5 THE MESSAGE by Eugene H. Peterson).

The trial of Jesus is not over, despite the fact that it started with the announcement of His birth. It wasn't over with his death on Calvary. The trial of Jesus was not over with his resurrection and ascension. After two thousand years of witnessing, the trial is not over, largely because of our unbelief. John says, "He came to what was His own, but His Own people did not receive Him. But to all who have received Him, those who believe in his name, he has given the right to become God's children" (John 1:11 NET). His Spirit, that was of God, and He was God, has ascended back to God in the Glorified Spiritual Body as it was in the beginning. David saw this Glorified Body of Jesus and told us to look at it. "Look up you gates. Rise up, you eternal doors! Then the majestic King will enter!" The Lord who is strong and mighty! The Lord who is mighty in battle! Look up, you gates! Rise up, you eternal doors! Then the majestic King will enter! Who is this majestic King? The Lord who leads armies! He is the majestic King (Psalms 24: 7-10 NET)!"

Since 1779, Christians around the globe have sung the so called National Anthem of Christendom." It is good to know that Edward Perronet, who was a missionary in India, half the way around the world, wrote the lyrics. This hymn grasps the symbolic meaning of the Glorified Lord of Glory. It seems fitting to me to share these words, following David's Affirmation in Psalms 24: "All hail the power of Jesus' Name! Let angels prostrate fall; Bring fourth the royal diadem, and crown Him Lord of all, Bring forth the royal diadem and crown Him Lord of all. Ye chosen seed of Israel's race, ye ransomed from the fall. Hail Him who saves you by His grace, and crown Him Lord of all. Hail Him who saves you by His grace, and crown Him Lord of all. Let every tribe and every tongue before Him prostrate fall. And shout in universal song the crowned Lord of all. All shout in universal song the crowned Lord of all."

Dr. Reid with Prayer Group in Richmond, VA.

EPILOGUE

When I was subpoenaed to appear before a select Blue Ribbon committee of the General Assembly in Virginia regarding remarks I made on voting fraud in Virginia, I immediately called my attorney, William Kuntsler, to represent me. He flew in from New York and I met him at the Richmond International Airport. When we arrived at the hearing room in the State Capitol, my attorney was not permitted to accompany me before the committee. Senator Gray, a staunch supporter of the Byrd machine, addressed me first and said, "Mr. Reid, we have checked your record, and so far as we are concerned, you have an 'impeccable' record for truth and veracity." My daughter Michelle would say, "Now, Daddy, that was a good thing." At the time, I wasn't so sure. I was not familiar with the term *impeccable* or the word *veracity*. What was foremost on my mind in that room was that I was appearing before the same racist Democrats who had stood behind the governor in his stand on 'interposition and nullification' of the Supreme Court's decision of May 1954, that called for the desegregation of the public schools in Virginia and in other predominantly Christian jurisdictions.

Now, fifty-plus years later, I find those words both comforting and reassuring. In the light of other writings and questions regarding the authenticity of the authors, I want to reassure the publishers and readers of this book that my record remains the same. My record is impeccable when it comes to truth and veracity. All of the churches that I was blessed to serve are still standing. All of the jails in all of the cities are still standing. The Holiday Inn in Danville, Virginia, involved in the incident previously mentioned in this work, has been rebuilt and is across the street on Riverside

Drive. Another motel, Strafford Inn and Conference Center, now occupies the grounds that were previously used by the Holiday Inn. The Southern Christian Leadership Conference is still moving on. (I resigned as a member of the National Board in 2002). IFCO/Pastors for Peace is still taking caravans of material supplies to Cuba and elsewhere. It is still operative in its dogged determination to break what we have called the "godless, illegal, lawless, immoral, and unjustified embargo placed upon it by the United States and three of its powerless allies, "propped up" by the United States against the people of Cuba and the overwhelming number of nations of the world.

While I believe that there are some saved, born again, sanctified and committed Christians in America, I would not describe America as being a "Christian Nation." As I see it, it is a nation that has secularized Christianity under a culture of Biblical corruption and theological misunderstanding and this has invited, permitted and been supported only by the man-made "God of the West, and not the Christ of Glory." However, the God of the Ages still has a faithful remnant. Jesus said, "Enter through the narrow gate, because the gate is wide and the way is spacious that leads to destruction, and there are many who enter through it. But the gate is narrow and the way is difficult that leads to life, and there are few who find it" (Matthew 7:13, 14, NET).

The fourteenth century Teresa of Avila has said; "God has no hands but our hands to do his work today. God has no feet but our feet to lead others in His way. God has no voice but our voice to tell others how He died and God has no help but our help to lead them to His side." Can the world see "His Image and His Likeness" in us today? Are we being Godly in words, thought and actions?

Milton, the Disciple, Author

More Stops along the Way

Dr. Reid with Abernathy
Francis Griffin & Wyatt T. Walker

Milton, the "Disciple"
with President LBJ

Gov. John Dalton assists
with Holy Communion

John Sengstacke, Virgin
Island Governor & Reid

With Mayor Roy
Martin-City Hall

Poor People's Campaign
Norfolk, Virginia

A Prayer Program at
the VA State Capitol

More Stops along the way

Statewide Pilgrimage
Prince Edwards County, VA

Reid, Abernathy,
Walker& William

"Daddy" King, Marian, Reid,
Harvey, and Curtis

1960-Marian's 1st Class
Petersburg, VA

Dr. Reid, Carlton Goodlette,
Eleanor Williams & Sherman
Brisco in San Francisco, CA

A Prayer Pilgrimage

www.ingramcontent.com/pod-product-compliance
Ingram Content Group UK Ltd.
Pitfield, Milton Keynes, MK11 3LW, UK
UKHW041431210726
13854UKWH00010B/1845

9 781412 088800